THE FEARLESS LION'S ROAR

NYOSHUL KHENPO'S THANGKA OF LONGCHENPA WITH
SAMANTABHADRA AND THE MASTERS OF THE
LONGCHEN NYINGTHIG DZOGCHEN NYEN GYUD LINEAGE.
(PHOTO BY AUTHOR.)

The Fearless Lion's Roar

Profound Instructions on Dzogchen, the Great Perfection

Nyoshul Khenpo Jamyang Dorje

With commentaries on Jigme Lingpa's
The Lion's Roar and Longchenpa's
Resting at Ease in Illusion

TRANSLATED BY
David Christensen

SNOW LION
BOSTON & LONDON
2015

Snow Lion
An imprint of Shambhala Publications, Inc.
Horticultural Hall
300 Massachusetts Avenue
Boston, Massachusetts 02115
www.shambhala.com

9 8 7 6 5 4 3 2 1

First Edition
Printed in the United States of America

♾ This edition is printed on acid-free paper that meets the
American National Standards Institute z39.48 Standard.
♲ Shambhala makes every effort to print on recycled paper.
For more information please visit www.shambhala.com.

Distributed in the United States by Penguin Random House LLC
and in Canada by Random House of Canada Ltd

Designed by Gopa & Ted2, Inc.

Library of Congress Cataloging-in-Publication Data
'Jam-dbyans-rdo-rje, Smyo-sul Mkhan-po, author.
The fearless lion's roar: profound instructions on dzogchen, the great
perfection/Nyoshul Khenpo Jamyang Dorje; translated
by David Christensen.—First edition.
pages   cm.
Includes index.
Translated from Tibetan.
ISBN 978-1-55939-431-4 (paperback)
1. Rdzogs-chen. I. Title.
BQ7662.4.J43 2015
294.3'444—dc23

Rest in natural great peace!
Your helpless mind, beaten back by karma,
thoughts, and emotions
Like incessant, pounding waves,
Here in the limitless ocean of samsara.

—Nyoshul Khen Rinpoche,
"Rest in Natural Great Peace"

CONTENTS

FOREWORD

———

PRINCE SIDDHARTHA attained enlightenment under the bodhi tree at Bodhgaya; he woke from the sleep of ignorance and was henceforth known as the Buddha, the Awakened One. He gave his first teachings at Sarnath, where he began guiding beings to their own awakening; and so it was that the Buddhist tradition came into being. In the eighth century of our era, when Buddhism was still flourishing in India, it was thanks to Guru Padmasambhava, King Trisong Detsen, the abbot Shantarakshita, pandita Vimalamitra, and other great masters, that the teachings were translated into the Tibetan language and were thus preserved.

These same teachings later gave rise to such great masters as Longchenpa and Jigme Lingpa and after them to our own teachers like Jamyang Khyentse Chokyi Lodro, the sixteenth Karmapa, Dudjom Rinpoche, Kangyur Rinpoche, Dilgo Khyentse Rinpoche, Minling Trichen Rinpoche, Trulshik Rinpoche, Drupwang Penor Rinpoche, Tenga Rinpoche, Tulku Urgyen Rinpoche, Kalu Rinpoche, and Nyoshul Khen Rinpoche and the great masters who are still with us such as the Dalai Lama, Sakya Trizin Rinpoche, Dodrupchen Rinpoche, and Taklung Tsetrul Rinpoche. It is thanks to these enlightened teachers that, to our great good fortune, the teachings of the Buddha are still so alive today. I am extremely happy to know that these teachings, and especially the commentaries and instructions of Nyoshul Khen Rinpoche, one of my most beloved teachers, are now accessible in English.

Khen Rinpoche was a most learned and accomplished master, especially in the theory and practice of Dzogpa Chenpo, the Great Perfection. He was very famous, and many of our present teachers were his students, including Dzongsar Khyentse Rinpoche, Dzigar Kongtrul Rinpoche, Neten Choling Rinpoche, Mingyur Rinpoche, Tsoknyi Rinpoche, Phagchok Rinpoche, Sogyal Rinpoche and many others such as my brother Jigme Khyentse Rinpoche and Khenpo Sonam Topgyal Rinpoche.

Not only was Khen Rinpoche extremely learned; his teachings were also based on his own immeasurable experience. As a person, he was incredibly kind. He always made us feel at ease; and I can say this because I had the great honor of knowing him and being his disciple for several decades. I had the good fortune to receive many teachings from him, in particular the complete empowerments, transmissions, and instructions for the entire works of Khenpo Ngawang Palzang, otherwise known as Khenpo Ngakchung—one of the most important holders of the Nyingma tradition in the lineage that came down from Jigme Lingpa, Jigme Gyalwai Nyugu, Patrul Rinpoche, and Nyoshul Lungtok, who was Khenpo Ngakchung's own teacher.

As well as being extremely kind, Nyoshul Khen Rinpoche was also a very strict and uncompromising teacher. As a preliminary to receiving his instructions, he made me reflect just on the four mind-changes for about five years. At the same time, he was also very approachable and ready to help others. This was true to such an extent that, when we were building the first retreat center in France, Rinpoche came in person to help us, building the walls of two of the retreat rooms with his own hands! Not only that, but he also gave teachings to the retreatants in the three centers in Dordogne: Thegchog Ösal Chöling (Chanteloube), Thegchog Drubpa Ling (Bois Bas) and Thegchog Rinchen Ling (Le Meyrat), under the guidance of both Kyabje Dudjom Rinpoche and Kyabje Dilgo Khyentse Rinpoche.

David Christensen came to Thegchog Rinchen Ling in France in the 1980s in order to follow the three-year retreat program. He has been working on this book for some years. I am grateful that through his efforts, these teachings, and especially Jigme Lingpa's *The Lion's Roar,* with detailed introduction and commentary by my precious teacher Nyoshul Khen Rinpoche, are now available for everyone. If we students and teachers feel confident that we understand Dzogchen and that we even have some realization and accomplishment, these teachings of *The Lion's Roar* will put us back on the right track. That is something that can never be unnecessary nor out of place.

I have confidence that every word of Nyoshul Khen Rinpoche comes from realization and that his blessings will reach to all those who have genuine bodhicitta and devotion. I close with the aspiration that whoever has the fortune to have contact with Rinpoche's teachings will reach the same level of realization as Nyoshul Khen Rinpoche.

Taklung Tsetrul Pema Wangyal Rinpoche
Written on the anniversary of Gyalwa Longchenpa, 2014

Translator's Preface

THESE TEACHINGS OF Nyoshul Khen Rinpoche were given during the three-year retreat at Thegchog Rinchen Ling, Le Meyrat, France. Due to Khenpo's ill health at the time, he very rarely taught from texts. Yet due to Rinpoche's kindness, we were still very fortunate to receive all the teachings and instructions included in this book that are not related to the three texts mentioned below. Also, when Khenpo did teach, it was literally like receiving a whispered transmission, as Rinpoche spoke very softly to ease his headaches. However in the final years of our retreat, when Rinpoche began to practice the yogic exercises of the channels and energies (*tsa lung; rtsa rlung*), there was a noticeable improvement in his health.

At this time Nyoshul Khen Rinpoche offered to teach from a text and asked me for some suggestions. I had a copy of Longchenpa's Trilogy of Resting at Ease (Ngalso Kor Sum; Ngal gso skor gsum) and suggested *Resting at Ease in Illusion (Gyuma Ngalso; Sgyu ma ngal gso)*. Khenpo agreed to summarize the essence of it and then also followed that with his teaching on Longchenpa's last testament, *Immaculate Light*. Upon completion of this, Khenpo asked if I had any shorter texts, so I offered him *The Lion's Roar (Senge Ngaro; Seng ge'i nga ro)* of Jigme Lingpa.

I would like to thank Nyoshul Khenpo for all his teachings. Looking at it from this point in time, what we received from him was truly amazing. Among all the teachings I have been fortunate to receive from many great lamas, Nyoshul Khenpo's instructions have especially seemed to remain indelibly in my mind. On one occasion during retreat, when I was translating orally as Khenpo was teaching, it seemed very easy to remember Khenpo's words, even after he spoke for long periods of time, and this still holds true to this day. Rinpoche replied that this was due to the blessings of the Dzogchen Nyongtri Chenmo, the Great Experiential Guidance of Dzogpa Chenpo.

Over the years some lamas have encouraged me to translate these teachings, as there is very little of Nyoshul Khenpo's teachings available. In more recent times, Gochen Tulku Sangngak Tenzin thought that the teaching of *The Lion's Roar* by Jigme Lingpa was greatly needed in the West these days, to point out the dangers of intellectualizing the teachings of Dzogchen, the Great Perfection.

I would also like to thank Pema Wangyal Rinpoche for his tireless effort in founding the three-year retreat centers in France, for giving teachings, and for bringing so many sublime lamas to teach our relatively small groups of retreatants. His kindness gave so many Westerners the opportunity to engage in deep practice under the guidance of great lamas. At Pema Wangyal Rinpoche's invitation, H.H. Dudjom Rinpoche spent a week in our retreat, offering empowerments and teachings, and granting personal interviews to all retreatants, especially concerning the understanding of the Dzogchen view, meditation, and conduct. We were fortunate to receive some of his very last teachings. Special thanks to H.H. Dilgo Khyentse Rinpoche for his clarifications of some points of *The Lion's Roar* root text, which are located in the notes to Nyoshul Khenpo's commentary on *The Lion's Roar.*

Thanks especially go to our editor, John Deweese, who spent a great amount of time checking and editing all of the translations included in this book and reworking the teachings into a form most accessible to readers. John and I compiled the book.

I would like to thank Corinna Chung for her original handwritten transcripts of my oral translations of the teachings, and Vyvyan Mishra and Pepe Trevor, who did some initial editing of some portions of the teachings. Also thanks to Corinna Chung and Madeleine Attar-Trehin for sharing the spontaneous songs that Khen Rinpoche wrote for them.

Appreciation is also due to all the Tibetan lamas who helped to clarify the root text of *The Lion's Roar:* Gochen Tulku Sangngak Tenzin, Tulku Rigzin Pema, Dagpo Tulku, Khenpo Orgyen Chowang, and Lopon Kalsang Dorje. Thanks to Andreas Kretschmar for reading the manuscript and offering his insights, and to Yvonne Rawsthorne and Noellina Christie Deweese for proofreading the manuscript and for their observations.

Also thanks to the sponsorship of Linda Pritzker, which enabled me to spend many months going back and checking word by word the original recordings of Nyoshul Khenpo's teachings.

Thanks to Shechen Monastery in Nepal for allowing the reprinting of my translation of Jigme Lingpa's *A Wondrous Ocean of Advice for the Practice of*

Those in Retreat in Solitude and for permission to use Dilgo Khyentse Rinpoche's comments in the notes to the root text of Jigme Lingpa's *The Lion's Roar*. Thanks to Rangjung Yeshe Publications for permission to use material for a note in the chapter "The Meaning of Meditation Deities."

I would like to acknowledge my daughter Uma Christensen, who is a shining light and inspiration in these troubled times, and Andrew Morris for his unwavering support for all my projects including this book.

Finally, many thanks to Nikko Odiseos, the president of Shambhala Publications, for embracing this project with such enthusiasm and encouragement. Also with appreciation to Michael Wakoff at Shambhala Publications for his care in copyediting the manuscript. Thanks to Lama Surya Das for connecting me to the publishers.

Chögyam Trungpa Rinpoche published an early version of *The Lion's Roar* in English more than forty years ago, in his book *Mudra*. Regarding *The Lion's Roar* and another Dzogchen teaching, Trungpa Rinpoche said, "I have included these translations in the book even though they are advanced teachings, because reading seems to have inspired many people. There is no danger representing them as they are self-secret, that is one cannot understand what one is not ready for. Also they are incomplete without a transmission from a guru of the lineage."[1]

In some small way, may the efforts of creating this book repay the kindness of our peerless teachers. May all be inspired by the simplicity and directness of the Dzogchen teachings in these complex times. May all sentient beings have the good fortune to receive the blessings of Nyoshul Khenpo Rinpoche and the lineage of the Great Experiential Guidance of Dzogpa Chenpo.

David Christensen
Melbourne, Australia, March 20, 2014

TECHNICAL NOTE

THIS BOOK INCLUDES in parentheses the Tibetan equivalents for many key terms. They are written in the Wylie system for transliterating Tibetan script, which enables one to accurately reconstruct the written form of a Tibetan word or phrase using English characters. This transliteration system is not designed to be a guide to pronouncing or reading Tibetan; that is, it is not a phonetic rendering of the Tibetan words, but a letter-by-letter transliteration. In some cases, following the English translation of a term or phrase, we provide in parentheses both the phonetic Tibetan and the Wylie transliteration, or occasionally, the phoneticized Sanskrit and then the Wylie transliteration, of the words Nyoshul Khen Rinpoche used.

When there are two terms separated by a semicolon in parentheses, the first is always either phonetic Tibetan or (rarely) phoneticized Sanskrit; and the second term is always the Wylie transliteration. The reason for supplying both phonetic and transliteration in some instances is that we want to give more people access to the Tibetan terms. This offers the general reader, who has received the teachings and is in the lineage but has not begun to learn Tibetan words in Tibetan script or Wylie transliteration, the opportunity learn some of the most commonly used practice terms. Readers can just remember that when there are two words or phrases separated by a semicolon, the first is always phonetic, usually phonetic Tibetan or occasionally Sanskrit; the second term or phrase always consists of the Tibetan words transliterated according to the Wylie system.

We chose this method because putting everything in phonetic Tibetan, while it would accommodate those who don't know how to read Tibetan script or Wylie transliteration, would not make clear exactly what Nyoshul Khen Rinpoche said in Tibetan. The only way to make Rinpoche's words clear for all readers is to include the Wylie transliterations. This is because some Tibetan words are similar in pronunciation, and the only way to know for sure which Tibetan terms or phrases are being translated is to include the Wylie transliteration. Providing only phonetic Tibetan would not allow one to understand which Tibetan phrases were being translated—it would be impossible to accurately trace all of the the phonetic renderings back to the actual Tibetan words and phrases if the Wylie transliteration were not provided.

THE FEARLESS LION'S ROAR

TRANSLATOR'S INTRODUCTION

THIS BOOK IS a compilation of the instructions Nyoshul Khen Rinpoche gave during our three-year retreat from 1982 to 1985, compiled in accord with the sequential model of classification of the nine *yanas* or nine vehicles of the Buddhist teachings taught by the Nyingma school of Tibetan Buddhism. The sequence of the teachings in this book thus follows the traditional order of presentation of the oral instructions according to the nine-vehicle system of the gradual path (*lam rim*) teachings of the Nyingma tradition.

In chapters 1 and 2, the teachings begin with biographies of the lineage masters Longchen Rabjam, or "Longchenpa," and Jigme Lingpa, to inspire faith and devotion in disciples. In Nyoshul Khen's presentation of the Buddhist path, the starting point is faith and devotion. Devotion to the spiritual teacher, lineage, and enlightened ones is one of most important themes that run throughout this book from beginning to end and unify the narrative of Rinpoche's teachings.

Next, one's guru traditionally imparts the mind training teachings (*lojong; blo sbyong*), which condense all the Mahayana Buddhist instructions into simple precepts that can be applied in one's practice. These are given in chapter 3, in the teachings contained in Longchenpa's last testament, *Immaculate Light*, which also includes further biographical details at the end of the text in the account of Longchenpa's passing away. Longchenpa is the most revered of the Tibetan masters of Dzogchen, and his last testament is an especially beloved poetic rendition of the essence of the Mahayana path. The Mahayana instructions are the basis for entering into the Vajrayana practices of deity yoga and Dzogchen, and so they come here, preceding the Vajrayana instructions. Khen Rinpoche clarifies the structure and contents of this teaching, elaborates on many of Longchenpa's instructions, and guides us through the text with insights into its meaning. As

Rinpoche points out, Longchenpa's particular presentation of the Mahayana mind training teachings in his last testament is specifically tailored toward those who follow the Dzogchen teachings.

In chapter 4, Rinpoche introduces the cycles of teachings of Longchenpa and Jigme Lingpa, the principal sources of Nyoshul Khen Rinpoche's lineage. These lead into a detailed account of the Longchen Nyingthig, which includes sutra instructions in mind training, but is mainly concerned with the Vajrayana practices of deity meditation and Dzogchen. Thus this chapter is the beginning of the in-depth presentation of the Vajrayana teachings that make up the rest of the book.

In this chapter, Rinpoche first puts Longchenpa's and Jigme Lingpa's writings in the context of the three turnings of the wheel of dharma as taught by the Buddha. Then he introduces the tantra system of the Nyingma, beginning with the original sources of the Indian masters Vimalamitra and Guru Padmasambhava and the traditions of *kahma* and *terma*. Rinpoche introduces the lineages and teachings that Jigme Lingpa received from his masters, upon the basis of which Jigme Lingpa became a *tertön* or treasure revealer. These are followed by a discussion of Jigme Lingpa's terma revelations, the Longchen Nyingthig, including the place that Jigme Lingpa's text *The Lion's Roar* occupies within the Longchen Nyingthig cycle. Thus Nyoshul Khen Rinpoche lays out his lineage in detail, and so the reader now has the foundation of knowing the sources and names of the principal teachings of Nyoshul Khen Rinpoche's instruction and practice lineage.

Next, in chapter 5, "How to Receive Dharma Teachings," the actual instructions of the Vajrayana and Dzogchen begin. Vajrayana instructions always start with the teachings on developing the proper attitude for receiving the practices of deity meditation and Dzogchen, and that is the subject of this chapter. These are the teachings Nyingma lamas traditionally give before offering empowerment into deity yoga and Dzogchen, and thus lead into the teachings on the nature of deities and Dzogchen practice that ensue in the following chapters. This is the natural sequence in which the oral instructions are given. In chapter 5, we have the introductory teachings that precede empowerment, and then the instructions on meditation deities that are given on the basis of empowerment follow in chapter 6.

Hence in chapter 6, "The Meaning of Meditation Deities," we come to the teachings on the meaning of buddhas and deities. Here, Khen Rinpoche unfolds the way to understand wisdom deities from multiple perspectives. Rinpoche's instructions follow and elaborate on chapter 13 of Jigme Lingpa's

Treasury of Precious Qualities, among other sources, so again these explanations are based firmly in the lineage teachings of Nyoshul Khen Rinpoche. This chapter begins with a detailed exposition of the relative and ultimate perspectives on the Buddha and deities. Rinpoche explains the ultimate meaning of Buddha and the ultimate meaning of deities "from the top down," from the dharmakaya perspective of the Dzogchen teachings. This is contrasted with the ordinary or relative understanding of buddhas and deities "from the bottom up," as proceeding from the relative level "upward" to ultimate enlightenment.

After introducing the dharmakaya, sambhogakaya, and nirmanakaya aspects of the Buddha, deities, and buddha fields, Rinpoche teaches some key points of the creation stage and completion stage of deity yoga meditation. This is followed with some insights into how one actually meets the deity. Finally, the last section of this chapter contains advice for retreatants when practicing deity yoga. At the end of the chapter, Rinpoche begins to point out the view of Dzogchen by introducing the illusory nature of phenomena and indicating the true nature of mind. This is because an important aspect of the practice of deity yoga is the meditation on all phenomena as illusory, and because the essential meaning of the completion stage of deity yoga is recognition of the nature of mind. This view is the basis for, and result of, the creation and completion stages of deity yoga.

Nyoshul Khen Rinpoche's teachings on deity yoga lead naturally into the next chapter, chapter 7, which presents Rinpoche's introduction to Longchenpa's Dzogchen text *Resting at Ease in Illusion.* Again, this is the natural progression of the teachings, as deity yoga practice is always combined with meditating on the illusory nature of phenomena in the postmeditation period. Rinpoche continues where he left off at the end of the deity yoga chapter, with more in-depth instructions on the nature of illusion. Such instructions bridge the practice of deity yoga with the practice of Dzogchen, and they are to be applied both in the practice of deity yoga and as the basis for Dzogchen practice; so this is a Dzogchen text that pertains to deity yoga, guru yoga, and Dzogchen practice proper. In the latter part of this chapter, Rinpoche begins to point out the Dzogchen view, leading us toward the instructions on *The Lion's Roar* of Jigme Lingpa.

Next, chapter 8, "The Importance of Mindfulness," lays out some of Rinpoche's key instructions on mindfulness in the form of a short commentary on Rinpoche's spontaneous song of realization "Mindfulness: The Mirror of Mind." Rinpoche explains both the common understanding of mindfulness as well as the extraordinary meaning, where mindfulness refers to recognizing and maintaining the Dzogchen view. This chapter introduces key precepts necessary for understanding the teachings in *The Lion's Roar* commentary, such as the practice of stillness, thought movement, and the noticing of stillness and movement. This practice leads into Dzogchen's main practice of recognizing and sustaining awareness (*rig pa*).

This chapter is also essential at this stage in the unfoldment of the oral instructions, as it introduces *shamatha*, or calm abiding meditation, and *vipasyana*, or insight meditation, which is necessary in order to understand *The Lion's Roar*. Khen Rinpoche will continue on with the explanation of these key points in his introduction to, and commentaries on, *The Lion's Roar* of Jigme Lingpa. There, Rinpoche further elaborates on the importance of unifying calm abiding and insight so as not to fall into errors in practice; and he distinguishes the practice of stillness, movement, and noticing taught in this chapter from the practice of recognizing and sustaining awareness. This chapter introduces mindfulness as the basis upon which one enters into the practice of Dzogchen, with instructions that are necessary in order to understand the teachings that follow in *The Lion's Roar* commentary.

Then we felt it best to have the root text of *The Lion's Roar* come next as chapter 9. This is because in chapter 10 that follows, the root text is broken up by Khen Rinpoche's commentary on it, so it is hard to get a sense of the text as a whole if one has not read it first. Thus, in chapter 9, one is able to read and get a sense and overview of *The Lion's Roar* teaching, which prepares one for the commentary, where the text is unpacked in detail by the guru's oral instructions.

In chapter 10, we arrive at *The Lion's Roar* with Rinpoche's commentary, reaching the final stage of the Nyingma oral instructions on practice, namely, those of Dzogchen, the Great Perfection. *The Lion's Roar* points out awareness, *rigpa,* the true nature of mind, as well as spelling out in detail the potential pitfalls and mistakes in Dzogchen practice. This chapter begins with Nyoshul Khen Rinpoche's introduction, where he references calm abiding and insight meditation, linking this teaching with the chapter on mindfulness, chapter 8, "The Importance of Mindfulness." Rinpoche explains that, in general, the errors in Dzogchen practice occur because of not being able to unite calm abiding and insight, as well as due to intellectualizing the meaning of Dzogchen and falling under the power of various hindrances.

Khen Rinpoche begins to point out the Dzogchen view in much more detail in the introductory section, leading into the profound Dzogchen instructions found in the root text itself. Rinpoche's commentary on *The Lion's Roar* is a unique teaching, and there is not much comparable to it currently available in English. While the pitfalls in recognizing and sustaining the view are explained in a few Mahamudra practice texts published in English, these points are explained differently in the Dzogchen teachings, which teach the eight errors, three diversions, and four ways of straying in relation to the practice of the view.

The teachings on the errors and pitfalls in practice are a major topic in the instructions given orally by Dzogchen masters, and there is a vast body of such oral instructions. Teachings like those in *The Lion's Roar* can be seen to lead one toward the Dzogchen teachings known as "making the distinction" (*shenjay; shan 'byed*), where one distinguishes awareness wisdom from the dualistic mind. The teachings in *The Lion's Roar* are thus an excellent starting point for critiquing and correcting one's practice under the guidance of one's teachers. They offer many entry points for dialogue with one's teachers regarding the correct understanding of the view, meditation, conduct, and result of the practice. Nyoshul Khenpo's commentary presents profound introductions to the Dzogchen view and meditation and offers a great many details about how one goes astray in Dzogchen practice and valuable advice on how to either avoid or resolve these errors, diversions, and ways of straying.

As a fitting conclusion to the book, Nyoshul Khen Rinpoche's spontaneous vajra songs come immediately after *The Lion's Roar*, in chapter 11, "Spontaneous Songs." Thus Rinpoche's teachings conclude with songs of realization that express the accomplishment and culmination of the path laid out by Khen Rinpoche throughout the book, welling up as songs of enlightened realization.

Appendix 1 is *A Wondrous Ocean of Advice for the Practice of Those in Retreat in Solitude*, a text containing Jigme Lingpa's teachings on *ri chos*, literally "mountain dharma," written during his first three-year retreat. It is included as appendix 1 since it does not have any commentary from Nyoshul Khen Rinpoche, though Rinpoche does refer to this text in his account of Jigme Lingpa's biography. Its inclusion is appropriate for a book of instructions given in a retreat setting that were intended to inspire listeners to practice diligently in daily life and in personal meditation retreats.

Finally, appendix 2, "The Tibetan Text of Jigme Lingpa's *The Lion's Roar*," is included for those who read Tibetan, and so that those who are interested can request the reading transmission (*lung*) for the text from their teachers in order to be better able to apply *The Lion's Roar* teachings to their own practice. Traditionally, it is taught that if one wishes to practice a text, it is important to receive the reading transmission. Having the text available, practitioners may also request from their gurus teachings on the text, as it relates to their own practice.

Chokyi Nyima Rinpoche, in his endorsement of this volume, advises us: "Living the life of a hidden yogi, Nyoshul Khen Rinpoche was a master of the teachings of sutra and mantra, both in terms of scholarship and spiritual accomplishment. His teachings are indeed a powerful treasure, yet to truly reap their benefit, one must study them under the guidance of a qualified teacher who holds the lineage. At best, one should endeavor to receive the empowerments, reading transmissions, and oral instructions related to such profound teachings."

As this book contains many oral instructions related to the practice of Vajrayana Buddhist meditation, Chokyi Nyima Rinpoche's advice is quite relevant. The tradition insists that it is impossible to actually understand, experience, and realize these teachings without receiving empowerment (*wang; dbang*), reading transmissions (*lung*), and oral instructions (*men ngak; man ngag*). Translations of Vajrayana oral instructions, such as those in this book, are usually published in restricted volumes requiring that one receive the permission of one's teacher before reading them. Without the guidance of a qualified lineage teacher, one will not be able to avoid the pitfall of intellectualizing the teachings, as outlined in great detail by Nyoshul Khen Rinpoche in his commentary to *The Lion's Roar* of Jigme Lingpa.

This volume of Nyoshul Khen Rinpoche's teachings offers an overview of the entire Nyingma tradition, with abundant material for newer practitioners and experienced yogins alike. It presents the Dzogchen teachings in their traditional context, laying the proper foundation for the practice, and then introduces profound Dzogchen teachings and indispensable instructions for correcting faults and misunderstandings in the practice.

1. LONGCHENPA'S LIFE STORY

LONGCHEN RABJAM (1308–63) was born in Yoru in the eastern part of central Tibet, near to the great Samye monastery built by Guru Padmasambhava in the eighth century. His father was a yogin named Lopon Tenpa Sung and his mother was Sonam Gyen. At the time of his conception, his mother dreamt of a huge lion with the sun and moon upon its forehead, radiating brilliant lights that illumined the entire world. The lion then melted into light, which dissolved into Sonam Gyen and merged with her mind. From that moment on, throughout her pregnancy, she had powerful experiences of bliss, clarity, and nonthought. Her body felt exceedingly light, and her mind became clear and lucid, and during her pregnancy she experienced neither discomfort nor pain. At the time of Longchenpa's birth, the Secret Mantra protectress, the wisdom dakini Mamo Remati, appeared. Lifting up the baby, she declared, "I shall protect him!" A few seconds later, she vanished into space.

From the age of three, Longchenpa began learning to read and write, and by the age of five, he had mastered reading and writing. From then on he gradually began to study all the other fields of learning. At the age of seven, Longchenpa received from his father the Nyingma cycle of treasure teachings and empowerments of the tertön Nyang Ral Nyima Ozer, known as the Eight Commands, Union of All the Sugatas (Kagyay Desheg Dupa; Bka' brgyad bde gshegs 'dus pa). When he was nine years old, his mother died.

Longchenpa's father passed away when he was twelve years old, and soon after he requested novice monk ordination at the ancient Samye monastery founded by Guru Padmasambhava. He received the name "Tsultrim Lodro," or "Disciplined Intelligence," and later he was also known as "Drimey Ozer," meaning "Immaculate Light Rays." From the time he was twelve until he reached the age of twenty-seven, Longchenpa learned the general subjects such as medicine, astrology, logic, and grammar. At the age of nineteen, he began studying for more than six years in the great Kadampa monastic college of Sangphu Neutok. In our present times, only the ruins of the college remain.

Longchenpa received and studied extensively all the teachings of buddhadharma including the Vajrayana teachings of many schools and lineages. As a result of his extensive studies, he became quite erudite and was awarded the name "Longchen Rabjam," meaning "Universally Learned Vast Expanse," or "All-Encompassing Vast Expanse." And as he resided near to the great Samye monastery, Longchenpa also came to be known at this time as "Samye's Recipient of Many Transmissions" (Samye Lungmangpa; Bsam yas lung mang pa). He could recite from memory all relevant quotations from the sutras and tantras, and other lamas could be heard to remark, "Don't even try to debate him; he knows all the scriptures by heart."

At the age of twenty-seven, Longchenpa found himself spontaneously filled with the thought of renunciation. He understood that being extremely learned was not enough and that the time had come to truly put into practice the extraordinary Mantrayana, the Vajrayana or "Vajra Vehicle" of Secret Mantra. So Longchenpa undertook the life of a wandering monk, freely roaming the areas surrounding Lhasa and its environs, carrying only a bag and a small tent. He was following the traditional style of *dra khor* (*grva 'khor*), the way of the pilgrim monk, which was to go on foot from monastery to monastery giving teachings and then engaging in debates and answering questions. When a lama was very successful at this, he would develop a venerable reputation, and would be revered as a living volume of Buddhist scripture. Just like a Tibetan book, such lamas would often wear boards resembling book covers fastened on their front and back that read, "A living volume of the dharma."

During this period of his life, Longchenpa was searching for a Dzogchen guru, and he experienced great hardships in the process. The master Melong Dorje, or "Vajra Mirror," had been highly regarded as a great Dzogchen master of the whispered lineage teachings (*snyan brgyud*) of the Secret Heart Essence of Vimalamitra (Bimai Sangwa Nyingthig; Bi ma'i gsang ba snying thig) tradition, but he had already passed away at this time. However, his heart disciple or dharma heir was Rigdzin Kumaradza Yeshe Shonnu, "The Awareness-Holder, Youthful Wisdom King," who had received all the transmissions of the tantras, commentaries, and pith instructions from Melong Dorje.

The awareness-holder Rigdzin Kumaradza was staying in the upper reaches of the Yarlung Valley at Yartodkyam, in an encampment with a hundred or so students who dwelt there in small tents made of yak felt. It might sound like staying in a mountain valley camp would be a pleasant situation, but living there was far from pleasant. In the winter months, there was deep snow piled high in drifts, and it was bitterly cold and so windy that it was impossible to light fires, imposing considerable hardships. Kumaradza himself also stayed in a one-man tent that was just big enough so that he could sit upright in it.

Rigdzin Kumaradza was teaching the natural Great Perfection according to the Heart Essence of Vimalamitra (Vima Nyingthig; Bi ma snying thig) to his entourage of disciples, who were like a natural mandala. They were all remaining in the meditative stability of the primordial nature (*ye babs kyi bsam gtan*), in the natural condition (*rang bzhin gzhi lugs*) of the Great Perfection, so they were not like ordinary beings. Although from the outside they appeared to be nothing but a camp of beggars, in that encampment was the accomplished and realized teacher Kumaradza who was inseparable from the Indian Dzogchen master Vimalamitra; the teachings were those of the Great Perfection; and there was the pure entourage of disciples practicing Dzogpa Chenpo.

When Longchenpa first met Kumaradza, he requested to receive teachings from him. Kumaradza was delighted and told him, "Last night I had an amazing dream with very auspicious signs that indicated your arrival and our interdependent connection. Then when I saw you, I instantly knew that you would be the holder of my dharma lineage." He asked Longchenpa to stay with him and said that he would teach him.

Throughout this period of his life, Longchenpa underwent all kinds of travails, hardships, and difficulties. For example, in earlier times, in Tibet as it was in India, when one received dharma teachings, it was obligatory to pay a dharma fee (*chos khral*) as an offering for the teachings received. Making offerings is a skillful means for the accumulation of merit, though nowadays in the East, there is no fee for the transmission of the teachings, which rely on the donations of the faithful. Nowadays we offer a mandala for a teaching or empowerment, but in those times, one would offer barley flour or grains. As we see in the life story of Marpa the translator, Marpa had to offer twenty-six yak loads of barley as a dharma fee to receive the Hevajra empowerment, and six loads of barley to receive Vajrayogini from a Sakya lama.

Thus when Longchenpa was with Kumaradza, it was the custom to offer a dharma fee to the guru, and though Longchenpa was extremely learned, he had no wealthy patrons. He was like us here in the retreat center, solely focused on studying the dharma, trying to receive teachings from the lamas and then to genuinely practice. Longchenpa was living like a beggar and had nothing to offer when Kumaradza was giving the Dzogchen empowerments. He stayed outside enduring the heavy snow and harsh elements, with only a burlap sack that he used for a meditation seat in the daytime and as his sleeping bag at night. Apart from his robes and this sack, Longchenpa had nothing; but internally he already possessed the wealth of Dzogpa Chenpo, the Great Perfection.

Of course, the offerings of the dharma fee of grain were not for Kumaradza personally but were to feed the entire gathering. It is like our situation when we enter retreat here, and we need someone to sponsor our living expenses and those of the retreat center, so that we can one-pointedly meditate according to the Dzogchen teachings. Longchenpa mentions in his writings that due to not having his dharma fees, he experienced a lot of difficulty. He thought, "My precious lama is giving teachings, yet I have nothing to offer. It seems I have no merit, so it is better if I leave early tomorrow morning before daybreak. Otherwise, the other students will just be displeased and will give me a hard time if I have nothing to offer for the teachings." But that night, Kumaradza saw through his clairvoyance what Longchenpa was planning. Kumaradza called his attendant and said that he would himself pay the fees of Lama Samyepa, as Longchenpa was commonly known.

When we consider that the humble Longchenpa had to sleep in an old burlap sack in the Tibetan winter, not to mention the hardships of Milarepa, we find that the great practitioners undertook severe difficulties. These days we might have romantic notions and think that it was not so difficult for Longchenpa to live as he did in Rigdzin Kumaradza's encampment. It is easy enough for us to talk about it, but those present had to survive the extreme conditions while practicing ceaselessly the natural state of the Great Perfection. Each day Longchenpa would get in and out of his sackcloth, with no thought as to whether or not he might die from the harshness of the elements. He bore immense hardships in order to receive the Dzogchen teachings and truly put them into practice.

Before we continue with Longchenpa's life story, it is worthwhile at this point to mention that throughout his life, Longchenpa offered many key pieces of advice for present and future disciples. For example, he wrote down three essential points for the benefit of practitioners in the future. Briefly, the three points are:

- to pray to one's spiritual teacher for blessings
- to regard one's teacher as the embodiment of the three jewels, and so pray to the teacher to purify one's obscurations and accumulate merit
- to keep the samayas, the spiritual vows of the Vajrayana teachings

For the first point, it is said that the king of all prayers is to express faith and devotion toward one's spiritual teachers. To understand the life of Longchenpa, it is helpful to know that when Longchenpa was practicing, he made constant, yearning supplications to Kumaradza and to the lineage gurus, diligently engaging his mind in guru yoga practice with fervent devotion (*mos gus drag po*). One day during Longchenpa's six-year retreat, an uncontrived experience of extraordinary devotion arose for him, and he experienced his mind and the wisdom mind of Rigdzin Kumaradza to be inseparably one. This is how Longchen Rabjam attained true realization of the natural state of the Great Perfection.

From that moment on, he was always in meditative absorption (*samadhi; ting nge 'dzin*) throughout all of his activities, whether he was sitting, moving around, or sleeping. Hence, we can understand the great importance Longchenpa gives to the first of his three essential points, which is to have faith and devotion toward one's teachers. This is how we receive the blessings of the guru and lineage gurus, which is the basis for realizing the dharma.

The second point is that one should pray to the guru as the embodiment of the three jewels, and in this way purify obscurations and accumulate merit. As the guru is the basis for accumulating great merit, it is very important to practice guru yoga to accumulate merit and purify all of our obscurations. The guru embodies the entirety of the sources of refuge, the three jewels of Buddha, dharma, and sangha; the three roots of guru, deity, and dakini; and the three kayas or "bodies of enlightenment." Hence, by supplicating and serving the guru, and by practicing dharma, making and visualizing offerings and so on, one accumulates the vast merit needed to attain enlightenment. Likewise, all one's karma, misdeeds, faults, and obscurations are purified through the blessings of the guru. Longchenpa is telling us in both his first and second points that if we wish to gain experience and realization, we should apply ourselves wholeheartedly to the practice of guru yoga.

The third point Longchenpa wrote about was in regard to the possibility of damaging one's *samayas,* the spiritual vows of the Vajrayana tradition of Secret Mantra. Longchenpa tells us in some of his teachings that one day he had an argument with one of his vajra brothers. Quarreling or fighting with one's vajra brothers and sisters is one of the tantric downfalls and will create karmic obscurations in one's mind. So Longchenpa immediately offered a confession and apologized to the vajra brother with whom he had a dispute.

Thereafter, in many of his teachings, Longchenpa mentioned that sometimes, through no fault of our own, there may be people who will dislike us. If we are famous, there may be those who are jealous of us and want to be like us, and who might resent or even denigrate us. Regardless of how others may feel toward us, Longchenpa encourages us not to argue or find fault with our vajra sisters and brothers, since we may be driven by malice, ill will, or bad feelings toward them. He counsels us to keep our spiritual vows well and to avoid conflict with our vajra siblings.

Returning now to the life story of Longchen Rabjam: Once he had been accepted as a disciple, Longchenpa stayed with Kumaradza for six years and received all of the major transmissions of the Dzogchen teachings. In particular, under Kumaradza's guidance, Longchenpa practiced the entire Dzogchen path of the Secret Heart Essence of Vimalamitra, from the foundation practices (*ngondro; sngon 'dro*) all the way up to the main Dzogchen practices of Directly Cutting Through (*trekchod; khregs chod*) and Directly Crossing Over (*thogal; thod rgal*). Kumaradza taught Longchenpa in accordance with the Oral Instructions of Great Experiential Guidance (Mengak Nyongtri Chenmo; Man ngag myong khrid chen mo), which guide the disciple's practice step by step through the stages of experience to realization. Following this tradition, Longchenpa would practice until he was able to truly experience the teachings of view, meditation, and conduct that he received through the great blessings of Rigdzin Kumaradza.

After Longchenpa received the Dzogchen teachings from his guru Kumaradza, Longchenpa set out to accomplish his practice in a six-year retreat at Chimpu, coming from time to time to see Rigdzin Kumaradza for blessings and advice. Later, at the sacred place of Gangri Thodkar, the White Skull Peak Snow Mountain, Longchenpa accomplished the stage of Dzogchen practice known as "consummate awareness" (*rig pa tshad phebs*). At a later time, Longchenpa attained the stage of "exhaustion of all phenomena into dharmata" (*chos nyid zad sa*), the level of the fourth vision according to the path of Directly Cutting Through to Primordial Purity (*ka dag khregs chod*). The uncontrived natural state of the Great Perfection (*rdzogs chen gnas lugs bcos ma ma yin pa*) was born in his mind. Longchenpa became a fully enlightened buddha through the path of Dzogchen, a living embodiment of the dharmakaya buddha Samantabhadra in person.

Once Longchenpa had gained realization through the practice of Dzogchen, at the age of thirty-one, he began to teach dharma, and continued to do so right up to the end of his life at the age of fifty-six. He taught Dzogchen to thousands of fortunate disciples in the regions surrounding Lhasa and the great Samye Monastery, and also in Bhutan. At Bumthang in Bhutan, Longchenpa founded the temple known as Tharpa Ling. It was called "Tharpa Ling," the "Sanctuary of Liberation," because so many beings entered the path to liberation at that holy place. In recent times, Dodrupchen Rinpoche has given many teachings and empowerments from the Heart Essence (Nyingthig; Snying thig) tradition at Tharpa Ling, which is near a village called Samling. All together Longchenpa founded eight places of dharma in Bhutan, and these retreat centers and monasteries are known as the "eight 'Ling' temples." As part of his karmic connection with Bhutan, Longchenpa's later incarnation, the great treasure revealer and tertön king Pema Lingpa, was also born in Bhutan.

After Longchenpa returned to Tibet from Bhutan, he continued to give empowerments and instructions to a great many fortunate beings. During this time he composed a vast array of texts and commentaries for all the schools of Buddhism in Tibet. However, in particular, through his writings, dialogues, and teachings, he preserved the doctrine and practice lineage of Dzogpa Chenpo, the Great Perfection. Among his many enlightened qualities, Longchenpa is regarded as being an emanation of Manjushri, the buddha of wisdom, who came to clarify and preserve the teachings of Dzogpa Chenpo. Once he had returned to Tibet, Longchenpa's main Dzogchen lineage of transmission was passed down through his disciple Khenchen Khyabdal Lhundrub and survives in an unbroken lineage to this day.

Longchen Rabjam passed from this world in 1363 at Samye Chimpu, the forest and retreat center of Guru Padmasambhava and his disciples, in the mountains above the great Samye monastery. At this time Longchenpa requested his students to arrange some offerings and asked to be left alone. When they requested to remain, Longchenpa told them they could stay but that they should not make any fuss and simply practice, as he was about to leave his worn-out illusory body. Then, assuming the dharmakaya posture of the lion, he was liberated into the primordial expanse (*gdod mai dbyings su grol*).

When great masters who have followed the Dzogchen path pass away, they are directly enlightened in the immediacy of the ground (*gzhi thog tu sangs rgyas*). There are two ways that they may demonstrate the attainment of buddhahood. One of these is called "fully manifest buddhahood" (*mngon par rdzogs pa'i sangs rgyas*), and the other is known as "true and complete buddhahood" (*yang dag pa'i sangs rgyas*). There is no difference in quality between these two ways of demonstrating enlightenment at the time of passing away, but they are different in the way they manifest.

Among the two, the former demonstrates many signs and leaves relics for the benefit of beings. The latter is where the master assumes the rainbow body that leaves no relics or remains. Instead of leaving remains, both the coarse impure constituent elements (*khams*) and the subtle pure constituent elements completely dissolve into an adamantine, vajra body of rainbow light, having the nature of vajra wisdom (*ye shes rdo rje'i rang bzhin*). Longchenpa passed away in the former manner, and so he left relics and remains for the benefit and inspiration of his disciples and for the disciples and sentient beings of the future.

Upon Longchenpa's passing into parinirvana, there were all the auspicious signs of the manner of passing known as "fully manifest buddhahood," including rainbows, lights, thunder, earth tremors, and showers of flowers raining from the sky. After his body was cremated, as the sign of passing into the primordial ground, the five kinds of relics (*sku gdung rigs lnga*) were found among the cremation ashes. Among these, there are the tiny jewel-like and pearl-like relics called *ringsel* (*ring bsrel*), and there are the larger remains known as *kudung* (*sku gdung*) or *dungchen* (*gdung chen*). There are five types of the latter, which are different kinds of remains that are known as *shari ram, serri ram, bari ram, nyari ram,* and *churi ram.* These are said to represent the five buddha families, and their presence indicates the master's realization of the five enlightened bodies (*kaya; sku*) and the five primordial wisdoms (*jnana; ye shes*). As well as all five of these types of larger remains, there were countless ringsel relics like tiny indestructible pearls that were found in Longchenpa's cremation ashes after they had cooled.

As a sign that Longchenpa's body, speech, and mind were fully enlightened as the three vajras and inseparable from dharmakaya Samantabhadra, his eyes, tongue, and heart all fused together as one mass, the size of a fist. This holy relic remained unharmed by the fire and was passed down through Longchenpa's disciples and is presently in the possession of the Queen Mother of Bhutan. Also, Longchenpa's skull remained intact after his cremation, producing a yellowish white stone-like holy relic. Thus all the auspicious signs of completely manifest buddhahood were present in the relics and remains of Longchenpa. It was exactly as it is taught in the *Tantra of the Blazing Bodily Remains* (*Ku Dung Bar Wai Gyud; Sku gdung 'bar ba'i rgyud*), one of the seventeen tantras of the Dzogchen Instruction Series (*mengakde; man ngag sde*), which describes the signs found in the cremation relics of one who has attained realization of the Dzogpa Chenpo. This is a brief account of the life and liberation of Longchen Rabjam.

2. JIGME LINGPA'S LIFE STORY

THE SUBLIME BEING Vidyadhara or "Awareness-Holder" Rigdzin Jigme Lingpa (1729–98) was born at Yoru in Tibet into very humble surroundings. It was a time when the view and practice of the Dzogchen teachings were becoming corrupted by intellectual assumptions and speculation. Jigme Lingpa was considered to be an emanation of the Indian Dzogchen master Manjushrimitra, the principal disciple of the original Dzogchen master Garab Dorje. Jigme Lingpa was also the emanation of Longchen Rabjam Drimey Ozer (1308–63). His birth was in accord with a prophecy of Guru Padmasambhava, as we find in this verse in praise of Jigme Lingpa from The Embodiment of the Guru's Realization (Lama Gong Du; Bla ma dgongs 'dus) cycle of treasure teachings (terma; gter ma):

> Omniscient one, treasure trove of great love for beings;
> Emanation of Drimey Ozer,
> Treasury of wisdom mind treasures;
> Sky Yogi of the vast expanse of luminosity,
> I pray to noble Jigme Lingpa.

At the age of six, Jigme Lingpa entered the monastery of Palri Thegchog Ling in southern Tibet at the Chongye valley, near to his birthplace. At Palri he received a general monastic education and entered into the Vajrayana path. At the age of thirteen, he came under the guidance of his accomplished guru Thugchok Dorje Tsal, the son of the great tertön Tsasum Lingpa. From Thugchok Dorje Tsal, Jigme Lingpa received the empowerments and instructions of the treasure cycle Bindu of Liberation: The Natural Freedom of Enlightened Mind (Drol Thig Gongpa Rang Drol; Grol thig dgongs pa rang grol), a terma of Tertön Sherab Ozer (1518–84), who was also known as Drodul Lingpa. This was the tradition followed at Palri Thegchog Ling monastery, and Jigme Lingpa spent twelve years mastering these profound instructions. Apart from studying poetics and practicing the Bindu of Liberation (Drol Thig; Grol thig) teachings, he did not engage in a great deal of study.

At the age of twenty-eight, Jigme Lingpa entered retreat for three years (1756–59) in the vicinity of his monastery at Chongye Palgi Riwo, practicing the Bindu of Liberation cycle of teachings. He writes about his retreat in a text in the treasure cycle revealed by Jigme Lingpa, the Heart Essence of the Vast Expanse (Longchen Nyingthig; Klong chen snying thig). In the Longchen Nyingthig, following the famed Dzogchen instruction text *Supreme Wisdom* (*Yeshe Lama; Ye she bla ma*), there is an advice from the genre known as "Mountain Dharma" (*ri chos*) called *A Wondrous Ocean of Advice for the Practice of Those in Retreat in Solitude* (see appendix 1). It is in this teaching that Jigme Lingpa tells us of his first three-year retreat, mentioning that during those three years he never a spoke a word to anyone. He had only the bare necessities, with just enough food to live on and only sufficient clothing to barely keep him warm.

Jigme Lingpa describes the rhythm of his practice throughout the cycle of day and night, outlining the style of practice he followed. He would begin the day with the preliminaries, supplicating with fervent, intense devotion. Then he meditated on the practice of the yoga of the channels and vital energies (*tsa lung; rtsa rlung*), carrying on to the subsequent sessions of the day where he practiced guru yoga, the creation and completion stages of deity yoga, the yoga of sleep, and the subsidiary yogas.

It was at the beginning of this first three-year retreat, at the age of twenty-eight, that Jigme Lingpa received the terma treasure revelations of the Heart Essence of the Vast Expanse. Having gone to sleep after fervently supplicating Guru Padmasambhava, he entered the luminosity of sleep. Within this, Jigme Lingpa had a vision of flying to the great Boudhanath stupa in Nepal, where he received the terma treasure cycle of the Heart Essence of the Vast Expanse from the dakinis. The entirety of the teachings of the Longchen Nyingthig burst forth within Jigme Lingpa's mind and great wisdom realization blazed.

During and after this first three-year retreat, Jigme Lingpa studied the writings of Longchenpa, such as the Trilogy of Resting at Ease (Ngalso Kor Sum; Ngal gso skor gsum), the Seven Treasuries (Dzo Dun; Mdzod bdun), and the Four Heart Essences (Nyingthig Yabzhi; Snying thig ya bzhi). Through reading all of Longchenpa's key works, Jigme Lingpa realized that Longchen Rabjam was truly an enlightened being. He experienced an overwhelming devotion to Longchenpa, vowing that he would never give up his efforts to practice dharma until he beheld Longchenpa's face, even at the cost of his body and life. Deciding he must accomplish and meet Longchenpa through prayer, supplication, and guru yoga (*lamai naljor; bla ma'i rnal 'byor*), Jigme Lingpa began a second three-year retreat at Samye Chimpu, above the great Samye monastery in Central Tibet. Samye Chimpu is where Guru Padmasambhava and his twenty-five disciples practiced in retreat together, and where disciples of the Indian Dzogchen master Vimalamitra also remained in retreat.

Jigme Lingpa stayed at Chimpu in retreat. He began his retreat in the Upper Cave of Nyang, and then soon moved nearby to a cave known as the "Lower Cave of Nyang." It was the place where the great master Nyang Tingzin Zangpo had practiced as a disciple of the Indian Dzogchen master Vimalamitra. The cave is also known as the "Flower Cave of Great Secrecy" (Sangchen Metog Puk), and Jigme stayed at these for three years in strict retreat.

Jigme Lingpa remained year-round in this cave, which was in fact nothing more than a rocky overhang. As it was not the kind of cave one could walk into and shelter in, Jigme Lingpa erected some thatched walls made from branches and cloth. He said that when it rained, the water would run down, completely soaking the cloth. Jigme Lingpa practiced there for three years, continuously supplicating Longchenpa with fervent, intense devotion (*mogu dragpo; mos gus drag po*). He had the great fortune of having in his possession one of the original "Looks Like Me" (*nga 'dra ma*) statues made in the actual likeness of Longchenpa and blessed by him, which Jigme Lingpa used as a support for his practice.

One day, Jigme Lingpa experienced the first of his three visions of Longchenpa, who appeared above and in front of Jigme Lingpa in the space of the clear sky, wearing the three monastic robes and appearing in perfect form and slightly advanced in age. To finally encounter Longchenpa after many years of devout supplication was to have the deepest wishes of his heart fulfilled, like a trader who finally acquires a long-sought treasure. At this time, Longchenpa spoke to Jigme Lingpa thus: "May the wisdom mind transmission of the meaning to be expressed be transferred. May it be transferred. May the transmission of the words that express be completed. May it be completed!" Through the blessings of this meeting with Longchenpa's wisdom body (*ye shes kyi sku*), countless qualities of Longchenpa's enlightened realization (*dgongs pa*) arose in Jigme Lingpa's mind.

In the second year of the same retreat, Jigme Lingpa remained in retreat in the Lower Cave of Nyang and was blessed with a second vision of Longchenpa. On this occasion, Longchenpa had no particular perceptible form that was visible to Jigme Lingpa. Longchenpa placed a text on Jigme Lingpa's head and handed it to him, saying, "This clarifies the meaning found in my work *The Great Chariot*. You must write a commentary on it, and this will benefit many beings."

The Great Chariot is Longchenpa's vast commentary on his work *Resting at Ease in the Nature of Mind* (*Semnyid Ngalso; Sems nyid ngal gso*). With this second vision of Longchenpa, Jigme Lingpa received the blessings of Longchenpa's speech. As a result, all the subtle knots in his throat chakra were released, and the power of wisdom speech blazed forth. Jigme Lingpa received Longchenpa's blessing to compose works of dharma. In accordance with Longchenpa's wishes, Jigme Lingpa later composed his renowned work *Treasury of Precious Qualities* (*Yonten Dzod; Yon tan mdzod*) to clarify the meaning of *The Great Chariot*.

In the third year of his retreat, Jigme Lingpa had another vision of Longchenpa, who appeared in the form of a youth, about twenty years in age, wearing the robes of a scholar monk and a pandita's pointed hat with long earflaps. With this vision, Jigme Lingpa was blessed with the realization of Longchenpa's wisdom mind, and his mind became one with the enlightened mind of Longchenpa. As a result, the power of Jigme Lingpa's wisdom and intelligence were greatly enhanced, and he spontaneously understood all the sutras and tantras, the tantric commentaries, and the oral instructions.

Jigme Lingpa attained his great realization and accomplishment through practicing guru yoga and receiving blessings. Earlier in Jigme Lingpa's three-year retreat at Chimpu, prior to his three visions of Longchenpa, he received the *Guru Practice of the Sealed Essence* (*La Drub Thigle Gyachen; Bla sgrub thig le'i rgya can*). Jigme Lingpa had a vision of a mandala ritual's being conducted, and the *Sealed Essence* (*Thigle Gyachen; Thig le'i rgya can*) arose in the depths of his heart. We now find this practice, which Jigme Lingpa received through Longchenpa's blessings, in the Longchen Nyingthig cycle of teachings. Jigme Lingpa writes that during this retreat at Samye Chimpu, the meaning of Longchenpa's writings The Three Chariots (Shingta Sum; Shing rta gsum) and the Seven Treasuries arose in his heart. He tells us that as a result, he wrote many key points of instructions, quintessential teachings on view and meditation, and the essentials of practice in brief works. These include *The Lion's Roar That Vanquishes Diversions and Errors* (*Seng ge'i nga ro*), which we will discuss later in our further teachings.

By blessing Jigme Lingpa with the transmission of the *Guru Practice of the Sealed Essence,* Longchenpa is saying, "If there is anyone who wishes to meet me, just as you have, then they may do so through this guru practice of the *Sealed Essence.* By visualizing me and praying to me with fervent devotion, meditating on me as inseparable from Guru Vimalamitra, it will be possible to either see me in actuality, hear my words, or meet me in dreams. By the blessings of any such encounters, the disciple's knowledge will spontaneously increase, and in particular his or her realization of Dzogpa Chenpo will become as vast as the sky."

Generally, if you wish to meditate on a deity such as Kalachakra or Vajra Kilaya, in order to be able to accomplish that deity and attain realization through the practice, you need to first receive the empowerment. Then you must go through all the detailed practices of the development and completion stages. You need to meditate on many different things, and it is a very elaborate process. In contrast to the approach of deity yoga, the "guru practice" (*la drub; bla sgrub*) of guru yoga is a special feature of the approach of Dzogchen, where the guru is considered to be the single "jewel that embodies all." All the sources of refuge such as the three jewels, the three roots, and the three kayas, and all the enlightened ones, are embodied in the form of the guru. This makes the method much simpler, with much less elaborate details and methods.

Devotion is one of the central key points mentioned in the Dzogchen tantras. If one has the kind of faith and devotion whereby one is able to see the guru as the embodiment of all the buddhas, then this approach is very simple but is also the most profound. The *Guru Practice of the Sealed Essence* bestows swift blessings that have the power to grant one realization and enlightenment through guru devotion alone, without going through the complexities of deity yoga practice. This is a unique feature of the ninth vehicle of Dzogchen or Atiyoga, as explained by Khenpo Ngaga, Ngawang Palzang, in his commentary on Patrul Rinpoche's *Words of My Perfect Teacher* (*Kunzang Lamai Zhelung; Kun bzang bla ma'i zhal lung*). Through the blessings of the guru practice, realization can quickly be born in one's mind. The guru practice (*la drub; bla sgrub*) accomplishes the essence of the guru and is an enhancement for all other types of dharma practices. It is also a remedy for all possible obstacles one may face on the spiritual path.

One Kagyu teacher, Gyalwa Yang Gon (1213–87), stated that he did not meditate on the blue Hevajra, which is one of the principle Kagyu deities and the main deity practiced by Marpa, the founder of the Kagyu tradition. He said that neither did he meditate on Green Tara as practiced by the

Kadampa lineage. Rather, through simply endeavoring in the guru practice, by meditating with intense devotion toward his root teacher, all his accomplishments (*siddhi; dngos grub*) and realizations arose. Gyalwa Yang Gon said he had no interest in whether Hevajra is blue or Tara is green, saying, "I have no need to meditate on them, since through meditating solely on my root teacher, praying with devotion, all my realizations were born."

Moreover, Milarepa's disciple Gampopa (1079–1153) said in his biography that during the degenerate times of the future, beings will not have the ability to realize the authentic meaning of Mahamudra. He said that in those times a way to remedy this situation would be to pray one-pointedly to him. Gampopa said that by meeting him through the power of devotion, beings of these times will be able to give birth to the realization of Mahamudra.

Also, the mahasiddha Lama Zhang Rinpoche (1122–93), who was a disciple of Gampopa, said in regard to the instructions for realizing the meaning of Mahamudra: "In Tibet these days, some instructions advise that meditation is to remain in equipoise on emptiness. Some say that meditation is to rest in the clarity of mind, and some say that meditation is to abide in bliss. There are so many different instructions on the ways to meditate. But for me, there is no more profound way to meditate than through devotion (*mogu; mos gus*). Yet these days there are few that believe it is possible to be liberated through the power of devotion."

After completing his retreat, Jigme Lingpa went on pilgrimage around central Tibet to all the holy places of accomplishment, carrying only a small bag and begging for food. In each of these holy places, he meditated and practiced. His conduct was like the words of the early Nyingma master Zurchungpa: "He was like a child of the mountains, wearing mist for clothing." This line from Zurchungpa means that the yogin stays away from towns and keeps to the solitude of the mountains.

Jigme Lingpa had realized the dharmakaya for his own benefit, so there came a time when a portent indicated that the time had come for him to teach the dharma and benefit others. On the tenth day of the monkey month of the male wood monkey year 1764, during the celebration of the feast offering, Guru Rinpoche and a host of dakinis appeared to Jigme Lingpa in person. With the compassionate blessings of Guru Rinpoche and the gathering of auspicious circumstances, such as the five certainties of sacred place, teacher, entourage, teaching, and time, Jigme Lingpa realized that the time was now ripe for him to teach the Longchen Nyingthig cycle. Jigme Lingpa first codified the outer guru practice *Gathering of the Awareness-Holders* (*Ladrub Rigdzin Dupa; Bla sgrub rig 'dzin 'dus pa*), and then gradually wrote out and arranged the sadhanas of the three roots and the various other practices.

Jigme Lingpa had four principal disciples, his heart sons, who disseminated his teachings throughout Tibet. They were the four named "Jigme" or "Fearless": Dodrub Jigme Trinlay Ozer, Trama Lama Jigme Gyalwai Nyugu, Lama Jigme Kundrol Namgyal, and Lama Jigme Ngotsar Tenzin. Thus the Longchen Nyingthig tradition became renowned throughout Tibet. The royal family of Derge in East Tibet sponsored the publishing of Jigme Lingpa's collected works. They also sponsored the publication of the Collected Tantras of the Nyingma (Nyingma Gyubum; Rnying ma rgyud 'bum), which Jigme Lingpa had collected, compiled, and introduced, and the publication of which he oversaw. The woodblocks for these printings still exist in the Derge Printing House to this day, where many great works have survived.

Finally, Jigme Lingpa settled in Tsering Jong, in the Donkhar valley at Chongye in southern Tibet, where he established a temple and continued to impart the nectar of hidden instructions to many fortunate beings. Apart from all the writings within Jigme Lingpa's treasure cycle of the Heart Essence of the Vast Expanse, he also composed many other works. These include the *Treasury of Precious Qualities* and the teaching known as *Replies to Questions on Meditation* (*Gom Chok Drilen; Sgom phyogs' dri lan*), which is a collection of advice Jigme Lingpa gave to his disciples on meditation and practice. There is also the *Collection of Talks* (*Tam Tsok; Gtam tshogs*), a collection of general advice he offered to various people, and the *Collection of Eulogies* (*Tod Tsok; Stod tshogs*), which is a collection of praises to the Buddha, Longchenpa, and others. In total, there are nine volumes in Jigme Lingpa's collected works.

At Tsering Jong, Jigme Lingpa mainly taught his own terma revelations and writings from the Longchen Nyingthig cycle, as well as the works of his omniscient father Longchen Rabjam; together, Longchenpa and Jigme Lingpa are known as "the omniscient father and son." Jigme Lingpa maintained a life of simplicity and imparted his teachings to the constant stream of fortunate beings that came into his presence. Among his extensive activities, Jigme Lingpa had great enthusiasm for saving the lives of animals, those animals who were to be slaughtered or who had been trapped by hunters.

As the time of Jigme Lingpa's death approached, his close disciples asked if they could be of any assistance at the time of his death. He replied, "I need no help as I am going directly to the Lotus Light. However, you can whisper in my ear and tell me, 'Now your time has come to go to the Copper-Colored Mountain.' That is all you need to do." In 1798, having reached the age of seventy and served the dharma and countless beings, Jigme Lingpa left his body. Amid miraculous signs, he departed for the Lotus Light of Chamara, the Copper-Colored Mountain (Zangdog Palri; zangs mdog dpal ri), the pure realm of Guru Padmasambhava. And so Jigme Lingpa passed beyond all sorrow into enlightenment, leaving the precious remains of his body at Tsering Jong.

3. COMMENTS ON LONGCHENPA'S FINAL TESTAMENT, *Immaculate Light*

LONGCHEN RABJAM, whose name means "All-Encompassing Vast Expanse," and who was also known as "Drimey Ozer" or "Immaculate Light Rays," was no ordinary person. He came to this world to spread the teachings of Dzogpa Chenpo, the Great Perfection. From the vast expanse of his wisdom mind, which was one with dharmata or "the true nature of all phenomena," his physical body manifested as a display of wisdom in order to benefit sentient beings. Then finally, at the end of his life, his wisdom mind dissolved back into the original ground, free of fixation (*thog ma'i gzhi 'dzin pa med pa*).

Longchen Rabjam is generally known as "Longchenpa," meaning "Vast Expanse." He transmitted his wisdom realization of the Great Perfection to his main disciples, including Tulku Dragpa Ozer and Khenchen Khyabdal Lhundrub. The transmission of Longchenpa's special Dzogchen practice lineage, which is known as the Hearing Lineage of Great Experiential Guidance (Nyengyu Nyongtri Chenmo; Snyan brgyud myong khrid chen mo), or as the Oral Instructions of Great Experiential Guidance (Mengak Nyongtri Chenmo; Man ngak myong khrid chen mo), or simply as the Great Experiential Guidance (Nyongtri Chenmo; Myong khrid chen mo), has been passed from teacher to student in an unbroken tradition right down to our present times.

To represent Longchenpa's body, his disciple Kunga Rinchen made thirteen "replica" statues of Longchenpa, intended to resemble him, and these were blessed by Longchenpa himself. In addition, all the five types of precious relics (*dung; gdung*) and many small pearl-like relics (*ringsel; ring bsrel*) were collected from Longchenpa's remains and have been passed down through the generations to bestow blessings on practitioners.

To represent his speech, Longchenpa wrote such works as the Seven Treasures (Dzo Dun; Mdzod bdun) and the three trilogies: the Trilogy of the Innermost Essence (Yang Thig Kor Sum; Yang thig skor gsum), the Self-Liberation Trilogy (Rang Drol Kor Sum; Rang grol skor gsum), and the Trilogy of Resting at Ease (Ngalso Kor Sum; Ngal gso skor gsum). Before his passing, he wrote his last testament, *Immaculate Light,* in verse to show future practitioners how to reflect and practice, urging them not to be attached to this life and not to cling to existence in the three realms of samsara.

In order for beings of the present and future to gain the same realization as Longchenpa, they have the opportunity to be blessed by the emanations of his body, speech, and mind, which have just been mentioned. When a realized being such as Longchenpa passes into the peace of nirvana, beings who possess sufficient spiritual merit are able to meet his wisdom body. Now, more than 670 years since Longchenpa passed away, there are lamas who have had visions of him, which were accomplished through praying to Longchenpa.

Although his physical body dissolved, Longchenpa's wisdom mind continues to remain as the dharmakaya vajra wisdom body (*chos sku ye shes rdo rje'i sku*). If we pray to him from this world—or even from the moon, or from anywhere, as his wisdom body is not subject to distances far or near—we will receive his blessings. Longchenpa attained the deathless state of the youthful vase body (*gzhon nu bum sku*), the realization of dharmakaya enlightenment, which is very different from the state in which an ordinary person dies.

Longchenpa transmitted the Hearing Lineage of Great Experiential Guidance (Nyengyu Nyongtri Chenmo; Snyan brgyud myong khrid chen mo) to his disciples. Thenceforth, this lineage has been passed down by imparting, in actual experience, the naked wisdom of empty awareness (*rig stong ye shes rjen pa*) from teacher to student. This has continued in an unbroken transmission to this present day. If this transmission of Longchenpa's wisdom mind were to be broken, the direct transmission would be lost. We would be left only with theoretical knowledge.

We cannot discover the self-originating wisdom of the Great Perfection (*rdzogs pa chen po'i rang byung ye shes*) by searching through books. As this is so, each lineage holder must have the power and blessings that arise from direct realization. Someone who truly has the experiential understanding of the Great Perfection can convey this experience to another, rather like handing an object from one person to another. When the transmission of the realization of the wisdom mind (*thugs kyi dgongs pa*) is broken, then this is the end of the Dzogchen teachings in this world. There are beings up to this present time who have received the transmission of realization of Longchenpa's wisdom mind and have established it through their own direct experience. The lineage of the practice for accomplishing this is unbroken. Those who have realized it are the regents of Longchenpa's wisdom mind.

Now we are receiving Longchenpa's last testament, known as *Immaculate Light* (*Drimay Oed; Dri med 'od*). It is therefore important that we have faith in Longchenpa, who left these words for the sake of his present and future disciples. Some weeks before his passing, Longchenpa told his attendant Gyalsey Zopa to bring a pen and paper, and he dictated these verses. Longchenpa said that this advice was for future generations, for those who follow the Buddha's teachings in general, and for those connected to the Dzogchen tradition in particular.

The last testament of Longchen Rabjam, *Immaculate Light,* is found in Longchenpa's Innermost Essence of the Dakini (Khadro Yangthig; Mkha' 'gro yang thig) collection, one of the three volumes of the Trilogy of the Innermost Essence (Yang Thig Kor Sum; Yang thig skor gsum). As the Victorious One, Longchenpa, was about to leave his body and pass into nirvana, he wrote this text as an encouragement, as a reminder to engage in practice, and as support for practice. This advice contains teachings on the impermanence of all compounded things and on the nature of the three realms of samsara as suffering. It also offers us the advice to abandon all worldly activities and to dedicate our life to meditation and spiritual practice.

As is explained in Longchenpa's *Resting at Ease in Illusion* (*Gyuma Ngalso; Sgyu ma ngal gso*), all phenomena pertaining to the ground, path, and fruition of the three realms of samsara are in fact illusory. Hence, the way we should listen to this teaching is with the view that the three realms of samsara do not truly exist. First, on the level of the ground, samsara does not truly exist; then in between, while we are on the path, it also does not truly exist; and finally, at the time of fruition, samsara does not truly exist. Whatever appears to our senses is like the experience in a dream, like an illusion, devoid of any inherent existence. With this perspective, therefore, we can see that samsara's very nature is suffering; it is a vicious cycle of sorrow. Worldly activities are ultimately futile and have no essential existence.

Longchenpa also takes the opportunity in his last testament to point out dharmata. Dharmata is the nature of the ground (*zhi; gzhi*), which we must understand as a basis for receiving the Dzogchen teachings. So in the beginning, we analyze dharmata, "the true nature of all phenomena," until an intellectual understanding of it arises in our mind. Otherwise, under the power of our habitual delusions, this building we are in appears to be solid and real. Indeed, we believe that whatever we perceive is stable and enduring. Then we become attached to these objective phenomena.

So first we need to think and listen with this point of view in mind, even though we may not fully understand at this stage. Based on this understanding, we will be able to gain a firm conviction in the truth of the words of our own teachers. Without this understanding, we will continue to misguidedly believe that our deluded perceptions are real and permanent, which only prevents us from gaining true understanding.

Now let's begin with the final testament of Longchen Rabjam, *Immaculate Light*.

> Homage to all sublime beings endowed with great compassion.
> I pay homage to those who are like the excellent sun, supreme and
>   brilliant.
> By the power of your compassion, you exhibit manifold displays,
> Unfolding activity and gazing upon all beings
> While remaining in the primordial ground expanse (*gdod ma'i
>   gzhi dbyings*).

Longchenpa pays homage to the holy beings, such as the primordial Buddha Samantabhadra, and to all his teachers.

> Homage to the one who, upon fulfilling his destiny,
> Traveled to Kushinagar,
> The holy and supreme city,
> To tame those who cling to the permanence of things.

Here Longchenpa pays homage to the Buddha Shakyamuni, who performed the twelve great deeds and finally passed into nirvana in Kushinagar, thus demonstrating the nature of impermanence.

> Having understood the nature of samsara,
> And that worldly things are futile,
> Now I am casting off my transient, illusory body.
> Listen as I impart this advice, which alone is of benefit.

Now Longchenpa declares his intention to leave behind his transitory, illusory body and exhorts practitioners to listen to his advice and take it to heart.

> Believing that this life is real, you are deceived again and again
> By its transitory, futile nature.
> Realizing with certainty that it is not to be relied upon,
> From today onward, practice the sacred dharma.

If we believe in the appearances of this life, we will find no certainty, as there are so many deceptions in our experience. Understanding this life's impermanent and ultimately futile nature, we should not be attached to this lifetime but should strive day and night to practice the dharma.

> Friends are not forever;
> Like guests they gather for a while and then part.
> So cut emotional ties to your illusory companions
> And practice the sacred dharma that brings you lasting benefit.

Our spouses, parents, and acquaintances are all transient guests, like visitors who appear in the three realms of samsara the way people meet and part in a large city. Therefore, Longchenpa urges us not to be attached to the illusory appearance of friends and companions, but to focus on the dharma and practice meditation.

> Accumulated and hoarded, wealth is just like honey;
> You have toiled for it, but it will be enjoyed by others.
> So while you have the chance, accumulate the merit of generosity,
> And thus make ready the provisions needed for the next life.

No matter how wealthy we are and how many possessions we may have accumulated, once we die, all of these things pass out of our dominion and into the hands of others. In addition, while we are alive, we experience threat and harm from enemies who would usurp our wealth and from thieves who would steal our possessions. This is comparable to the great effort bees expend to make honey, only to have it taken from them for others to enjoy. Longchenpa urges us not to be attached to wealth and possessions, but rather to dedicate our lives to practicing the dharma.

> Your well-constructed homes are perishable by nature and are
>   merely on loan to you.
> When your time comes, you cannot remain there.
> So give up your clinging to the bustle of busy places,
> And from now on rely upon a place of solitude!

No matter how wonderful and comfortable we make our home—even if it is like a divine palace—it is still really only something that we have borrowed for a time. When we die, we cannot take it with us, so ultimately it really isn't so important. And up until we die, our home and property can cause us a great deal of strife from enemies, competitors, and many other things. As a result of all these kinds of problems, we cannot really completely enjoy being there, since there is still a sense of unease within us. Therefore, we should give up thinking about enjoying our home, and abandon all attachments and aversions to home and community. In an isolated place of meditation blessed by the former buddhas, we should endeavor to practice the dharma.

> Likes and dislikes are akin to children's games.
> They are a blazing inferno of futile attachments and aversions.
> So abandon all your quarrels and enmities,
> And from now on subdue your own mind!

We indulge in loving or unkind feelings, in likes and dislikes. Yet all thoughts and emotions toward our worldly companions are like viewing the spectacle of children at play. All of our preferences are unreliable and cause us to accumulate the karma of meaningless attachment and aversion. We need to give up all strife and hostility and instead without delay subdue our own mind and practice the dharma.

> Deeds are futile and illusionary;
> However much you strive, in the end they bring you no reward.
> So abandon the activities of this life, all worldly concerns,
> And from now on seek the path to liberation!

All our worldly activities are actually empty, like the illusions created by a magical illusionist. However long we may persist in these illusions, whether they last only briefly or for a long period, in the end we still find no reward in them. Let us give up our worldly activities and seek the path to liberation, endeavoring with diligence in spiritual practice.

> Having obtained this favorable body,
> Like a precious boat it grants the power to liberate you from
>   the ocean of sorrow.
> Hence, cast off laziness, indolence (*snyoms las*), and discouraged
>   indifference (*sgyid lug*),
> And from now on develop the vigor (*stobs*) of diligence.

Just as a boat can transport us across the seas, in the same way this precious human life gives us the opportunity to cross the ocean of samsara and reach the city of liberation and attain buddhahood. Let us not be indolent and idle, but always practice the dharma with diligence.

> The holy lama is your escort through frightening places,
> A guide who protects you from worldly foes.
> Effortlessly expressing great reverence with your three doors,
> Venerate and rely upon him from now on!

A spiritual teacher is a guide who escorts us and delivers us from fear of the suffering of the three realms. We need to venerate (*mchod*) and rely on our teacher and devote ourselves wholeheartedly to the dharma.

> Profound advice is like ambrosial medicine,
> The supreme remedy for the malady of afflictive emotions.
> By relying on it and becoming well trained in it,
> Master your emotions from now on!

The sacred dharma is like medicinal nectar, and we should accept this precious medicine from our teacher and endeavor in dharma practice.

> The pure three trainings, like a wish-fulfilling jewel,
> Are the excellent path that brings you happiness in this life and
>   the next,
> As well as the ultimate happiness of attaining the sacred peace
>   of enlightenment.
> So let your mind rely upon them from now on!

The three higher trainings of the path of the sacred dharma are ethical discipline (*shila; tshul khrims*), concentration (*samadhi; ting nge 'dzin*), and intelligence (*prajna; shes rab*). They are like a wish-fulfilling jewel, for in this life and the next they will cause us to attain the joy of liberation. Thus we need to apply ourselves immediately to the wish-fulfilling jewel of the three higher trainings without delay and give up laziness and indolence.

> Hearing a variety of teachings is like being given a precious
> lamp
> That removes ignorance and illuminates the path to liberation.
> Opening your wisdom eye, you shine with the light of benefit
> and well-being.
> So from now on, be impartial and free from bias.

Hearing a wide range of teachings is like a precious lamp, like the sun or the moon that has the power to remove darkness. The manner of eliminating the darkness of ignorance is to train oneself in the vast and profound hearing and contemplation of the buddhadharma.

> Excellent contemplation is like a skilled goldsmith;
> It clears away all your misconceptions and doubts.
> So through the intelligence that stems from reflection,
> Assimilate and master it from now on!

Next, in relation to view, meditation, conduct, and fruition, the Victorious One, Longchenpa, teaches us thus:

> The nature of meditation is like tasting nectar.
> Meditating on the meaning of hearing and contemplation,
> afflictive emotions are cured.
> Crossing the ocean of existence, you reach the shore of
> the essence.
> Meditate in the deep forest from now on!

> The view is by nature like the immaculate space,
> Free of all concepts of high and low, without limits or bias,
> Dimensionless, inexpressible by thought or word.
> Find a way to realize this from now on!

Meditation is by nature like the mountains and oceans,
Without fluctuations, transitions, and changes, limpid and
    untarnished.
Pacifying all concepts and distractions,
Meditate exactly like this from now on!

Conduct is by nature like a wise person
Who knows the exact time and most opportune way to help.
Since obstacles, accepting and rejecting, affirming and negating,
    are illusory,
Liberate subject-object fixation from now on!

Fruition is by nature like a ship's captain discovering treasure;
Your own spiritual wealth will spontaneously benefit others.
Naturally at ease, without hope or fear,
Try to acquire this from now on!

Regarding view, meditation, conduct, and fruition, it is said that the view is like space; meditation is like the ocean; conduct is like a wise person; and the fruition is like a wish-fulfilling jewel. We should rely on view, meditation, and conduct as Longchenpa exhorts us and apply ourselves to training in the methods that benefit ourselves and others.

The nature of mind is the dharmadhatu, like space,
Since the nature of space is akin to the meaning of the innate
    nature of mind,
Ultimately nondual and perfectly equalized.
Realize this with certainty from now on!

Phenomena in their diversity are like reflections in a mirror.
Apparent yet empty, the "empty" is not something separate
    and distinct [from appearances].
How delightful to be free of judging them as either identical
    or separate.
Know this with certainty from now on!

The grasped object and the grasping subject are dreamlike.
Though in truth they are nondual, habitual tendencies create
    dualistic perception.

> Moreover, one's mental designations are empty of self-nature.
> Understand nonduality from now on!

> Samsara and nirvana are by nature like a magical display.
> Though things appear as good and bad, in essence they are
>   equivalent.
> All is unborn and has the nature of space.
> Understand this with certainty from now on!

All phenomena in samsara and nirvana—within the sky of our mind's nature—are like reflections in a mirror. Whatever appears is no more real than children's games. All things are like apparitions, so we shouldn't be attached or cling to them! The view is like the vast space of the infinite sky, without limits or extremes of duality. We must not fall into duality, but within the great equality of the dharmadhatu, rest in the meditative equipoise of the view.

> Deluded appearances, happiness and sorrow, are all like
>   phantoms.
> Although virtuous and negative causes and results arise
>   individually,
> Their nature is unborn, and their essence is without transitions
>   and transformations.
> Understand this with certainty from now on!

> All mentally labeled phenomena are like children's games.
> In reality they do not exist, but they are differentiated by thoughts,
> And there is clinging to good and bad, or to one's individual
>   biased beliefs.
> Understand the equalized sameness [of everything] from now on!

Happiness, sorrow, good and bad—all phenomena in the three realms of samsara are deluded appearances, like objects in a dream. In dreams we feel that we ourselves and everything else are all real, solid, and substantial. But we should not cling to the dream as being true, nor should we be attached to it. Without clinging with bias to whatever appears in our mind, we should remain in the realization of unbiased equality (*phyogs med mnyam par nyid kyi dgongs pa la gnas*).

In brief, our perceptions (*nangwa; snang ba*) and thinking process (*bsam blo*) are very limited. We see our world as something huge, and we think it is permanent and stable, indestructible like a diamond, immovable like a great mountain. But in fact this way of thinking is only our concepts about it. From the ultimate point of view, there are infinite worlds filling limitless space. They are all like illusions in a dream; they arise due to circumstances but are neither permanent nor stable. Therefore, in order to understand the lack of true existence of the phenomena to which we are so attached, we need to have a vast, open mind.

Moreover, we who perceive everything as being real are ourselves not in the least bit real or permanent; we too are like an illusion or a dream. Both the objects of our perceptions and ourselves as the perceiver or subject have an illusory nature. From the viewpoint of a sublime being, the infinite myriad appearances of the universe are perceived as easily fitting on the top of a tiny particle; this is the actual size they perceive our universe to be!

In other words, the natural state (*nay lug; gnas lugs*) of the Great Perfection is vast, so vast that a being of lesser capacity, one with less development of intelligence and faith, is unable to embrace this vastness. Thus Dzogpa Chenpo, the Great Perfection, is the practice for beings of superior capacity. It is as vast as the open space of the sky. That is why it is called "Dzogpa Chenpo," the "Great Perfection" or "Great Completeness."

This has all been in relation to the view. The subsequent verses relate to the ten perfections of a bodhisattva.

> Furthermore, generosity is like a precious treasure,
> And the cause for ever-increasing, inexhaustible riches.
> So, to the lesser, middling, and superior fields of merit,[2]
> Give what is suitable from now on!
>
> Immaculate discipline is like a fine chariot,
> The vehicle to carry you to the city of higher destinies and the
>   excellence of enlightenment.
> Practicing self-restraint and gathering virtuous actions for
>   beings' benefit,[3]
> Let your mind rely on discipline right now!
>
> Patience is like a supreme, imperturbable ocean.
> To remain unshaken by harm is the greatest spiritual challenge.

To be able to willingly accept suffering, and [to cultivate] the
    mind of compassion,
Become acquainted with patience from now on!

Diligence is like a great blazing fire,
Destroying all undesirable things, totally delighting in virtue.
So without discouraged indifference, indolence, or laziness,
Follow the path to liberation from now on!

Immovable meditative stability is like supreme Mount Meru,
Focused, unmoving, and undistracted by objects.
Whatever the meditation, nothing else disturbs it.
From now on let your mind become accustomed to it!

Vast transcendent intelligence is like the orb of the sun,
Dispelling the darkness of ignorance and illuminating the holy
    dharma,
Cultivating the sublime land of liberation and drying up the
    ocean of faults.
So develop it from now on!

Skillful means is like a sea captain guiding one to treasures,
Carrying beings across the ocean of suffering to the land of great
    bliss,
Where they attain the supreme three kayas[4] and spontaneously
    fulfill the two aims.
So benefit others with skillful means from now on!

Great strength is like a brave warrior defeating his enemies,
Destroying the hordes of defilements and setting you on the
    path to enlightenment.
Since it completes the accumulation of merit without obstacles,
Let your mind rely on it from now on!

Aspirational prayer (*smon lam*) is like a supreme wish-fulfilling
    jewel.
All wishes are spontaneously granted, and great bliss
    automatically flourishes.

One's mind is peaceful, one's aspirations fulfilled.
So pray with powerful waves of blessing (*rlabs chen*) from now on!

Primordial wisdom is like rain clouds gathered in the sky.
Beneficial rain falls from the clouds of meditative absorption and
    perfect recollection,
Propagating crops of virtue for all beings.
Endeavor to attain it from now on!

While remaining in the natural state of the view, we should perform gen-erosity, maintain discipline, practice patience, strive with diligence, remain in meditative stability, and actualize transcendent intelligence; these are the six perfections (*paramita; phar phyin*). Then, through skillful means, strength, and aspirational prayer, we progress higher and higher until we reach the city of primordial wisdom. These are the ten qualities Longchenpa exhorts us to develop. We must devote ourselves to our practice!

Now, the following verses relate further to these ten perfections of a bodhisattva, which are categorized either as belonging to the aspect of skill-ful means (*upaya; thabs*) or transcendent intelligence (*prajna; shes rab*).

Skillful means and transcendent intelligence are like a fine vehicle.
One neither falls into worldly existence nor into the peace of
    nirvana.
One accomplishes the twofold aim for oneself and for others.
Completing the five paths, the three kayas are spontaneously
    present.
So strive to practice them from now on!

The factors of enlightenment are like an excellent highway,
The route traversed by all buddhas of the past and future,
Encompassing the four foundations of mindfulness[5] and the
    thirty-seven factors.
Dedicate yourself to meditating on them from now on!

Skillful means and wisdom and the thirty-seven factors of enlightenment pertain to the five paths or stages of the Mahayana vehicle. Following this great highway, we must devote ourselves to practice now.

Now, the subsequent verses relate to the four immeasurable thoughts.

Furthermore, love is like good parents,
Bestowing compassion unceasingly upon their children, the beings
    of the six realms.
By serving others with such great love, benefit always ensues.
So let your mind rely upon love from now on!

Compassion is like a bodhisattva, a child of the victorious ones,
Who feels the pain of all beings as if it were his own.
Wishing them to be free of it, wear the armor of effort.
Let your mind rely upon compassion from now on!

Empathetic joy is like the lord of a noble family,
Who delights in the good deeds of others
And rejoices for their sake.
Become supremely accustomed to empathetic joy from now on!

The nature of equanimity is like level ground,
Free from torment, free from attachment and aversion to those
    near and far,
Always abiding in evenness and great bliss.
Become naturally accustomed to this from now on!

The two facets of bodhicitta are like a holy leader,
A guide to take you to the all-virtuous land of liberation.
Unwearied by worldly existence, serving others perfectly,
Cultivate these again and again from now on!

Devotion (*mos pa*) is like a great oceanic reservoir,
Filled with all that is good,
Always of a single taste as waves of faith well up unfailingly.
Let your mind rely upon it from now on!

Dedication is like an inexhaustible sky treasury.
Dedicating [merit] in the dharmadhatu, it never diminishes but
    only increases.
In the single taste of dharmakaya, the rupakaya bodies are
    spontaneously present.
Dedicate within the purity of the three spheres[6] from now on!

Rejoicing is like the realm of space,
Bringing limitless nonconceptual merit,
Free of covetousness, unwavering, and utterly pure.
Constantly rely upon it from now on!

We must practice the four immeasurables of compassion, love, empathetic joy, and equanimity; as well as bodhicitta, devotion to the dharma, the dedication of merit toward perfect enlightenment, and rejoicing in this; and try as much as possible to be unattached to the activities of this life.

The subsequent verses teach us how to meditate with mindfulness (*dran pa*), attentiveness (*shayzhin; shes bzhin*), and conscientiousness (*bag yod*).

Mindfulness, moreover, is like a virtuous hook
That catches the crazed rampant elephant of the mind,
Leading it away from all faults and toward what is
   virtuous.
Rely on this from now on!

Attentiveness is like an undistracted watchman
Who affords the thief of nonvirtue no opportunity,
And protects the supreme wealth of virtue.
Let your mind rely on it with certainty from now on!

Conscientiousness is like a well-constructed moat,
Which prevents brigand bands of afflictive emotions from
   striking.
It leads an army to victory over the foes of karma.
Strive to guard your mind from now on!

We must keep the virtuous practices of love, compassion, rejoicing, and so forth, in our minds. Mindfulness is like a hook that can subdue the wild elephant of mind, and attentiveness is like a guard who protects the wealth of our virtuous practice. So we should never separate from them. In essence, we must always practice with mindfulness, attentiveness, and conscientiousness.

Faith, moreover, is like a fertile field,
Granting all wishes and yielding the harvest of enlightenment,

Thus creating happiness and continual benefit.
So let your faith develop and increase from now on!

Generosity is like an exquisite lotus pond,
Attracting the sacred and delighting beings,
Rendering material objects fruitful, and wealth useful.
So give joy to others from now on!

Pleasing speech is like the drumbeat of the gods,
Captivating beings, agreeable in every way.
Since it subdues and delights sentient beings,
Offer them praise to delight them from now on!

Peaceful conduct is like a holy sage
Who halts nonvirtue and increases the faith of beings.
Giving up hypocrisy, abiding in natural serenity,
Engage in perfect conduct from now on!

The sacred dharma is like a mighty sugata,[7]
In harmony with all, yet transcending all,
Equal to all, yet unlike anything.
Let your mind rely on the dharma from now on!

This body of freedoms and opportunities is like an illusory house,
Which appears and exists for an uncertain duration.
Since its nature is to form and then disintegrate, there is no
    time in this life to waste.
Remember this constantly from now on!

The above six verses refer to six means to attract disciples, such as speaking pleasantly without anger or pride, that naturally bring benefit to disciples and to ourselves. When we act in a harmonious way in accord with the dharma, such as giving gifts and so on, this will benefit both ourselves and others. This is how we will be able to avoid actions that are contrary to the dharma.

Wealth is like fleeting autumn clouds.
The nature of possessions is to decline,

They have no true essence at their core.
Realize this with certainty from now on!

All beings are ephemeral, like past and future guests.
The former generations have already gone, as in time the younger
   generations will.
After one hundred years, all those presently alive will have
   disappeared.
Realize this with certainty right now!

The experience of this life is like today's daytime;
The bardo appearance is like tonight's dream time;
The next life is like tomorrow, which will soon be here.
Practice the holy dharma from now on!

This human body is like an illusory house. Our life is impermanent, no
matter how long we live. Our wealth and possessions are like clouds in the
sky; there is no certainty how long they will last . . . until tomorrow, or
maybe the day after? Who knows? All beings in this world are like guests.
Those who have already passed were like guests, those who are present now
are like guests, and those who will come in the future will be like guests. No
one of them is in any way permanent or stable. So as they cannot be relied
upon, we must devote ourselves to the practice of dharma.

Whether our life is short or long, happy or sad, it will pass. The experiences of this life are just like a single day. Then, after we die, the bardo[8]
state is like tonight's dream. Whether our dream experiences are good or
bad, they will all quickly pass; not even one will remain. And the next life
is like tomorrow, without any permanence, stability, or certainty. This life,
the bardo, and the next life are just like the experiences of a mere two days.
Since there is neither permanence nor stability in what we experience, we
must practice to "capture the citadel of awareness," to achieve stability in
awareness, which is permanent and stable.

Thus I have shown [the nature of] all things through examples.
Now I have one further exhortation for you, my devotees:
As the nature of all composite things is to fall apart,
Likewise I shall not remain; I am departing to the land
   of liberation.

Since samsaric phenomena cannot be relied upon in any way,
Capture the permanent domain of the unborn dharmakaya!

The appearances of this world are illusions that deceive you,
Deceptive in nature like a flirtatious person.
Since they remove you from virtue and increase your emotional
    afflictions,
Keep well away, and practice the sacred dharma!

However wealthy you may be, without contentment you are poor.
A greedy mind's desires can never be fulfilled.
Contentment is the greatest of riches.
Having just a little, your mind is overwhelmed with happiness.

As alcohol and lovers are the source of afflictive emotions,
Abandon the mind that craves and obsesses over them.
Emulating the way of the sages,
Meditate in solitude and discover peace!

With no time to lose, focus solely on virtue, day and night.
Give up your faults, and do what is beneficial.
In keeping with these words,
Without being distracted for a moment, practice the dharma.
So that you have no regrets at death, do what will benefit your
    future from now on!

As the time was approaching for Longchenpa's departure to the dharma-kaya land of liberation, the peaceful dharmakaya, the youthful vase body, the pure realms, he leaves this testament for future beings who have not been able to meet him. As Longchenpa exhorts us, we must devote ourselves to practicing the dharma!

Longchenpa teaches us here that worldly things do not last. Even if we are the wealthiest person in the world, if we lack contentment we are like a beggar. Contentment is the greatest wealth. We can use whatever wealth we have to carry out positive activities and practice the dharma.

Those who drink too much alcohol and are always drunk obviously cannot practice meditation. Longchenpa also advises us not to go chasing after lots of men or women, because that will lead to quarrels and strife that will destroy our practice of meditation. We should be content with the partner we have. If we behave carelessly and frivolously, this will be an obstacle to practice. Hence we should not go stirring up our desires, but instead meditate in places of solitude.

Longchenpa counsels us not to stay in towns and cities, because this will cause us to lose our peace of mind. We will be endlessly distracted and will not be able to practice. We should always stay in places of solitude and devote ourselves to dharma practice. Then, at the time of our death, we will have no regrets. The best outcome will be enlightenment in this very lifetime; and if we don't attain that, at least we will have no regrets. So we must be clear about what we are doing!

> One further point for you, who are my longtime disciples:
> Due to our [shared] karma and pure aspirations,
> We have been connected through the dharma and our sacred
>   commitments.
> But since it is in the nature of gatherings to part, master and
>   disciples will separate.
> Understand that we are like traders meeting in the marketplace.

> I have given this advice from my heart solely to benefit you.
> Abandon your country, possessions, loved ones and relatives,
> All of this life's distractions and busyness,
> And meditate in a peaceful place in order to stabilize
>   your mind!

> When your time comes to die, nothing can prevent it.
> To be fearless at death, you need the dharma
> And your teacher's oral instructions on the profound essence
>   of practice.
> So take them to heart and practice right now!

> Among all practices, those of the luminous essence—
> And among those, the secret meaning of the Nyingthig,
>   the most essential of all—
> Are the supreme path to buddhahood in a single lifetime.
> Dedicate yourself to accomplishing the great bliss of
>   Samantabhadra.

As the Victorious Longchenpa's wisdom mind is dissolving into the expanse of the dharmakaya, he imparts this advice: If we always stay in towns and cities, we will only spin our heads with busyness, work, and an abundance of worldly activities. True benefit comes only from the dharma. So from our hearts, we must abandon concern for our body, friends, loved ones, companions, wealth, possessions and position, all of which bring no ultimate benefit. We need to give up all the things of this life, which are fleeting and unstable like illusions or dreams. Their transient nature means that they can never be finished or bring us true satisfaction. For this reason, we should practice developing meditative absorption (*samadhi; ting nge 'dzin*) in a peaceful place. Whether this is in a place of solitude or simply within our own home, we should meditate there with the aim of stabilizing our mind.

Meditation to stabilize the mind (*bsam gtan sgom pa*) is the ultimate of all practices; it brings us to the level of the holy sages. There are a great many teachings on this kind of meditation. However, among them all, the supreme teaching is the instruction of our guru. And among all the instructions of the guru, the most supreme instructions are those of the Luminous Vajra Heart of the Great Perfection (Dzogchen Osel Dorje Nyingpo; Rdzogs chen 'od gsal rdo rje snying po), the Secret Heart Essence (Sangwa Nyingthig; Gsang ba snying thig). This is the vital quintessence (*snying po'i bcud*), like drops of the heart's blood. For in one lifetime, it can grant us the wisdom mind of a buddha. In fact, Victorious Longchenpa is advising us to meditate on Dzogchen, the Great Perfection.

> Furthermore, seek teachings from the lineages of the holy sages
> Who possess the quintessential nectar of the profound meaning.
> Then, with the power of your diligence, practice these in
> solitude!
> Swiftly, you will attain the level of the victorious ones.
>
> The sacred dharma accomplishes all supreme bliss right now in
> this very life,
> As well as bringing you benefit in future times.
> It is endowed with great qualities, both apparent and unseen.
> Be diligent in understanding the meaning of the essence from
> now on!

We should receive teachings from teachers of all traditions impartially and put them into practice. Without being sectarian, we should request the teachings and practices that benefit our mind and put those into practice. The essential sacred dharma will benefit us in this life as well as in the next one.

Thus ends Gyalwa Longchenpa's actual advice. The last section relates to Longchenpa personally. Longchenpa indicates that his reincarnation, Pema Lingpa, is soon to be born to the east, at Bumthang in Bhutan.

> In the cloud-free sky,
> The lord of stars, the full moon,
> Is soon to rise.

The "lord of stars" is the moon that is soon to rise. The moon is a metaphor for Longchenpa's reincarnation Tertön Pema Lingpa,[9] whose manifestation in the eastern direction draws near.

> Canopies, parasols, banners, and music;
> And all is beautified by the presence of a host of dakas and
> dakinis, . . .

Now the wisdom dakinis are coming to escort Longchenpa from the world, holding canopies, parasols, and banners, and playing music.

> [Behold] the lord imbued with compassion, the face
> of Padma.

Longchenpa now beholds the face of the compassionate lord, Guru Rinpoche, Padmasambhava, telling Longchenpa that his time has come to depart from this world. So for this reason, he says:

> By his confirmation,
> My time has now come, like a traveler setting off.

Longchenpa's time to depart has come, just as a traveler sets off on a journey. As his physical body begins to dissolve into the space of the dharmakaya, Longchenpa expresses his joy.

In death I have more delight
Than a seafaring merchant who has found what he sought;

Longchenpa experiences more delight than a sea trader who has discovered a wish-fulfilling jewel, and so fulfilled the goal of his journey.

Than Indra victorious in battle;

When the gods defeat the demigods, Indra has achieved his purpose.

Than the bliss from accomplishing meditative stability.

A yogi who can remain in immovable one-pointed meditative stability (*bsam gtan rtse gcig gyo ba med par*) has accomplished his meditation, and his objective is completed. These examples all indicate that Longchenpa is abiding continuously in the unchanging dharmata, gazing at the face of Guru Padmasambhava, and being invited and escorted by the wisdom dakas and dakinis. As the pure visions of the buddha fields unfold, Longchenpa experiences inexpressible joy. Like the victorious lord of the gods Indra, or the yogi who has accomplished his meditation, or the trader who has discovered a treasure, Longchenpa is filled with sublime bliss and joy.

Now I, Pema Ledrel Tsal,[10] will not remain;
I am going to capture the deathless citadel of great bliss.

Longchenpa is dissolving into the expanse of space (*ying; dbyings*), capturing the citadel of the deathless state of great bliss, the stronghold of the wisdom body, the dharmakaya. Longchenpa now attains enlightenment within dharmadhatu, "the expanse of the true nature of phenomena."

Up to this point the text had been written down by Victorious Longchenpa's attendant Gyalse Zopa, but at this point Longchenpa's disciple becomes too upset to write down anything more. Longchenpa continues:

My life is finished, my karma exhausted; prayers are now of
**   no further benefit.**
All my worldly work is done, and the experiences of this life
**   have ended.**
In the bardo, as the buddha fields unfold,

In a flash I will recognize that in essence they are my own
   manifestations,
And that I am close to reaching the omnipresent primordial
   ground.

My gifts have made others happy.
My reincarnation will benefit Tharpa Ling.
I pray that my future sacred disciples will meet him at that time,
And that his teachings will bring them joy and satisfaction.

Now, as my connections to this life are ending,
I shall die happily like a homeless beggar.
Do not feel sad, but always pray to me!

As he is preparing to pass away, the Victorious One, Longchenpa, tells
his disciples that he will be enlightened in the expanse of the dharmakaya
and that his reincarnation will appear. From that state, Longchenpa's emanation body (*nirmanakaya; sprul sku*), blessed by Longchenpa's light rays
of compassion and prophesied by Guru Padmasambhava, will appear as the
one known as Tertön Pema Lingpa. He will be born at Longchenpa's seat of
Tharpa Ling in Bumthang, central Bhutan. Finally, Longchenpa prays that
all his future disciples will be able to receive teachings from his reincarnation and that they will all have an auspicious connection with him.

These altruistic words of heart advice
Are a multitude of lotus flowers to delight the faithful bees.
By the virtue of these excellent words,
May all beings of the three realms
Transcend sorrow within the primordial ground.

This completes the advice by "Immaculate Light Rays," Drimey Ozer.

4. Introduction to the Heart Essence of the Vast Expanse, a Dzogchen Terma Cycle

In regard to what we are going to be listening to, there are the innumerable teachings given by the Buddha. If we wish to condense these, there are the teachings of the general vehicle and those of the extraordinary vehicle. In some contexts within the Nyingma tradition, the extraordinary vehicles are the three inner tantras of Mahayoga, Anuyoga, and Atiyoga or Dzogchen. At other times, the "extraordinary vehicle" refers to Dzogchen alone. As Longchen Rabjam explained, in the first eight vehicles of Buddhist training, we practice by engaging the dualistic mind, but in the ninth vehicle of Atiyoga, or the Great Perfection, we do not practice with our dualistic mind but actually engage our primordial wisdom nature.

In relation to the general and extraordinary teachings, we first need to understand that during the three stages of his life, Buddha Shakyamuni gave different categories of teachings with different emphases, known as the three turnings of the wheel of dharma. One may wonder at what stages in his life the Buddha actually taught the three turnings of the wheel of dharma. We find in the long biography of Guru Padmasambhava, *The Chronicles of Padma* (*Pema Kathang; Pad ma bka' thang*), that from the age of thirty-six to forty-six, the Buddha primarily taught the approach of the first turning of the wheel of dharma. Following this, for the next fifteen to twenty years, the Buddha principally taught according to the second turning of the wheel of dharma. Then during the remaining latter part of his life until his passing away into parinirvana at the age of eighty-two, Buddha Shakyamuni emphasized the teachings of the third turning of the wheel of dharma.

In the early part of his life, Shakyamuni remained within the kingdom of Kapilavastu and lived the life of a prince. Following this, Shakyamuni spent six years practicing austerities, finally demonstrating enlightenment under the bodhi tree in Bodhgaya, India. Then at Sarnath the Buddha Shakyamuni taught the four noble truths of the arya, or sublime, beings, which form the basis of the Root Vehicle of the Buddha's teachings. This was the beginning of the first turning of the wheel of dharma.

Also at the beginning of the first turning of the wheel of dharma, Buddha entered into retreat in the sixth month of his thirty-sixth year. This retreat was carried out annually by the Buddha and came to be known as the "summer rainy season retreat" (*Varshika; g.yar gnas*), and the tradition of monastic retreat at this season is still maintained to the present day. During the first turning of the wheel of dharma, Buddha also gave extensive discourses on monastic discipline (*Vinaya; 'dul ba*) to his entourage of close disciples, at Varanasi in northern India.

In general, it is said that the Buddha's teachings can be understood as the dharma of the scriptures and the dharma of realization. An example of the dharma of the scriptures is the Tripitaka, which is the "three baskets," or collections of scriptures of the Root Vehicle, the teachings of the first turning of the wheel of dharma. The Tripitaka is like something that we can take hold of so we do not become lost or separated from the path. Through these three collections, we can attain realization of the dharma. The Tripitaka is the "handle" that enables us to take hold of the dharma of realization, the three higher trainings of ethics, concentration, and wisdom.

The approach taught in the first turning of the wheel of dharma is called the "Root Vehicle" of the Buddha's path, as it is the basis for the other two vehicles of the Mahayana, or "Great Vehicle," and the Vajrayana, or "Diamond Vehicle." For the teachings of the first turning of the wheel of dharma, it is preferable for us to use the term "Root Vehicle," as opposed to the term "Lesser Vehicle" (*Hinayana; theg dman*). The latter term is a way that the Mahayana tradition referred to the teachings of the Root Vehicle, and it arose in order to contrast this approach with the path of the Mahayana, or "Great Vehicle," which includes the teachings of the second and third turnings of the wheel of dharma. "Root Vehicle" is better for us to use nowadays, to avoid any possible sectarian connotations.

Then following this initial period, in the middle part of his life, the Buddha gave teachings at Vulture Peak, near Rajgir in northern India, to an assembly of arya, or noble, beings. These noble ones included Buddha's disciples such as Ananda and Subhuti and a host of sravakas, pratkeyas, and bodhisattvas. At this time, the Buddha imparted to those present the Mahayana teachings on emptiness (*shunyata; stong pa nyid*). This was the second turning of the wheel of dharma.

Finally, the teachings of the third turning of the wheel of dharma were given by the Buddha at Vaishali in northern India, as well as at Mount Malaya in south India, and on the island of Sri Lanka. At this time and in these places, the Buddha revealed the teachings on *sugatagarbha,* the buddha nature or "enlightened essence," to gatherings of gods, humans, and nonhumans.

The third and final turning of the wheel of dharma, expounding the teachings on buddha nature, was the basis for the Vajrayana or Secret Mantrayana of the awareness-holders (*vidyadhara; rig 'dzin*). The Nyingma tradition divides the teachings of buddhadharma into nine vehicles, nine distinct spiritual approaches and paths taught in Tibet by Guru Padmasambhava. In the Nyingma school's system of Secret Mantra, there are the three outer tantras of Kriya, Upaya or Charya, and Yoga tantra; and then there are the three inner tantras of Mahayoga, Anuyoga, and Atiyoga or Dzogchen. Within Atiyoga there are three divisions of teachings, the Mind Series (*semde; sems sde*), the Space Series (*longde; klong sde*) and the Instruction Series (*mengakde; man ngag sde*). According to the system of Guru Padmasambhava, Atiyoga is divided into general yoga (*chiti; spyi ti*) and quintessence yoga (*yangti; yang ti*). Quintessence yoga corresponds to the Instruction Series of Dzogchen; and Jigme Lingpa's text *The Lion's Roar,* which we will be learning later, belongs to this highest and most essential level of instruction.

The main Dzogchen transmissions came to Tibet through the Indian masters Guru Padmasambhava and Vimalamitra, the Tibetan translator Vairocana, and Longchen Rabjam, and these transmissions flourished throughout all of Tibet. The lineage for these teachings that has been passed historically from lineage holder to lineage holder down to the present day is called the "oral lineage" (*kahma; bka' ma*), or sometimes it is also known as the "long lineage" (*ringyu; ring brgyud*). This lineage reaches back in an unbroken succession, all the way to the original gurus who initially received the teachings within our human realm. For example, due to the teachings and blessings of Vimalamitra transmitted through the kahma "oral lineage," the kahma collection known as the Secret Heart Essence of Vimalamitra (Bimai Sangwa Nyingthig; Bi ma'i gsang ba snying thig) appeared in Tibet.

In general, the terma treasure teachings are known as the "short lineage," since they are taught after being newly discovered, received, and revealed by a *tertön* or "treasure revealer." Furthermore, within the treasure teachings, there are both long and short lineages of transmission. The long lineage of treasures are the teachings of earlier treasure revealers handed down through a succession of lineage gurus to one's present gurus. The short lineage of treasure teachings refers to the transmissions received by tertöns in pure vision from the greatest masters, principally from Guru Padmasambhava, Vimalamitra, and Longchenpa.

From the tradition of Guru Padmasambhava, there are various terma or treasure teachings such as the Heart Essence of the Dakinis (Khadro Nyingthig; Mkha' 'gro snying thig); the Open Transparency of Realization (Gongpa Zangthal; Dgongs pa zang thal); the Black Quintessence (Yang thig nag po), and so many others. These teachings were all given by Guru Padmasambhava, and although they were revealed at different periods in history, they are all synthesized and united in the experience and realization of Longchenpa.

In fact, both the terma tradition of Guru Padmasambhava and the canonical kahma lineage of Vimalamitra and Padmasambhava, as well as the Dzogchen Mind Series and Space Series lineages of the Tibetan translator Vairocana, are all gathered in the writings of Longchen Rabjam. These writings include the Seven Treasuries (Dzo Dun; Mdzod bdun), the Trilogy of Resting at Ease (Ngalso Kor Sum; Ngal gso skor gsum), the Self-Liberation Trilogy (Rangdrol Kor Sum; Rang grol skor gsum), and the Trilogy of the Innermost Essence (Yang Thig Kor Sum; Yang thig skor gsum), which is part of the Four Heart Essences (Nyingthig Yabzhi; Snying thig ya bzhi). Thus Longchenpa gathered the essential meaning of all the traditions of kahma and terma in his writings.

To illustrate, Longchenpa had visions of all of the eight principal manifestations of Guru Padmasambhava. Longchenpa's Self-Liberation Trilogy has eight works that relate to his visions of the eight manifestations. These eight works are the three root texts of the Self-Liberation Trilogy, together with their three autocommentaries, plus the prayer of the *Self-Liberation of the Nature of Mind* (*Semnyid Rang Drol; Sems nyid rang grol*), one of the three root texts, and also Longchenpa's commentary on the *All-Creating King Tantra* (*Kunje Gyalpo; Kun byed rgyal po'i rgyud*), totaling eight texts. These writings emerged spontaneously from Longchenpa's wisdom mind as mind treasures (*gongter; dgongs gter*), inspired by the blessings of the eight manifestations of Padmasambhava.

All of these lineages came down from Longchenpa to Jigme Lingpa. When we refer to the "long lineage" of the teachings coming from Long-chenpa, there were fourteen main lineage teachers between Longchenpa and Jigme Lingpa, and this is Jigme Lingpa's long lineage for Longchenpa's writings. The transmission and realization of all of Longchenpa's works was passed down from Longchenpa through the succession of lineage gurus to the great awareness-holder Jigme Lingpa, and this line of transmission is also called "the long lineage."

Thus Jigme Lingpa received from his gurus both the long lineage kahma teachings, as well as the long lineage of the terma treasure teachings of Longchenpa and other tertöns. The majority of the traditions Jigme Lingpa received from his teachers were from the long lineage of the kahma rather than being treasure teachings. Jigme Lingpa collected, compiled, and was instrumental in the publication of the kahma teachings of the Nyingma Gyubum, the Collected Tantras of the Nyingma.

Jigme Lingpa also received long lineage transmissions of terma. Here "long lineage" does not refer to the ancient teachings of kahma, but in this case it means earlier terma treasure cycles, passed down through the lineage gurus from earlier treasure revealers (tertön) such as Longchenpa. As an example, among the long lineage of terma cycles, Jigme Lingpa received the transmission of the terma cycle Essence of Liberation, the Self-Liberation of the Wisdom Mind (Drol Thig Gongpa Rangdrol; Grol thig dgongs pa rang grol), which was one of the principal terma revelations of Tertön Sherab Ozer (1518–84).

In addition to such long lineages of terma cycles, Jigme Lingpa also received the direct or short lineage of terma teachings by way of his pure visions of Guru Padmasambhava and Longchenpa. For example, as a result of Jigme Lingpa's visions of Guru Padmasambhava and Longchenpa, he received the direct transmission of the terma cycle that came to be known as the "Heart Essence of the Vast Expanse." Thus, just like Longchenpa, Jigme Lingpa received the long lineage of the kahma teachings as well as both the long and the short lineages of the terma treasure teachings.

Jigme Lingpa had visions of Longchenpa's wisdom body on three occa-sions. On the basis of Jigme Lingpa's direct encounter with Longchenpa, a cycle of Longchenpa's treasure teachings was revealed to Jigme Lingpa. He called his terma cycle the "Heart Essence of the Vast Expanse" (Longchen Nyingthig; Klong chen snying thig). Prior to Jigme Lingpa, these teach-ings of the Dzogchen Instruction Series were generally known as the "Heart

Essence of Secret Luminosity" (Osal Sangwa Nyingthig; 'Od gsal gsang ba snying thig). The great terma cycle of the Heart Essence of the Vast Expanse, or Longchen Nyingthig, encompasses the combined view and realization of Vimalamitra, Guru Padmasambhava, and Longchenpa. Also, the Longchen Nyingthig is distinguished as a major terma cycle because it contains three key elements essential for a cycle to be considered "major": the practice of the guru; the practice of the "Great Compassionate One," or Avalokiteshvara; and the practice of Dzogchen. If all three key aspects of the guru, Avalokiteshvara, and Dzogchen practices are not present, then a terma cycle is usually counted as a minor one.

Among the three key aspects, in the Heart Essence of the Vast Expanse, there are both peaceful and wrathful sadhana practices of the guru, involving visualization, recitation, and so on. The sadhana practice of Avalokiteshvara is called *The Compassionate One Who Naturally Liberates Suffering* (*Thukje Dugngal Rangdrol; Thugs rje sdug bsngal rang grol*). And for the Dzogchen practices, there is, for example, the guidance manual *Supreme Wisdom* (*Yeshe Lama; Ye shes bla ma*). In the great terma cycles such as Heart Essence of the Vast Expanse, there are also a variety of practices of the three roots of the guru, the meditation deity (*yi dam*), and the dakini.

Among the collected writings contained within the Heart Essence of the Vast Expanse cycle are a number of terma revelations, as well as other kinds of texts that were written by Jigme Lingpa himself. The terma revelations include a root tantra called *The Wisdom Expanse of Samantabhadra Tantra* (*Kunzang Yeshe Long gyi Gyud; Kun bzang ye shes klong gyi rgyud*), which is a tantra coming directly from the wisdom mind of the dharmakaya Buddha Samantabhadra. Accompanying this root tantra, there is also the *Subsequent Tantra of Great Perfection Instructions* (*Gyud Chima; Rgyud phyi ma*), which supplements the root tantra.

Following this is an explanatory text or "scriptural transmission" (*lung*), known as *Samantabhadra's Enlightened Realization* (*Lung Kunzang Gong Nyam; Lung kun bzang dgongs nyams*). This explanatory text was written in order to clarify the meaning of the root tantra. There are also two main texts of oral instructions (*men ngak; man ngag*) called *Distinguishing the Three Key Points of the Great Perfection* (*Dzogpa Chenpoi Nesum Shenjay; Rdzogs pa chen po'i gnad gsum shan 'byed*), and the *Vajra Verses on the Natural State* (*Nelug Dorje Tsig Gang; Gnas lugs rdo rje'i tshig rkang*). Finally, there are the practice commentaries on the oral instruction, the "guidance manuals" (*tri; khrid*) elucidating these instructions, such as the principal guidance manual of the Longchen Nyingthig, known as the *Supreme Wisdom* (*Yeshe Lama; Ye shes bla ma*).

Here we can see that there are three main types of teachings that make up the core of the Heart Essence of the Vast Expanse: the tantras, the scriptural transmissions, and the oral instructions (*gyu lung men ngak; rgyud lung man ngag*). Among these, the root tantras (*gyu; rgyud*) are spoken by Buddha Samantabhadra or Buddha Vajradhara. The scriptural transmissions (*lung*) are explanatory commentaries on the tantras and are written by highly realized masters to clarify the meaning of the tantras. Then the oral instructions (*men ngak; man ngag*) gather and elucidate the key experiential meanings of the instructions found in the scriptural transmissions. In Dzogchen, it is important to receive the tantric empowerments that ripen the mind stream, the scriptural transmissions that are the support of the tantras, and the oral instructions that liberate our minds.

In addition, there are three main types of oral instructions: the detailed explanations of the learned ones, the experiential instructions of the yogins, and the general instructions for public gatherings. Among the experiential oral instructions of the yogins, we have in the Longchen Nyingthig, the oral instruction teaching *Distinguishing the Three Key Points of the Great Perfection* (*Dzogpa Chenpoi Nesum Shenjay; Rdzogs pa chen po'i gnad gsum shan 'byed*). This short work presents the key points that enable the yogin to make three important distinctions essential for the practice of Dzogchen, and thus to practice authentically and to correct faults and mistakes in the practice. One must learn to distinguish between the all-ground or "foundation of all things" (*kun zhi; kun gzhi*) and the dharmakaya or "body of reality" (*choku; chos sku*), between dualistic mind (*sem; sems*) and awareness (*rig pa*), and between calm abiding meditation (*shamatha; zhi gnas*) and insight meditation (*vipasyana; lhag mthong*).

As mentioned, among the experiential instructions of the yogins, the principal Dzogchen guidance manual (*tri; khrid*) of the Longchen Nyingthig is called *Supreme Wisdom* (*Yeshe Lama; Ye shes bla ma*), which was written by Jigme Lingpa. The *Yeshe Lama* gathers all the key meanings of the tantras, scriptural transmissions, and oral instructions together in a form that can be practiced and directly experienced by the yogin. As our minds have gone astray, circling endlessly in the three realms of samsara, we are not able to recognize the true nature of our mind. In our current condition, we are like a blind person deprived of sight, and we need guidance in order to see our primordial wisdom nature (*yeshe; ye shes*). We are like a blind person on the road, and the guidance manuals are what enable the practice lineage to take us by the hand and lead us to liberation. The purpose of Dzogchen guidance manuals is to lead us to self-originating wisdom (*rangjung yeshe; rang byung ye shes*) and guide us steadily along the path to liberation and omniscience.

If we wish to truly put into practice the teachings of the *Yeshe Lama*, we need to first train in the general Buddhist teachings; otherwise we will not have the capacity to fully realize the meaning of dharma. Applying the general teachings, we purify our mind so that we can successfully enter into the practices of Secret Mantrayana and Dzogchen. In order to purify our minds through the general teachings of the sutra vehicles, we have in the Longchen Nyingthig a teaching on the preliminary practices called *The Seven Mind Trainings Manual, Steps to Liberation*. This text by Jigme Lingpa clearly lays out the heart of the teachings on the seven-point mind training as taught by the great Indian Dzogchen master Vimalamitra in the Heart Essence of Vimalamitra (Vima Nyingthig; Bi ma snying thig).

On the basis of the seven-point mind training, we continue to purify our mind through the Mahayana teachings and Vajrayana preliminaries (*ngondro; sngon 'gro*). For this, in the Longchen Nyingthig, there are two preliminary practice teachings. The *Applications of Mindfulness* (*Drenpa Nyerzhag; Dran pa nyer bzhag*) covers the general preliminaries. Then the *Instructions on the Way to Apply the Practice* (*Tri kyi Laglen la Deblug; Khrid kyi lag len la 'debs lugs*) covers the extraordinary preliminaries of the four times hundred thousand practices: refuge and bodhicitta, Vajrasattva recitation, mandala offering, and guru yoga.

Then for the main practice, there is the special guidance manual *Supreme Wisdom* (*Yeshe Lama; Ye shes bla ma*), which contains the experiential meaning of the Dzogchen teachings from both the kahma and terma lineages. Within the Longchen Nyingthig terma cycle, the actual meaning of the root and subsequent tantras of the Longchen Nyingthig are synthesized into the *Yeshe Lama* in a very clear manner. Also the *Yeshe Lama* distills the essential meaning of Longchenpa's writings found in the *Treasury of the Supreme Vehicle* (*Theg Chog Dzod; Theg mchog mdzod*) and the *Treasury of Word and Meaning* (*Tsig Don Dzod; Tshig don mdzod*). These two texts, in turn, encompass the experiential guidance (*nyongtri; myong khrid*) and complete meaning of the seventeen Dzogchen tantras, especially as contained within the Dzogchen root tantra *Reverberation of Sound* (*Dra Thalgyur; Sgra thal 'gyur*). The *Reverberation of Sound* is considered the principal among the seventeen Dzogchen tantras, the other sixteen tantras being regarded as secondary tantras. Thus the *Yeshe Lama* imparts the condensed essence of the tantras, scriptural transmissions, and oral instructions needed for Dzogchen practice.

In the *Yeshe Lama,* there are the instructions on the special preliminary practices unique to Dzogchen, for which there are three sections. The first section is for those who like more elaborate yogic practices and wish to gain ordinary signs of relative accomplishments (*siddhi; dngos grub*), the yoga of the sounds of the four elements. It should be noted that this first set of preliminaries is not generally practiced these days. The second section of Dzogchen preliminary practices, the practices of separating samsara and nirvana (*khordey rushan; 'khor 'das ru shan*), is for those who have great energy and diligence. These are related to our body, speech, and mind and are practices that meditate upon the six realms of sentient beings and on the three jewels and deities (*yidam*).

The third section of special Dzogchen preliminaries teaches the three methods for training the body, speech, and mind. The latter of these three is the training of the mind, the practice of investigating the arising, abiding, and ceasing (*byung gnas 'gro gsum*) of thoughts. This practice is important for everyone but is said to be especially important for those who are more inclined toward mental analysis and less inclined toward activities and energetic endeavor. By first establishing an analytical notion of emptiness through this practice of searching for the place of the arising, abiding, and ceasing of mind and thoughts, certainty in the view of emptiness will develop. In summary, these three sections of the special Dzogchen preliminaries are different skillful means that lay the proper foundation for the direct introduction to awareness (*rig pa*) and for enhancing the recognition of awareness.

Overall, the *Yeshe Lama* has three main sections or groups of instructions. The first is for individuals of highest capacity to be liberated in this very life and makes up most of the text. It includes the three principal instructions of Dzogchen: the preliminary practices of separating samsara and nirvana (*khordey rushan; 'khor 'das ru shan*); the practice of the view of Directly Cutting Through (*trekchod; khregs chod*); and the practice of the meditation of Directly Crossing Over (*thogal; thod rgal*). The second main section of the *Yeshe Lama* is the group of instructions for those of middling capacity to be liberated either in the bardo of dying or in the bardo of dharmata and also includes general explanations regarding the bardo of rebirth. The third main section of the *Yeshe Lama* contains the instructions whereby those of lesser capacity can be liberated in the bardo of rebirth and includes the teachings on the transfer of consciousness (*phowa; 'pho ba*) to a nirmanakaya buddha field of the nature (*rang bzhin sprul pa'i zhing khams*).

Jigme Lingpa writes in the colophon of the *Yeshe Lama* that he had condensed the essential points of the most secret and supreme teachings of Dzogchen into this guidance manual. He also alludes to Longchenpa's writings known as the "Seven Treasuries" for those who wish to study the Dzogchen teachings in a more elaborate way. Jigme Lingpa later told his disciples that the *Yeshe Lama* was a replica of his realization and understanding, condensing the essence of both the kahma and the terma traditions, and so they should practice according to its instructions.

There are further teachings in the Longchen Nyingthig, in particular a cycle of supportive teachings (*gyabcho kor; rgyab chos skor*) related to the *Yeshe Lama* and written by Jigme Lingpa. This includes *Drops of Nectar, Words of the Omniscient One* (*Kunkyen Zhal Lung Dudtsi Thigpa; Kun mkhyen zhal lung bdud rtsi'i thigs pa*), which is a commentary on one of the principal oral instruction texts of Longchen Nyingthig called *Vajra Verses on the Natural State*. Jigme Lingpa also wrote other important texts of supportive teachings such as *White Lotus* (*Pema Karpo; Pad ma dkar po*), *Seeing the Natural State in Its Nakedness* (*Nay Lug Cher Thong; Gnas lugs cer mthong*), and also a teaching included here together with our commentary, *The Lion's Roar* (*Seng ge'i nga ro*). These four supportive texts present additional oral instructions that elaborate on the meaning of the special guidance manual *Yeshe Lama*. We will return to one of these later, in our teachings on *The Lion's Roar* of Jigme Lingpa.

5. How to Receive Dharma Teachings

As it states in the *Vajra Pinnacle Tantra* (*Vajra Sekhara Tantra; Rdo rje rtse mo'i rgyud*):

> Collect all your thoughts
> And listen with a noble motivation.

In this world there are many different fields of knowledge. There are innumerable arenas of learning, both ancient and modern. There are fields of knowledge related to the outer world and those related to the inner spiritual paths such as the buddhadharma. Among those relating to inner spiritual paths, there are systems of knowledge taught by the non-Buddhist teachers, traditions that propound a belief in an external god or external reality as being the ultimate truth. There are those of the teachers and traditions of the buddhadharma, with their own understanding of the ultimate.

According to the ordinary way of studying and comprehending the outer world, for our education we enter school from the first grade and progress until gaining an educational degree, perhaps right through to university. Then we become doctors and scientists, lawyers, business people and office workers, schoolteachers, any of the fields that are based on worldly knowledge. In these sciences and fields of learning, our minds are directed toward understanding outer objects and applied to the conditions of the outer world.

In contrast, the Buddha has taught that the purpose of dharma, the spiritual teachings, is to look within and subdue one's own mind. The Teacher, the sublime Buddha, said, "Whatever dharma activity we are undertaking, whether teaching, listening, or meditating, we should begin by turning our attention within." The Buddha has taught that the purpose of dharma is to subdue one's own mind, which from the very beginning has been afflicted by emotional disturbances and has become obscured.

The Buddha taught that the root of everything we perceive and experience is the mind. For this reason, the way of the Buddha is that one must turn one's attention inward, toward the mind itself. It is important that we examine our own minds and interact with the teachings when we engage with the buddhadharma. If we do not do so and simply receive the teachings passively, then although it will create positive impressions in our minds, it will certainly not enable us to attain enlightenment in one lifetime or within a relatively short number of lives.

When we direct our attention inward and look at our mind, we find that there are three types of thoughts that form, which may be classed as positive thoughts, neutral thoughts, and negative thoughts. We all have positive thoughts, such as love and compassion, patience, and so on, all of which are positive thoughts related to virtuous qualities. The buddhadharma teaches practitioners to also cultivate thoughts related to the Buddhist teachings. What are these positive thoughts that are so important for practitioners? According to the dharma, we have the potential for giving rise to three essential positive mental attitudes, which are faith, the thought of renunciation, and the "mind of enlightenment," or bodhicitta.

In addition to positive thoughts, we have all of the ordinary, neutral thoughts related to everyday pursuits such as eating, sleeping, coming and going, and conducting our daily lives. There are also two general types of neutral mental states: an unconscious state without any mental activity, and a conscious state endowed with mental activity. Likewise, each of us has negative thoughts, and these can all be included within three categories of thoughts related to the three central psychological poisons that afflict the mind: anger (*zhe sdang*), attachment (*'dod chags*), and delusion (*gti mug*). Negative thoughts are those that stem from these three categories of afflictive emotions (*klesha; nyon mongs*). The first category includes aversion, aggression, and anger; the second includes craving, desire, and attachment; and the third includes stupidity, ignorance, and delusion.

When listening to and learning buddhadharma, it is very important that we engage the teachings on the basis of the three positive mental attitudes. Otherwise, if we listen to dharma teachings with an indifferent, neutral state of mind, the meaning of the dharma will not be able to enter and penetrate our mind. Also if we listen with a distracted mind, we will not be able to hear and receive the teachings, so it is very important to practice attentive mindfulness (*dren shay; dran shes*) when listening to the dharma.

It should be clear that if we listen to the teachings with a negative mental attitude, our frame of mind will not be in accord with the dharma. In such a case, receiving teachings can even create negative karma rather than positive, since negative karma will be the outcome of negative states of mind. Thus it is explained in the buddhadharma that all of our negative thoughts and actions should be abandoned, that all of our neutral thoughts should be transformed into something positive and meaningful, and that only positive attitudes and intentions are to be adopted.

For practitioners, this means that we should try to cultivate the three kinds of positive thoughts. As mentioned, these are first, faith and devotion toward the Buddha, dharma, and sangha, the three jewels. Second, we grow in the thought of renunciation by seeing the defects of samsara, the faults of worldly existence. Third, we cultivate positive thoughts related to bodhicitta, the "mind of enlightenment." To give rise to the thought of bodhicitta, we develop the aspiration to establish all beings in a state in which they are free from any suffering and have reached the level of perfect buddhahood. This is what is also known in the buddhadharma as the thought of compassion.

In order to listen to and properly receive the dharma teachings, these three positive thoughts and intentions are essential. If we cultivate the three positive attitudes well, then the dharma will enter and merge with our mind; so it is fundamental to cultivate and maintain the three thoughts while listening to and learning the teachings.

How are we to understand the three positive mental attitudes necessary for a dharma practitioner? To begin with, the gateways to the dharma are faith and renunciation. In general, the sutra teachings speak of four types of faith: inspired faith, aspiring faith, confident faith, and irreversible faith. The Buddha said in the *Sutra of the Vast Display* (*Lalitavistara Sutra; Rgya cher rol pa'i mdo*) that it is impossible to truly enter the path of dharma without faith and devotion. For example, without faith the way is blocked for us as we will not be able to trust in the teachings. Thus it is very important that we listen to the dharma with an open heart filled with faith and devotion.

For example, the *Sutra of the Fortunate Aeon* (*Bhadrakalpika Sutra; Bskal pa bzang po'i mdo*), which relates the twelve deeds of the life of the Buddha, begins with the teachings on the precious wheel of faith. The reason faith is referred to as a precious wheel is because in the ancient scriptures of the Vedas, there is a legend about a universal ruler or *chakravartin* who through his great merit is endowed with the seven precious royal possessions. One of these seven possessions is a precious golden magical wheel, which always spontaneously proceeds ahead of the universal ruler wherever he advances in order to prepare the way for him. Due to the presence of the precious wheel, wherever the universal ruler goes, people automatically fall under his power, and he naturally gains mastery over every place.

Similarly, when the Buddha taught, he always began his teachings by introducing the precious wheel of faith, which opens the way to the dharma teachings like the precious wheel of a universal ruler. Faith is to have trust and confidence in the dharma, and without this trust we cannot penetrate the profound depth of the teachings. If we place vegetables in front of dogs, they will normally show little interest in eating them. Likewise, if we lack faith and have little interest in the dharma, we won't partake of the teachings and enter the path.

When we speak of the second of the three positive mental attitudes, the thought of renunciation, we need to begin by gaining a definite understanding of the nature of suffering in the three realms of samsara. In important sutras such as the *Supreme Dharma of the Application of Mindfulness Sutra* (*Saddharma-nusmrityu-pastana; Dam pa'i chos dran pa nyer bzhag pa'i mdo*), the *Sutra of One Hundred Karmas* (*Karma Shataka Sutra; Mdo sde las brgya pa*), and others, the main theme is renunciation.

The Tibetan term for renunciation is *ngepar jungwa; nges par 'byung ba,* which literally means "certainty of release." *Ngepar* is short for *ngepar shepa,* meaning to have certain, decisive knowledge from within; in this case, it refers to having certainty that the nature of worldly existence is suffering. In addition to this certainty, there is the heartfelt wish to be released, *jungwa,* from this suffering. One must gain confidence in the fact that the nature of cyclic existence in samsara is suffering, together with having the powerful wish and intention to be free of this suffering. This is what is known as the thought of renunciation.

The third of the three positive mental attitudes is bodhicitta, the "mind of enlightenment." Bodhicitta especially concerns our motivation for listening to and learning the buddhadharma teachings. In regard to motivation, there are two general kinds of impure, flawed motivations for listening to the dharma. The first of these is listening in order to be protected from fear or harm, such as, for example, listening to the dharma in order to receive safe haven from punishment and retribution. The second is listening to and learning the dharma for material gain such as money, food, clothing, and possessions.

Most importantly, there are the three levels of positive motivation one may give rise to in order to hear and receive the dharma teachings, which are the lesser, middling, and superior motivation. The lesser motivation is wishing to obtain higher rebirths in the worldly realms of gods and men and to escape the suffering of the lower realms. The middling motivation is aspiring to attain the level of an arhat solely for one's own benefit. The superior motivation is to listen to the teachings with the bodhicitta motivation, the intention to bring all beings to the level of buddhahood. Thus we should listen to the buddhadharma while generating the great motivation and expansive attitude of bodhicitta.

Bodhicitta has two aspects, the first of which consists of wishing that all beings as vast as space may be free from suffering and from the causes and effects of suffering. This is known as the compassion aspect of bodhicitta. Second, bodhicitta includes the wish that all beings may be established at the level of perfect enlightenment, that they may all experience the supreme happiness of enlightenment. This is known as the loving-kindness aspect of bodhicitta. So in essence, bodhicitta is endowed with both compassion and love. This is the state of mind in which we listen to dharma teachings, according to the Mahayana Buddhist sutra tradition.

Bodhicitta also has two principal facets, the relative and the ultimate. As just mentioned, relative bodhicitta is having the wish to liberate all beings from the suffering of worldly existence, as well as actually engaging in practice for this same purpose. These are the two aspects of relative bodhicitta, known as the bodhicitta of aspiration and the bodhicitta of application. Then we speak of ultimate bodhicitta, which is a selfless state beyond all conceptual views. Ultimate bodhicitta is uncontrived (*chomay; bcos med*). It is the natural state (*naylug; gnas lugs*) of emptiness, the true nature of mind. In brief, whenever we listen to and contemplate dharma teachings we should keep these three positive thoughts of faith, renunciation, and bodhicitta at the forefront of our mind. This will allow the dharma to truly penetrate our heart.

Furthermore, in order to avail ourselves of the vast skillful means of the Vajrayana teachings of Secret Mantra, we must first be able to properly hear and contemplate Vajrayana and Great Perfection teachings. This means being able to receive the teachings in a state of pure vision. When receiving the teachings of the Vajrayana and Dzogchen, the attitude of bodhicitta is to be conjoined with the pure vision of seeing the world and beings as pure wisdom. In particular, it means to maintain the pure perception of the teaching situation as being endowed with the five certainties of the Sambhogakaya or "complete enjoyment body," the pure realm of buddhahood.

According to the Vajrayana tradition, when receiving empowerments and teachings, we visualize that the five certainties of the sambhogakaya buddha field are present. This entails visualizing and imagining that we are experiencing pure manifestations of five aspects of our environment: the pure appearance of the form of the teacher, of the place in which we are, of the time of the teaching, of the teaching being given, and of the entourage receiving the teaching. We cultivate the pure vision of seeing the guru and disciples as buddhas, bodhisattvas, and deities. Although we imagine the pure setting through visualization, in fact appearances are already pure, so we are not inventing anything.

Finally, when receiving the Dzogchen teachings, we should view all phenomenal existence as an infinite all-encompassing purity (*dag pa rab byams*), a great mandala that is spontaneously present. We are to regard all of phenomenal existence as infinite purity, which is the natural and spontaneously present mandala of Buddha Samantabhadra. In the approach of the Great Perfection, we don't simply visualize the five certainties of the sambhogakaya and try to transform something that is thought to be impure into something pure. We do not mentally visualize pure appearances and try to transform the impure into the pure, in the way we normally would when receiving the teachings of Secret Mantra while applying the creation stage (*kyerim; bskyed rim*) visualizations.

Instead, from the point of view of Dzogchen, the Great Perfection, everything already has the nature of innate purity. This is the key distinction regarding how we listen to the teachings according to the unique understanding of Dzogchen, the pinnacle of the path of buddhadharma. According to the Great Perfection, the primordial purity of dharmata, the true nature of phenomena, is already innately present. For this reason, we are to regard all that appears and exists in the phenomenal world as a mandala of pure appearances. Everything is a naturally present, all-encompassing purity from the very beginning.

How then should we understand the five certainties when receiving Dzogchen teachings? We should know that the teaching environment embodies the spiritual qualities of the Sambhogakaya. Thus, the place where the teaching is being given is the supreme Sambhogakaya buddha field, the Akanishtha realm of all-encompassing purity. The teacher is to be regarded as the glorious dharmakaya Buddha, Samantabhadra in person. The entourage is filled with self-appearing (*rang snang*) dakas and dakinis, buddhas and bodhisattvas; all those present are seen to be pure wisdom beings. The teaching being presented is the Great Perfection of natural luminosity (*rang bzhin od gsal rdzogs pa chen po*). The time at which the teachings are being given is the continuously revolving wheel of eternity (*dus rtag pa rgyun gyi 'khor lo*), also known as the "fourth time of equality," or the "natural time of dharmata."

The sacred place, teacher, entourage, teaching, and time are the five certainties that are understood by the Dzogchen teachings to be intrinsically present from the very beginning. We remember this well in order to acknowledge the purity of the Sambhogakaya buddha field within the view of the Great Perfection.

The way we are to conduct ourselves during the teachings is to listen respectfully, abandoning all disrespectful thoughts and actions. We listen with a one-pointed mind free from distraction. Regarding our conduct (*spyod pa*) when receiving the teachings, we should avoid the three defects of the vessel and the five wrong ways of remembering, as well as the six stains. The six stains are pride, lack of faith, lack of effort, outward distraction, inward tension, and discouragement. All of these teachings on conduct just mentioned are detailed in the teachings on the preliminary practices (*ngondro; sngon 'gro*). They are found in Patrul Rinpoche's *Words of My Perfect Teacher* (*Kunzang Lamai Zhelung; Kun bzang bla ma'i zhal lung*), in the section on how to listen to teachings, which explains in detail both the appropriate and the inappropriate ways of listening to dharma teachings.

Also, when receiving teachings, we should adopt the virtuous qualities of the six perfections (*paramita; phar phyin*) of the Mahayana Buddhist teachings, as well as taking to heart what are known as the four considerations. In the *Flower Array Sutra* (*Gandhavyuha Sutra; Sdong po bkod pa'i mdo*), the final chapter of the renowned Mahayana scripture the *Avatamsaka Sutra* (*Mdo phal po che*), the Buddha is conversing with the bodhisattva Sudhana and explains the four considerations:

> Noble one, consider yourself as an ill patient,
> The dharma as a remedy,
> The spiritual teacher as a wise physician,
> And the unremitting practice as the treatment that cures you.

As a final key point for giving rise to the proper conditions for listening to teachings, in the Nyingma tradition the teachers place great emphasis on remaining in the view (*tawa; lta ba*), the true nature of mind or mind essence (*sem ngo; sems ngo*); and so one's motivation and conduct are related to the view. This is in contrast with some traditions of the New Translation schools such as the Gelugpa, where more attention is paid to manifesting the correct ritualized form in order to create the proper conditions for listening to teachings. For example, in their tradition, when teachings are held, there are great offerings of flowers, water bowls, and lamps, arrayed very precisely, for the accumulation of merit. In the Nyingma tradition, all dharma teachings are to be understood within the meaning and practice of the view.

6. The Meaning of Meditation Deities

In our retreat program, at this time we are learning the practice of meditation deities (*yidam*). These meditation deities are not worldly divinities or gods but are known as wisdom deities (*yeshe lha; ye shes kyi lha*) and are all understood to be the emanations of the primordial buddha, Samantabhadra. In a general sense, there are two ways of understanding a buddha or an enlightened one, depending on whether one considers a buddha from the ultimate point of view or from the relative point of view. A buddha may be understood from the ultimate point of view as manifesting from the absolute "downward" into the relative realms of experience out of compassion for beings. On the other hand, a buddha may be understood from the relative point of view, as one who begins from the relative condition of an ordinary sentient being in samsara and gradually progresses "upward" along the path in order to realize the ultimate.

Please note that in these teachings, when we speak of "downward" and "upward," we are not speaking of directions in physical space, like "up" and "down." The term "downward" refers to an enlightened buddha's manifesting from the formless dharmakaya, the "body of truth" that is empty like space, into the relative realms where the buddha assumes form. The term "upward" refers to the process by which an embodied sentient being progresses on the dharma path and realizes enlightenment as the dharmakaya buddha.

When we speak of the Buddha according to the relative viewpoint of the general vehicles of Buddhism, we are speaking from the perspective of the ordinary dualistic mind (*sems*). In this case, the teachings speak of the outer buddha nature. From the standpoint of the outer buddha nature, Buddha Shakyamuni became enlightened under the bodhi tree at the "outer Bodhgaya," the place where the thousand buddhas of this fortunate aeon are enlightened.

On the other hand, if we want to understand Buddha Shakyamuni according to the ultimate viewpoint of Dzogchen, the Great Perfection, then we are speaking from the perspective of the dharmakaya. Dharmakaya means "absolute body" or "truth body," and refers to the wisdom mind (*dgongs pa*) of an enlightened being; it is an empty body that is like space. This is known as the inner buddha nature, and from this perspective, it is said that the Buddha became enlightened in the "inner Bodhgaya." Here, the dharmakaya is also known as the inner Bodhgaya, because it is the ultimate place of enlightenment of the Buddha. The inner Bodhgaya is the Bodhgaya of one's own self-knowing awareness (*rang gi rig pa*).

Thus, according to this extraordinary point of view, when it is taught that the Buddha was enlightened within the state of the dharmakaya, it means that he was enlightened within the vast expanse of the wisdom mind of the primordial buddha Samantabhadra. According to the teachings of Dzogpa Chenpo, the pinnacle of all paths, it is taught that when one realizes the buddha nature internally, then one's buddha nature is known as the glorious primordial buddha Samantabhadra.

The one who has fully realized buddha nature from the very beginning is known as the primordial buddha Samantabhadra. Many aspirations and prayers address a seemingly "external" Samantabhadra, and "internally," there is the factor of one's faith and devotion with which one approaches Samantabhadra. However, conventions such as external and internal do not really exist as substantial things (*dngos po*), as actual places and entities. The teachings are only expressed in these terms for our intellectual understanding, as on the relative level there is no other way to communicate without making use of such concepts.

Buddha Samantabhadra is enlightened in the primordial ground, the vast expanse of the dharmakaya. From this wisdom mind, Samantabhadra manifests infinite sambhogakaya buddha fields, arrayed in the vastness of the expanse of space (*dhatu; dbyings*) like infinite lights, as numerous as there are atoms in all of existence. From that state of dharmakaya enlightenment, and due to its blessings, compassion, and power, the infinite sambhogakaya buddha fields naturally manifest. These appear for the sake of male and female bodhisattvas, for the dakas and dakinis of either worldly or wisdom origin, for yogins and yoginis, for any beings who have attained the first to the tenth spiritual levels (*bhumi; sa*). Then similarly from the sambhogakaya buddha fields, Samantabhadra displays infinite nirmanakaya emanations such as Buddha Shakyamuni, who appear in the worldly realms of existence for the benefit of sentient beings.

DHARMAKAYA

If we wish to understand the dharmakaya Buddha for ourselves, let us consider the example of space (*namkha; nam mkha'*). To begin with, we need to contemplate well, repeatedly, what is meant when it is said that the natural state of mind (*sems kyi gnas lugs*) is similar to space. In the Dzogchen teachings, space is the principal example given in order to understand dharmata, the ultimate reality or "true nature of phenomena." Reflecting well on the analogy of space will be very beneficial for our practice. For example, it is impossible to go beyond the limits of the sky, to go beyond space. Even if one wishes to do so and travels for thousands of years, one will never be able to pass beyond the farthest limits of space.

Think about the fact that we can never arrive at some place that exists outside of space. Wherever we find ourselves, we will always be within space. It makes no difference if we go to enormous efforts, building great structures like the Eiffel Tower, or even building thousands of them one on top of the other in an effort to reach the limits of the sky. No matter how far we go, we can never go beyond the sky. Fortunately, in order to realize dharmata, we don't have to go to any particular place or head off in some direction out into space.

Whether we remain somewhere or travel, eat or drink, we are never for a moment separate from space. Whether we are happy or sad, space is always present, and we are always within it. Whether we desperately want space to be near to us and try to hold on to it, or if we really don't like space and attempt to reject and discard it, space can never change and we will still find ourselves within it. However much we may exclaim "I love space!" and "I want space!" and even make great efforts to venerate space and invite it to dwell with us, we can neither increase space nor decrease it; space never changes, as space always is as it is. Although we may throw fits, screaming at space for a thousand days, shouting "I don't want you, space!" or "I don't need you, space, go away!" space will still always remain with us.

Whatever may happen, the nature of space is always present. For example, even when we sleep, space is still present. The true nature of our mind, dharmata, is similar to space. We are always inseparable from the nature of dharmata, which literally means "the true condition of all phenomena." Like space, the true nature of our mind is always present whether we like it or not. Like the example of space, the empty luminous dharmata (*chos nyid stong gsal*) has always been with us in samsara, from time without beginning, right up to the present moment. Thus the key difference is that the nature of mind is not a blank emptiness like ordinary physical space. While mind is empty like space, it also has the quality of clarity (*salwa; gsal ba*), which gives mind the ability to know and to experience.

From the very beginning, and from now until we may attain enlightenment, we are continually inseparable from the nature of mind, just as we will never be separate from space. Thus we don't need to create something that did not previously exist in order to discover dharmata, since we all have this ultimate nature. Like space, we ourselves and all phenomena are always included within the wisdom mind of dharmata (*chonyid kyi gongpa; chos nyid kyi dgongs pa*).

Dharmata, the great self-existing wisdom (*rangjung yeshe chenpo; rang byung ye shes chen po*), is always present within us and can be recognized through the pointing-out instructions of one's guru. Although this is so, the ability to realize it for oneself depends upon each person's faith and devotion and on the blessings of one's teachers. When these are present in conjunction with one's past karma and pure aspirations, through the combination of these conditions one's own great wisdom can be actualized. But for this to occur, we need to practice and meditate.

Why is this necessary if self-existing wisdom is already present within us? Normally, we are completely under the power of phenomenal appearances. First, from ignorance, the notion of an external existence arises. Then, related to these perceived "external" objects, we develop many hopes and fears, grasping at and fixating upon the phenomena we experience. It is due to the strength of our delusions that we think that what appears to us really exists. Phenomena seem to exist, but this is only because of the dualistic way in which we currently perceive appearances.

However, when speaking of the realization of the ultimate natural state of Dzogpa Chenpo, the Great Perfection, rather than being overpowered by phenomena, phenomenal appearances are actually under one's own power. Samantabhadra's wisdom mind of dharmata is neither confused nor tainted by the appearances of this world. They are mastered through one's realization of dharmata, the ultimate natural state (*gnas lugs mthar thug*). But for ordinary beings such as ourselves, realization can take place only through training and practice. Merely knowing about dharmata is not enough, since for realization to occur, it must be actualized in one's own experience. This is why we need meditation and practice.

When we speak of realization, we are speaking of the inconceivable secret nature (*gsang ba bsam gyis mi khyab pa*) of the tathagatas, which is also known as the "inconceivable secret nature of the Buddha's wisdom mind." Buddha Samantabhadra's wisdom is all-pervading and omniscient, and so all the phenomena of samsara and nirvana are included within Samantabhadra's wisdom mind (*thugs kyi dgongs pa*). In the blink of an eye, the wisdom mind of Samantabhadra can see everything within samsara and nirvana. And yet for us, pure realms such as Samantabhadra's Akanishtha buddha field, and even this world which is the pure realm of Buddha Shakyamuni, seem unimaginably vast and infinite. They seem to be far beyond what we can encompass with our mind. This is why we have to practice, as there is simply no other way for us to experience the wisdom mind for ourselves and actually realize it.

In our present condition, we can only imagine things in terms of our own ordinary experience of the world. For us, the world does seem to exist, but this is only due to our deluded perception. We have continuously pursued our delusions, and from this cloud bank of dualistic thoughts, we have created external objects as though they really exist, just as we do when dreaming. When a person is sleeping, all kinds of objects appear to him or her that seem completely real. But in the realization of the inconceivable secret of the tathagatas, the natural state of Dzogpa Chenpo, this world and all that appears to us doesn't even exist.

The inconceivable secret mind of Samantabhadra is the secret nature beyond thought, so it cannot be conceptualized but must be embraced by our own experience. The inconceivable secret mind of Samantabhadra is not an object like a house that has an outside and an inside; it is the secret nature that cannot be conceived of by conceptual thought. We can try to analyze it in an intellectual fashion, asking "What is Samantabhadra in the external world? What aspects of Samantabhadra do we have within us?" It may be helpful in the beginning, but we will not reach any genuine understanding through this kind of reasoning alone.

All beings have the same true nature of mind, the very same essence (*ngowo; ngo bo*) as Buddha Samantabhadra. This essence we share with Buddha Samantabhadra is the inseparability of space and awareness (*ying rig yermey; dbyings rig dbyer med*). The difference between ourselves and Samantabhadra is that our awareness has not been actualized and enlightened. We have not realized it for ourselves; and the only way we can understand it is if we ourselves experience and realize the inseparability of space and awareness.

How are we to understand buddha fields or pure realms (*zhing khams*) according to the point of view of Dzogpa Chenpo, the pinnacle of all paths? In works such as the *Treasury of Precious Qualities* (*Yonten Dzod; Yon tan mdzod*) by the awareness-holder Jigme Lingpa, we find many details regarding the three kayas and their respective buddha fields.

In order to understand buddha fields from the Dzogchen viewpoint, we need to consider all pure realms from the perspective of the dharmakaya buddha. As we have said, the inner realization of buddha nature is known as the primordial buddha, glorious Samantabhadra. Buddha Samantabhadra is enlightened in the primordial ground (*gdod ma'i gzhi*) as the dharmakaya. The infinite space itself is the example for the dharmakaya of the buddha. The pure realm of Buddha Samantabhadra is the dharmadhatu, the "expanse of the true condition of all phenomena" or "sphere of ultimate reality." Whatever pure realms, places, times, and inhabitants may exist, all of these are included within the pure realm of Buddha Samantabhadra.

Being enlightened within the state of dharmakaya, Samantabhadra manifests boundless sambhogakaya buddha fields. Buddha Samantabhadra's empty aspect (*tong cha; stong cha*) is the limitless expanse of space (*dhatu; dbyings*), and Samantabhadra's clarity aspect (*sal cha; gsal cha*) is the sambhogakaya buddha fields, appearing as lights in space. They are arrayed like lamps in the expanse, like infinite lamps manifesting limitless buddha fields as vast and many as there are atoms in the universe. All these sambhogakaya realms, each possessing the five certainties of the sambhogakaya, are displayed like the sun, moon, and the immeasurable stars within the infinity of space.

Samantabhadra's dharmakaya pure realm is also known as the "Akanishtha Realm of All-Encompassing Purity," or as the "Luminous Vajra Heart" (Osal Dorje Nyingpo;'Od gsal rdo rje snying po). Samantabhadra has fully awakened to his own awareness, and as a result of this, all that exists appears to him as the Akanishtha buddha field. We too have the same awareness (*rig pa*), but we don't recognize it, and for this reason Samantabhadra shows us the path through his emanated wisdom forms, which appear in limitless worlds.

The way Samantabhadra gradually or "indirectly" benefits sentient beings is by appearing as all of the different enlightened beings and teachers, while at the same time displaying various pure realms suitable for training sentient beings. Emanating in this way, we have all of the three kaya pure realms of Samantabhadra, namely, the dharmakaya, sambhogakaya, and nirmanakaya. The dharmakaya buddha fields are known as "Pure Realms of the Luminous Vajra Heart," the sambhogakaya buddha fields are known as "Pure Realms of Brahma's Thundering Drumbeat," and the nirmanakaya buddha fields are known as "Aeon of the Great Brahma," which encompasses all possible nirmanakaya pure realms.

All of the buddha fields of the three kayas share the same essence and are not separate, since all are included within the dharmakaya buddha field, just as the three kayas are contained within the dharmakaya. Hence, the buddha appearing in each pure realm is not separate from dharmakaya Samantabhadra. In the dharmakaya buddha field, the buddha is Samantabhadra; in the sambhogakaya pure realms, the buddha is Vajradhara and the buddhas of the five families; in the nirmanakaya realms, the buddha is the supreme nirmanakaya such as Buddha Shakyamuni. Buddha Shakyamuni is never separate from Samantabhadra and Buddha Vajradhara, as all are enlightened in the dharmakaya.

In brief, the pure realms of the three kayas encompass the entirety of all pure realms beyond measure. They are created through Samantabhadra's aspirational prayers and activity for the purpose of teaching, training, transforming, and liberating sentient beings. In these places and times, there appear the buddhas of the five families as well as all possible deities of the five families, all of which are included within what are known as the "one hundred peaceful and wrathful deities." The totality of all the limitless deities is inseparable from the wisdom mind of Samantabhadra. They are the display (rol pa) and emanation (sprul pa) of the inconceivable secret nature of Samantabhadra. They are Samantabhadra's manifold skillful means, through which beings become able to recognize and realize their own awareness wisdom (rang rig pa'i ye shes).

In the same way as the process of display and emanation unfolds from Buddha Samantabhadra, every buddha manifests pure realms within the worldly universes for the sake of liberating sentient beings. Thus when we speak about the enlightened ones unfolding from above to below, we also say that our teacher Buddha Shakyamuni was enlightened in the expanse of the dharmakaya and is identical with Buddha Samantabhadra. From that state, sambhogakaya buddha fields beyond measure appeared, arrayed like infinite lights within space. From these in turn, there arose manifold nirmanakaya emanations, such as Buddha Shakyamuni arising in our world.

Thus it is said that whatever teachings exist in any possible realm, they are the continuous expression of the vast sphere of Samantabhadra's wisdom mind (*kun bzang dgongs pa'i klong*). Samantabhadra has fully realized the final, natural state of all phenomena (*chos tham cad kyi gnas lugs mthar thug*), and it is through the blessings of this realization that all of the tantras of the Secret Mantrayana and the scriptures of the Mahayana arise. For example, according to the Great Perfection, there are the 6,400,000 principal stanzas of the Dzogchen tantras; and among the immense range of tantras such as Sri Guhyasamaja, Chakrasamvara, and Sri Hevajra, there are said to be seven hundred thousand or five hundred thousand root verses. Within the general Mahayana vehicle of teachings, there is the treasury of all the eighty-four thousand sutras, and then the one hundred thousand sections of the *Buddhavatamsaka Sutra*, the one hundred thousand sections of the *Heap of Jewels Sutra* (*Ratnarashi Sutra; Rin po che'i phung po'i mdo*), and so on.

Whatever spiritual qualities Buddha Samantabhadra has, we also possess the same qualities in our buddha nature or enlightened essence (*sugatagarbha; bde gshegs snying po*). The difference is only that we need to actualize these spiritual qualities within ourselves, through receiving teachings and blessings and by practicing meditation. Through practice, we will come to realize our mind nature, and when we do so, we will discover that we have the same nature as Samantabhadra. We meditate and practice in order to actualize the inseparability of expanse and primordial wisdom (*dbyings ye shes dbyer med*), the wisdom mind of Samantabhadra. Then we can manifest realms without limit for the sake of training beings. Like Samantabhadra, we can guide and teach the dharma to incalculable sentient beings and manifest an inestimable display of peaceful and wrathful deities.

For example, in this world there are limitless waters great and small, from ocean and lakes down to small puddles of water. In each of these, the reflection of the sun and moon appears, so that there are countless reflections appearing in a single instant. The emanations of Samantabhadra appear in the same way, an infinite number of reflections appearing simultaneously. Based on these enlightened emanations, all the various teachings in all possible aspects are revealed to the sentient beings to be trained.

In brief, if we condense the meaning of all these teachings about Samantabhadra, then among the three jewels of Buddha, dharma, and sangha, they are related to the jewel of the Buddha. It is very important that we learn about the enlightened qualities of the dharmakaya buddha Samantabhadra. In order to practice dharma, we must have trust and confidence in the precious jewel of the Buddha.

SAMBHOGAKAYA

In order to benefit sublime beings on the spiritual levels (*bhumi; sa*) as well as all sentient beings, the dharmakaya Buddha emanates in a form that can be perceived and experienced by beings. For this, the rupakaya or "body of enlightened form" is emanated, as the display of the dharmakaya buddha. The rupakaya refers to both the sambhogakaya and the nirmanakaya buddha emanations. First, from the vast expanse of the dharmakaya, due to the blessings, compassion, and power of that state of enlightenment, the boundless sambhogakaya buddha fields appear, arrayed like lights throughout infinite space.

If one would ask what purpose and benefit the sambhogakaya buddha fields serve, they manifest for the sake of beings who are on the first to the tenth spiritual levels. They appear for the sake of male and female bodhisattvas, dakas and dakinis, vidyadharas, yogins and yoginis, the noble beings on the first to the tenth spiritual levels. Those who have attained any of the first through tenth levels have reached the third and fourth of the five paths or stages of enlightenment, and thus they abide on the path of seeing or on the path of meditation.

Within the sambhogakaya buddha fields are the five buddha families and their entourages of bodhisattvas, dakas, and dakinis. All these infinite buddhas and buddha fields of the sambhogakaya realms are complete and perfect, endowed with the five certainties of the sambhogakaya. If we speak of the five certainties (*nges pa lnga*) of the sambhogakaya buddha field, it means that the sambhogakaya possesses five special attributes that make it ideal for the attainment of complete enlightenment. These five are the perfect place, perfect form of the teacher, perfect teaching, perfect entourage, and perfect time.

The first of these five is the perfect place, which is Ghanavyuha Akanishtha, the Unexcelled Abundantly Arrayed Buddha Field (Ogmin Tugpo Kodpa; 'Og min stug po bkod pa). It is called "Abundantly Arrayed" because it displays an infinite abundance of manifestations of the spiritual qualities of enlightenment. This is not the same level of Akanishtha as the dharmakaya buddha field of Samantabhadra, which can be perceived only by tenth-level bodhisattvas. Ghanavyuha Akanishtha is a buddha field emanated into the form realm (*gzugs khams*) of samsara that can be perceived by noble beings on the first through tenth spiritual levels. The sambhogakaya also possesses the perfect form of the teacher, which is the sambhogakaya buddha adorned with all the marks and signs. The perfect form of the teacher is the sambhogakaya buddha such as Buddha Vajradhara.

Since the perfect entourage is made up of the male and female bodhi-sattvas and the dakas and dakinis on the ten spiritual levels, the perfect entourage is made up of beings who have reached the third and fourth of the five paths, the path of seeing and path of meditation. It does not refer to ordinary beings, since the beings still on the first two of the five paths, the paths of accumulation and union, don't have a sufficient accumulation of merit and wisdom to enable them to perceive and meet the sambhogakaya buddhas.

The sambhogakaya buddha field is also endowed with the perfect teaching, which is the teaching emphasizing the ultimate meaning and not simply the relative, provisional meaning. Finally, the ultimate, perfect time is without interruption or cessation, the ongoing continuum of eternity (*dus rtag pa rgyun gyi 'khor lo*) that continues until samsara is exhausted.

NIRMANAKAYA

The Nirmanakaya Buddha

From the compassion of the sambhogakaya buddhas, the nirmanakaya emanations appear for the sake of those beings on the beginning stages of the dharma path. From the vast expanse of dharmakaya Samantabhadra, out of the blessings and compassion of his wisdom mind, the limitless sambhogakaya buddha fields manifest, arrayed like lights throughout infinite space. Within these buddha fields are the buddhas of the five families and their entourages of bodhisattvas, dakas, and dakinis. All of these infinite buddhas and buddha fields are complete with the five certainties, and they arise naturally due to the blessings and compassion of the dharmakaya buddha.

Then from the sambhogakaya buddha fields, the nirmanakaya emanations arise for those who are on the first two of the five paths or stages to complete enlightenment. This means that the beings who are still on the first and second of the five paths, the path of accumulation (*tshogs lam*) and the path of joining (*sbyor lam*), do not have the fortune to perceive these [sambhogakaya] realms, as they have not yet reached the first of the ten spiritual levels. Until one has the necessary accumulation of merit, it is not possible to perceive and meet the sambhogakaya buddhas. The beings that are still on the paths of accumulation and joining do not yet have the fortune to perceive the sambhogakaya realms.

There are limitless places where the nirmanakaya emanates, as there are an inconceivable number of nirmanakaya buddha fields. Our world is not the only one; there are innumerable world systems and universes within the nirmanakaya realms. All nirmanakaya pure realms are the emanations of the sambhogakaya, arising from the compassion and light rays emanating from the sambhogakaya buddhas. When we say nirmanakaya realms have been created or manifested, the creator of these are the dharmakaya and sambhogakaya buddhas. The nirmanakaya realms arise from the compassion of the buddhas based on the positive karma and merit of the sentient beings to be born in these nirmanakaya fields.

The nirmanakaya buddhas naturally manifest from the sambhogakaya when the two primary conditions of the positive merit of sentient beings and the blessings of the dharmakaya and sambhogakaya meet. From those rainbow light appearances of the sambhogakaya, there emanate light rays causing incalculable enlightened nirmanakaya incarnations to appear throughout the three realms of samsara, just as Shakyamuni Buddha appears in our world.

Likewise, countless nirmanakaya pure realms arise due to causes and conditions. It is just like when the conditions of sun, moisture, and so forth, come together and a rainbow naturally appears. The rainbow manifestation will remain as long as the appropriate interdependent conditions are in place, and when the conditions are exhausted, it will disappear. The multifarious nirmanakaya manifestations are not definite in their forms nor fixed in the places, times, and duration of their appearance. Just as a rainbow will remain only as long as the conditions are in place, so when the interdependent conditions are exhausted, the nirmanakaya will disappear. Like rainbows, which appear but are intangible displays of light in space, the nirmanakaya are magical displays (*cho 'phrul*) appearing for the sake of sentient beings. Hence the physical manifestation of nirmanakaya emanations is known as an "illusory body" (*gyulu; sgyu lus*).

On the nirmanakaya level, the enlightened emanations don't have the five certainties of the sambhogakaya; in fact, they actually have five uncertainties: those of place, form, teachings, entourage, and time. There are an infinite multitude of places of nirmanakaya emanation, and the place is uncertain in the sense that it can be either pure or impure. The place may be either a nirmanakaya pure realm or an impure realm anywhere in the three worlds of samsara. Just as the rainbow only manifests where the conditions come together, there is no fixed place or time the nirmanakaya manifests, and thus it is said that the nirmanakaya manifestations are not certain or fixed.

The nirmanakaya *form* of the teacher is uncertain in the sense that it can manifest in myriad forms according to sentient beings' fortune and capacity, due to the presence of the necessary causes and conditions. There are an endless variety of the forms of emanations in the impure worlds to train beings, and yet all are of an illusory nature. The entourage is uncertain as the disciples are ordinary sentient beings. The teachings are uncertain because they expound the relative, provisional meaning in addition to the ultimate meaning taught in the sambhogakaya buddha fields.

The rupakaya or body of enlightened form emanates from the buddha's dharmakaya, and the rupakaya has two aspects, the sambhogakaya and the nirmanakaya. In general, there are three types of nirmanakayas. First there is the nirmanakaya of the nature (*rang bzhin sprul pa*), the nirmanakaya teachers emanated in the ten pure realms of the ten directions, which are all included within the buddha fields of the five families that liberate beings. Second, there is the nirmanakaya that guides beings (*'gro 'dul sprul pa*), and this includes all nirmanakaya buddhas known as the "six munis," who take birth in the form of human beings or any of the beings of the six realms. Thus this kind of nirmanakaya first refers to what are known as supreme nirmanakaya emanations (*chok gi tulku; mchog gi sprul sku*), such as Buddha Shakyamuni. Also among this kind of nirmanakaya are the secondary emanations that benefit beings of the six realms, such as sravakas and pratyekabuddhas, bodhisattvas, kings and rulers, and so on.

The supreme nirmanakaya benefits sentient beings through enlightened body, speech, and mind. Buddha Shakyamuni is a perfect buddha whose body possesses all of the thirty-two major and eighteen minor marks of perfection, the same enlightened qualities with which the sambhogakaya buddhas are endowed. With his body, he enacts the twelve deeds of a buddha. Also, the speech of the supreme nirmanakaya has all the perfect qualities of the dharma and continuously turns the three wheels of dharma and the Secret Mantrayana teachings in all of the languages of sentient beings. The mind of the supreme nirmanakaya is enlightened in the dharmakaya, possessed of all the qualities of omniscience, endowed with perfect knowledge and intelligence.

The third category of nirmanakaya refers to the diverse nirmanakaya emanations (*natsog tulku; sna tshogs sprul pa*) that appear both as beings and as inanimate objects. This is the nirmanakaya that manifests in various forms, including both animate beings and inanimate objects. For example, this refers to manifestations of beings such as craftsmen or artists who manufacture statues and paintings; and also in some cases, statues themselves are seen as nirmanakaya emanations.

In order to understand the supreme nirmanakaya buddha, let us first briefly recount the general explanations of the manner in which Buddha Shakyamuni and Buddha Amitabha made aspirations, practiced the path, and finally attained enlightenment. Here we will consider the nirmanakaya both from the viewpoint of the general explanations, which understand nirmanakaya buddhas as coming from the relative to the ultimate, from below to above, and also from the viewpoint of the extraordinary explanations, which understand buddhas as coming from the ultimate to the relative, from above to below.

According to the general way of explanation given for ordinary beings, it is not taught that Buddha Shakyamuni was in fact already enlightened and emanated into this world as a nirmanakaya buddha in order to benefit sentient beings. Rather, it is taught in many of the general sutra teachings that Shakyamuni was an ordinary sentient being who gradually attained enlightenment through a series of lifetimes spread out over aeons of time.

These sutras tell us that aeons before he became a buddha, Shakyamuni was born in a worldly realm as an ordinary sentient being. At that time there was a buddha known as Shakya Mahamuni dwelling in the world. Shakyamuni made offerings to the buddha, praying that he would be able to follow him, attain enlightenment, and greatly benefit sentient beings. At another point after many lifetimes, Shakyamuni was able to be reborn in the hell realms for the purpose of making further prayers there to be able to benefit and liberate sentient beings. Then after countless more lifetimes over aeons of time, Shakyamuni was born in this world and finally attained buddhahood under the bodhi tree at Bodhgaya in India.

Like the account of Shakyamuni's previous lives, there are similar accounts concerning Buddha Vajradhara. When he was still an ordinary being, Vajradhara met a buddha for the first time. He offered the Buddha Pushpa Maharoca a golden vajra and developed the wish to become enlightened for the benefit of all beings. In his final birth, he received the dharma teachings from the Buddha Kalyanamati and he stayed on the summit of a mountain known as "Array of Gem Clusters" practicing the teachings. As a result, he attained complete enlightenment and became known as Buddha Vajradhara, meaning "Holder of the Vajra," since he had previously offered a vajra to a buddha.

Likewise, there is a similar account of how Buddha Amitabha gradually attained enlightenment. The sutras recount that many aeons before he became a buddha, Amitabha was a fully ordained monk called Dharmakara, "Source of Dharma." In the presence of the Buddha Lokeshvaraja, he made the aspiration that whoever would hear his name or would pray to him, even without ever having met him, would be reborn in his pure realm. Dharmakara made this aspiration and cultivated bodhicitta, the thought of enlightenment.

As taught in the *Karuna Pundarika* or *White Lotus Sutra*, many lifetimes later the bodhisattva Dharmakara was born as the chakravartin or universal ruler known as Arenemin (Tsibkyi Mukyu; Rtsib kyi mu khyud). This king had a thousand sons who would become the thousand buddhas of this fortunate aeon. In those times there dwelled among them a buddha named Ratnagarbha, "Jewel Essence." The emperor and his sons, one of whom was in fact a previous incarnation of Buddha Shakyamuni, made aspirations in front of Buddha Ratnagarbha to be able to benefit the beings in our Jambudvipa world. On this basis, they will become the 1,002 buddhas of this fortunate aeon that will be born in our world, the southern continent of Jambudvipa.

At this time, the monarch Arenemin prayed that he would be able to manifest a pure realm in which sentient beings could be born, receive teachings, and attain enlightenment. As King Arenemin was actually a previous birth of Amitabha, upon attaining enlightenment, Buddha Amitabha manifested Sukhavati, the pure realm known as "Endowed with Bliss."

Thus, it is taught in the general sutra teachings that Amitabha met buddhas over many lifetimes, making aspirations and finally becoming enlightened. Through the power of his former prayers and aspirations, he was able to manifest the pure realm of Sukhavati, made of a great variety of precious substances. From the conventional point of view, it is said that the pure realm of Sukhavati exists many thousands of universes from this world, in the western direction. By praying to Buddha Amitabha, sentient beings can be born in that pure realm.

During the same time as the universal ruler Arenemin was offering his aspirations before Buddha Ratnagarbha, his brother, who was a previous incarnation of Buddha Shakyamuni, made his own aspirations. In the presence of Buddha Ratnagarbha, Shakyamuni gave rise to the wish to be able to benefit in particular those beings who were burdened with afflictive emotions, short life spans, and manifold illnesses. He prayed to be able to actually and directly benefit sentient beings right within the impure worlds of samsara, rather than waiting until after they had been born in a pure realm. Thus it came to be that after many more lifetimes, Shakyamuni came to this world and benefited countless beings as the nirmanakaya buddha, both here in Jambudvipa and with billions of emanations spread throughout a vast range of worldly universes and realms.

According to the point of view of Dzogpa Chenpo, Buddha Shakyamuni was enlightened in the primordial ground, the wisdom mind of Samantabhadra. In Dzogpa Chenpo, we see everything as manifesting from above to below, from the dharmakaya Samantabhadra downward, from the absolute to the relative. When we speak of the Buddha's unfolding from the absolute, we say that our teacher the Buddha was enlightened in the expanse of the dharmakaya. From that realization there arose the display of the infinity of lights of the limitless sambhogakaya buddha fields. From there the incalculable nirmanakaya emanations appear, such as Shakyamuni Buddha and so many others beyond measure.

In contrast, according to the general teachings, the Buddha was a sentient being who became enlightened in Bodhgaya, and his awakening proceeded from the relative to the ultimate. So there are these different perspectives, since the former speaks of the ultimate point of view that understands the Buddha proceeding from the above to the below, the other is the relative way of understanding the Buddha, where one proceeds from lower to higher. The former perspective is that of the dharmakaya, the viewpoint of primordial wisdom (*ye shes*). The latter perspective is that of the rupakaya body of enlightened form, the standpoint of the ordinary, dualistic mind (*sems*) taught for the benefit of those on the beginning stages of the path.

If we explain the enlightenment of Buddha Shakyamuni from the perspective of coming from below to above, then we say that Buddha Shakyamuni was enlightened under the bodhi tree at Bodhgaya, in India. Thus it is said that at the Vajra Seat under the bodhi tree at Bodhgaya, Buddha Shakyamuni was enlightened after accumulating merit for three incalculable eons. The place of Bodhgaya is called the "Vajra Seat" (*vajrasana; rdo rje gdan*) because it has been blessed by the enlightened ones and because of this it cannot be destroyed even at the end of the eon when this whole world is destroyed. Having thus purified all obscurations, finally under the bodhi tree, the place of enlightenment of the 1,002 buddhas of this fortunate eon, Buddha Shakyamuni attained complete enlightenment. This is what is known as the outer aspect of enlightenment.

Buddha Shakyamuni remained in the state of meditation and was able to pacify and overcome all his delusion and inner demons (*mara; bdud*) and achieve perfect enlightenment. At that time he made the following declaration:

> I have found a dharma that is like nectar;
> It is uncompounded clear luminosity,
> Profound and peaceful,
> And beyond all conceptual elaborations.
> Were I to explain it, others would not understand;
> And so I will remain in the forest without speaking.

From the point of view of the general teaching of the lower vehicles, after attaining enlightenment in Bodhgaya, Buddha Shakyamuni taught successively the sutra teachings of the three turnings of the wheel of dharma, followed by the general outer tantras and then the anuttaratantras, all the teachings below the level of Dzogpa Chenpo. Starting from below, from the outer introductory teachings, the Buddha progressively and sequentially revealed the higher inner teachings, and the dharma flourished in this world. The three turnings of the wheel of dharma by the Buddha are thus known as the nirmanakaya buddha teachings. In the first part of his life, Buddha Shakyamuni turned the first wheel; in the middle part, he turned the second wheel; and in the later part the third. This condenses the teachings of all the vehicles.

In the first turning, the Buddha taught the sixteen divisions of the four truths of the noble beings. In the early part of his life, Buddha gave many teachings on karma and renunciation, taught the monastic rules of the Vinaya, and so on. The teachings of the second turning of the wheel of dharma are related to emptiness, the shunyata nature of all phenomena, and specifically to the truth of how all things lack characteristics and attributes.

The third turning of the wheel of dharma is related to the teachings on *sugatagarbha,* the buddha nature. The sutra teachings are part of the teachings given from the perspective of the outer buddha nature. These teachings don't completely reveal the buddha nature, but they certainly indicate that all beings do have this nature. In the many sutras explaining the buddha nature, Buddha teaches the general qualities of the buddha nature in a more external way, but without the inner method of how to accomplish it or realize it for oneself. Within the sutra teachings of the third turning, there is little in the way of methods or oral instructions given openly. There are no detailed, step-by-step methods or oral instructions (*men ngak; man ngag*) for practice given. There is no inner methodology taught that actually enables one to swiftly accomplish the buddha nature and realize it for oneself.

If we want to go into this subtle aspect of how to practice and accomplish buddha nature, then we come to the Secret Mantrayana or Vajrayana, the "Diamond Vehicle," the teachings of the Buddhist tantras. The sutra teachings of the third turning of the wheel of dharma are the basis for the Vajrayana, since the teachings on buddha nature are the basis on which the outer tantras are taught. The manner of practicing and accomplishing the buddha nature is explained in the Vajrayana teachings of the outer tantras that were transmitted by Buddha Shakyamuni in the later part of his life, as the fulfillment of the teachings of the third turning.

Within the tantric teachings, there are the more coarse methods of the outer tantras and the more subtle approach of the inner tantras. Starting from the outer tantras, we can proceed to the higher or inner tantras, as the practice becomes increasingly profound and subtle. If we want to go into the subtle aspects of how to really practice in order to realize buddha nature for ourselves, we need to rely on the Vajrayana teachings of Secret Mantra.

From the viewpoint of the inner tantras, true nature of mind is known as dharmata, which is like space; it is our buddha nature or enlightened essence. This is actually the final key point of all Buddhist teachings on transcendent intelligence (*shes rab*) and primordial wisdom (*ye shes*). When the teachings speak of the vastness of the realization of the buddhas, it is known as the "secret of the buddhas and bodhisattvas," as the "secret of all phenomena," or as the "secret of the way things are in reality" (*dngos po'i gnas tshul*). There are many descriptive terms for the secret of the buddha, such as the "secret nature of dharmata." Similarly, it may be known as the "inconceivable secret of the dharmadhatu," which is without limit. At times, it is called the "inconceivable secret nature of wisdom mind" (*dgongs pa gsang ba bsam mi khyab*), or simply, the "natural state" (*naylug; gnas lugs*) of mind. The nature of each of these secrets is inconceivable (*sam mi kyabpa; bsam mi khyab pa*), as vast as the expanse of space.

The sutras give various outer examples of the qualities of the Buddha to help us understand the inconceivable vastness of enlightenment. As an

example of this, the *ushnisha* or "top knot" of the Buddha is an actual forma-
tion at the crown of the Buddha's head that is a manifestation of the vastness of his realization. When the tenth-level bodhisattvas among Buddha's
disciples wanted to see how far the Buddha's subtle ushnisha extended, they
would use their miraculous powers to follow it, flying through thousands
and thousands of world systems. Even then, they could never reach the limits of the space through which the Buddha's ushnisha extended. Finally the
range of their miraculous abilities was exhausted, and those bodhisattvas
returned back to Varanasi, where the Buddha had remained. This is one
example of the inconceivable secret nature of the Buddha.

Just as they had wished to investigate the Buddha's ushnisha at the crown
of his head, the greatest of the bodhisattvas also wanted to see how far the
light extended from the Buddha's body. Even when the bodhisattvas, by
their miraculous powers, traveled in a western direction through thousands
and thousands of world systems, they still could not find the end of the light
that emanated from the Buddha's body. Finally, when their abilities were
exhausted and they couldn't travel any farther, the light emanating from the
Buddha's body still surrounded them in the space. They discovered that
the light emanating from the Buddha's body is boundless and infinite, just
as the pure realms of the dharmakaya buddha Samantabhadra are.

This is another aspect of the inconceivable secret nature of the Buddha. If
we wonder what is meant here by "the inconceivable secret of the buddha,"
the term "secret" refers to being beyond all limits. This inconceivable secret
is not an object of our dualistic mind. It is not and cannot be something we
can comprehend or realize through logic or reasoning. The nature of dharmata is completely beyond concepts, so therefore it is said to be "beyond
thought" or "inconceivable" (*bsam mi khyab*). When one meditates, one
needs to have faith and confidence in that inconceivable nature of dharmata.

When speaking of the nature of the secret body of the tathagata, we
can refer to either the dharmakaya Samantabhadra, the sambhogakaya
Vajradhara, or Buddha Shakyamuni, who is the nirmanakaya emanation
of Samantabhadra. All the three kayas—dharmakaya, sambhogakaya, and
nirmanakaya—have the same nature. The wisdom bodies (*ye shes kyi sku*) of
Buddha Samantabhadra, Buddha Vajradhara, and Buddha Shakyamuni are
all the same in essence. As the nirmanakaya Buddha, Buddha Shakyamuni
appeared in the form of a human being, so that sentient beings could meet
and see him.

For example, in the city of Varanasi, one can still see the remains of small bone relics of the body of the Buddha and gain great merit by paying respect to them, making offerings, and so on. Similarly, during the Buddha's lifetime, he and his entourage spent time at a place in India called Rajagriha, in order to do a three-month summer monsoon retreat. At that time there was a king in that area who was their sponsor and had promised to provide the food and alms for their retreat. The king, however, failed to keep his word. The Buddha and his followers did not receive their food and instead had to eat food from the horses' stables. This example shows that the Buddha appeared as a human being who ate food like other human beings. The Buddha manifested as such due to his skillful means in benefiting sentient beings, so that people could gain merit by making food offerings to him. All enlightened emanations and the appearances of pure realms are for the benefit of the beings to be trained. This illustrates some of the enlightened aspects and qualities of the buddha's body.

The inconceivable secrets of the Buddha's enlightened speech are likewise beyond measure and conception. The Buddha gives teachings to all of the bodhisattvas in his entourage, who listen to the dharma in infinite worlds and universes. For instance, when Buddha Shakyamuni is dwelling in this world, his speech remains free from the slightest notion of outer or inner. It is free of any designation of distance; it is limitless like space. When the Buddha even so much as clears his throat or coughs, it is for the benefit of sentient beings. When he gives teachings to the gods, nagas, and human beings, each will be able to understand him in their own tongue. Even if there are thousands of different varieties of sentient beings present, each will understand the Buddha in their respective languages without the need to depend on translators.

The nirmanakaya buddha Shakyamuni abides in the expanse of wisdom wherever he travels or dwells. Throughout all of his actions, such as when stretching his body or bending and folding his arms, he is never separated from the realization of this ultimate nature, not even for the time span of the blink of an eye. In every single exhalation and inhalation of his breath, he never separates from the nature of dharmata. Merely through the movements of his breath, Buddha Shakyamuni has the power to benefit beings in worlds without end. This is the inconceivable secret of the Buddha's speech. It is beyond the conceptual framework of the human mind, beyond all possible intellectual conventions.

Also in relation to the Buddha's speech, Buddha Shakyamuni expounded the eighty-four thousand different teachings of the general vehicle of the sutras in three turnings of the wheel of dharma, as well as all of the vast teachings of the Secret Mantrayana. Likewise, the 6,400,000 stanzas of the Dzogchen tantras were taught by Buddha Samantabhadra. Thus all the infinite tantras of the Mantrayana were taught by the Buddha as the expression of his vajra speech. And yet the Buddha has said, "Following my enlightenment and until my parinirvana, I did not speak a single word, but pervaded all beings with my presence." Buddha did not speak one word of teaching, and no one listened. Yet whatever the extent of the nature of the dharma expressed by the Buddha, it was permeated by the wisdom mind of all buddhas. Each of these points shed light on the secret inconceivable nature of the Buddha's speech.

As it is for his body and speech, so the Tathagata's mind has the inconceivable secret nature. The primordial Buddha is the one who has never moved nor strayed from the state of dharmakaya, who has always remained in the realization of dharmata. The nature of buddhahood is beyond effort, beyond doing anything, beyond existence itself; it is beyond all of these things. The different dharma teachings are given and manifested for each being's benefit according to his or her individual fortune and merit, the different dharma teachings are given and manifested for their benefit.

In brief, whether we speak of Samantabhadra or Shakyamuni, they are actually identical in nature, with Shakyamuni being the emanation of Samantabhadra. Although in our sadhanas and pujas we may visualize Buddha Samantabhadra above and Buddha Shakyamuni below Samantabhadra, this is just convention and in accord with our ordinary, dualistic way of thinking. In reality, Samantabhadra and Shakyamuni are not two. The dharmakaya or "absolute body" and the rupakaya or "body of enlightened form" are always a unity.

Nirmanakaya Pure Lands: Amitabha and Sukhavati

If we wish to understand more concerning the nirmanakaya pure realms and the manner in which they come about, let's consider the example of Buddha Amitabha, whose name in Tibetan means "Infinite Light." On the ultimate level, Amitabha is the dharmakaya buddha. The meaning of his name "Infinite Light" refers to his infinite awareness wisdom (*rig pa'i ye shes*) that is without mental distortions, afflictive emotions, and habitual tendencies, and thus free from all stains and obscurations. The "infinite light" is in fact our infinite naturally luminous awareness (*rang gsal rig pa*). It does not mean ordinary physical light, but refers to the luminosity (*osal; 'od gsal*) of our true nature that possesses all of the qualities of enlightenment. In this sense we may understand that Buddha Amitabha is the same in essence as Buddha Samantabhadra.

The dharmakaya buddha Amitabha sometimes manifests on the sambhogakaya level as Buddha Amitayus, whose name in Tibetan means "Infinite Life." He is represented with the thirteen jewel ornaments and silk robes of the sambhogakaya deities. If we pray to Amitayus for the blessings of longevity and endeavor well in his long-life practices, we can receive the accomplishments (*siddhi; dngos grub*) of longevity and deathless immortality.

On the level of ultimate truth, Amitayus is inseparable from the dharmakaya, free from birth and death, and transcends samsara and nirvana. Thus, when we consider the enlightened body, speech, and mind of Amitayus, then it is said that the mind aspect is the realization of Amitayus as a state that never wavered from the wisdom mind of Samantabhadra; this again is simply awareness wisdom. If we practice the enlightened body of Amitayus, then to accomplish the sambhogakaya Amitayus is to realize the immortal vajra body.

Similar to his manifestation as Amitayus, the dharmakaya Buddha Amitabha also manifests as the sambhogakaya buddha Amitabha in the sambhogakaya buddha field. In this case, he is one of the five central buddhas of the five buddha families of sambhogakaya deities, the buddha of the western direction.

Then once again Buddha Amitabha also manifests as Amitabha on the nirmanakaya level. From the dharmakaya and the sambhogakaya, Buddha Amitabha is emanated into the nirmanakaya realm of Sukhavati or "Endowed with Bliss" (Dewa Chen; Bde ba can), the pure realm said to be in the western direction. In Sukhavati, Amitabha manifests the nirmanakaya form of Buddha Amitabha. And so it is said that the nirmanakaya Amitabha is in the western pure realm, seated with hands in the meditation mudra, wearing dharma robes, having the buddhas' ushnisha at the crown of his head, and the various other attributes. Similarly, Amitabha emanates into the nirmanakaya realm as the bodhisattva Avalokiteshvara, as Guru Padmasambhava, and as any other form.

Thus Buddha Amitabha manifests as all three kayas or "buddha bodies." There is dharmakaya Amitabha, who is the realization of ultimate truth. There is the sambhogakaya level, where Amitabha is one of the five buddhas of the five families, whose consort is Pandaravasini, and there is also his sambhogakaya manifestation as Amitayus. Both the sambhogakaya and the nirmanakaya form of Buddha Amitabha who resides in the Sukhavati pure realm are the manifest aspect (*snang cha*) of dharmakaya buddha, appearing for the benefit of beings.

The three kayas of Buddha Amitabha are all in fact identical in essence with dharmakaya Samantabhadra. The dharmakaya buddha Samantabhadra is the ultimate wisdom mind, the natural state of awareness free from all delusion. When we speak of the mandala of emanations of dharmakaya Samantabhadra, we refer to his sambhogakaya aspect as Buddha Vajradhara or as the five buddhas of the five families such as Vairocana, Amitabha, and all of the incalculable sambhogakaya deities. Then on the nirmanakaya level, there are Buddha Shakyamuni, the thousand buddhas of this fortunate aeon, and all of the other nirmanakaya buddhas.

Ultimately, all places, all times, and all phenomena within samsara and nirvana are nothing more than the wisdom display of Samantabhadra. In addition to this, all the enlightened nirmanakaya manifestations such as Shakyamuni, Avalokiteshvara, or Manjushri are the same single essence as Samantabhadra, manifested from his enlightened mind for the sake of training beings. The key point to be clear about is that when understood in their ultimate nature, they are each enlightened in the same unique essence, which is none other than awareness wisdom.

The general explanation in the sutra vehicle teachings about how the realms of enlightened activity of various buddhas unfold tell us that Amitabha practiced the path and made aspirations. Then upon attaining enlightenment, he emanated Sukhavati, the pure realm "Endowed with Bliss." There are a great many known examples of beings who have been born in Sukhavati by the power of their aspirations. The Indian master Nagarjuna, the teacher Araga, and so many other gurus have been reborn in Sukhavati through the power of their practice and aspirations. In fact, even an ordinary person may train in the transfer of consciousness (*phowa;* '*pho ba*) practice where one meditates on Buddha Amitabha on the top of one's head. Through praying to Amitabha frequently and fervently with great faith, and then practicing the transfer of consciousness at the time of passing away, it is possible that we too can be reborn in Sukhavati.

Seen from the ultimate point of view of the mandala of dharmakaya Samantabhadra, there is no "place" somewhere "out there," such as the western pure realm of Sukhavati, to which one "goes." Rather, whoever is able to purify the obscurations of his or her mind and endeavors in the practice of Buddha Amitabha will be blessed with the ability to directly behold the face of Amitabha. Since one's essential awareness (*rang ngo rig pa*) is ultimately identical to Amitabha's, by praying to, and meditating on, Amitabha, one will be able to meet and realize this awareness, and will see the face of Amitabha.

Chakrasamvara and the Twenty-Four Sacred Lands

In addition to the general Mahayana pure realms such as Sukhavati, there are an infinite variety of types of nirmanakaya pure realms that appear due to the skillful means of various buddhas. For example, according to the general explanations given in the Secret Mantrayana teachings of the tantras, there are twenty-four sacred lands of the dakas and dakinis. All of the twenty-four sacred lands are conventionally said to be in India. It is said that when one goes to those holy places, one will be able to meet dakas and dakinis, enter their realm, and attain both the relative and supreme spiritual accomplishments (*siddhi; dngos grub*). In biographical accounts, we find that many great masters and siddhas such as mahapandita Naropa actually went to these holy places.

We may have heard that one of the principal disciples of the great yogi Milarepa, whose name was Rechungpa Dorje Drakpa, also went to the twenty-four sacred lands. Yet when it is said that Rechungpa went to the twenty-four sacred lands, it is meant for the understanding of ordinary beings. We can begin with a general idea that there are twenty-four lands such as Oddiyana, Jalandadhara, and so on. We might think that Rechungpa flew to them like one would fly in an airplane or like a bird across the ocean.

Everyone can understand this way of speaking, and from the relative point of view, it is true; we are not being untruthful. However, these descriptions are in accord with the general way of understanding, for the benefit of disciples on the beginning stages of the path, and do not reflect the highest point of view. For the sake of ordinary beings, these sacred lands are explained as places one can go to, but this is just by way of explanation so that ordinary persons can gain some general understanding of enlightened activity.

In the various anuttaratantras, there are different versions of the general explanations regarding the twenty-four sacred lands. Some tantras say that the twenty-four lands are exclusively in India, others say that some of them are also in China, and others say that they are spread throughout the whole world, or that they are in both the human and the nonhuman realms. Still other tantras explain the twenty-four places on a higher, more internal level, saying that they are all found within the psychic channels of one's own subtle vajra body.

For example, in one account, there was once a fierce demon, or according to other tantras, a zombie, who was very powerful and was taking the lives of an enormous number of sentient beings. He was perhaps someone similar to Hitler, since he was a commanding leader who had many demon generals and deputies in twenty-four different lands, and thus had control over great regions. Through the blessings of the buddhas, various deities, dakas, and dakinis were able to subdue these demons. First the male demons were annihilated and their consciousnesses liberated into a pure realm, and then the females and their children were liberated, until finally no demons remained in those twenty-four lands. When one army defeats another, it must leave someone in charge, and so the dakas and dakinis took control of these twenty-four regions, transforming them into sacred lands.

In the version of the Chakrasamvara Tantra, what is now the manifestation of the mandala of Buddha Chakrasamvara was once the realm of the demon lord Bhairava. Buddha Vajradhara emanated and subdued the demon, and Vajradhara himself then arose in the wrathful form of Bhairava. Vajradhara appeared in Bhairava's form as the wisdom deity Chakrasamvara and transformed Bhairava's formerly demon-infested realm into a mandala of twenty-four sacred lands.

It is said that there are four principal dakinis within the twenty-four sacred lands that were once the realms of Bhairava. They are emanations of Buddha Vajradhara in forms that were previously those of fierce demonesses who had been living in the charnel grounds of those realms. One demoness was called Khandaroha or Dum Kye Ma in Tibetan. *Dum* means "piece," *kye* means "to be born"; so she is known as the one "born from a piece." The way she received her name is that when people went to one of the charnel grounds in Bhairava's realms, they would see a piece of a hand, an arm, or another body part. When they looked upon such a body part, the "piece" would immediately transform into a fierce demoness who would begin to devour them.

Once this demoness was subdued and her consciousness liberated into a buddha field, an enlightened emanation of Buddha Vajradhara and Chakrasamvara arose in Khandaroha's form, as a wrathful dakini. This emanation assumed the form previously held by the female demon, wearing bone ornaments and holding skull cups and other fierce and terrifying implements. In a similar manner, daka and dakini emanations of Chakrasamvara took control of the twenty-four blood sacrifice places of Bhairava, transforming them into the holy places of twenty-four sacred lands, where beings can meet with the buddhadharma and attain enlightenment. This is a brief account of how the enlightened emanations of dakas and dakinis came to manifest in the twenty-four places, according to the Chakrasamvara Tantra.

What is the reason for the buddhas, dakas, and dakinis to manifest in this way? Chakrasamvara is an emanation of the primordial buddha Samantabhadra. All the infinitude of possible wisdom deities, all of whom are included within Samantabhadra's dharmakaya pure realm Luminous Vajra Heart (Osal Dorje Nyingpo; 'Od gsal rdo rje snying po), are Samantabhadra's emanations. These include all the heruka wisdom deities such as Chakrasamvara and all the wisdom dharma protectors such as the various Mahakalas. Because ordinary beings cannot see or hear the wisdom form of Buddha Samantabhadra, we need to have these emanations such as Chakrasamvara and the dakas and dakinis, so that those within the realms of samsara are able to perceive them and enter the dharma path.

For example, the deity Chakrasamvara manifests nirmanakaya buddha fields for the sake of training beings, so that they may encounter his emanations, accomplish the wisdom form of Chakrasamvara, and attain buddhahood. It is for this reason that we have the creation and completion stage practices of the peaceful and wrathful deities of the Secret Mantrayana.

Based on the various accounts, we see that there is an outer way of explaining that the wisdom form of the Buddha must manifest in order for sentient beings to be trained. For this reason, one finds in the traditions of all the heruka deities of the anuttaratantra such as Chakrasamvara, Kalachakra, and Hevajra historical accounts relating to powerful demons that were subdued and liberated, and whose realms were appropriated by the buddhas. Wrathful heruka wisdom deities were emanated by Buddha Vajradhara, in order to rescue countless sentient beings from the terrors of birth in the lower realms due to the malevolent influence of the demons. This is why one sees those same powerful demons such as Bhairava under the feet of the wrathful wisdom deities, to indicate that they have been subjugated and their realms appropriated.

All such histories are taught from the relative point of view of ordinary beings. Ultimately, to understand the heruka deities according to the Dzogchen teachings, we must refer to the viewpoint of dharmakaya buddha Samantabhadra. All of the limitless deities of the infinite tantras of the Secret Mantrayana, such as Kalachakra, Yamantaka, Vajrakilaya, and so on—in fact, the entirety of the deities of the three kayas—all arise from dharmadhatu, the vast sphere of Samantabhadra's wisdom mind (*kun tu bzang po'i dgongs klong*).

Thus we have seen that there are histories for the wrathful deities, as well as for the peaceful deities such as the accounts of Shakyamuni and Amitabha. Usually the histories relating to the path of the peaceful deities teach that a great being gave rise to bodhicitta and accumulated enormous merit; and further, that they made aspirations that upon becoming enlightened, he or she would be able to manifest pure realms for the sake of sentient beings. In the vast sutras and tantras, one finds the accounts of the liberation and enlightenment of these great beings through a succession of lives. All of these accounts are according to the general explanations.

In summary, according to the extraordinary level of teachings, if the true nature of mind is realized, this is called the "dharmakaya buddha." It is also known as the "inconceivable secret of the Buddha," and among the body, speech, and mind, it is understood in relation to the aspect of mind. The wisdom mind of the dharmakaya buddha Samantabhadra needs to manifest emanations in order to display a path for sentient beings to follow. All of these emanated nirmanakaya buddha fields are manifestations of Samantabhadra and came into existence for the benefit of the beings he wishes to tame.

At this point we may wonder what is actually meant when the teachings speak of pure realms as though they were external places. When we say that Rechungpa went to the celestial realms (*khechara; mkha' spyod*) or that the great Jamyang Khyentse Wangpo went to the pure realm of Padmasambhava, the Copper-Colored Mountain, or that Panchen Lama Lobsang Chokyi Nyima went riding on a horse to the Shambhala pure realm, what does it really mean? If we think these are actual places out there in the universe, we might experience some confusion. In reality, these masters did not go to some external place. It is only explained in this conventional manner so that ordinary beings can gain a general idea of the pure perception (*dag snang*) of buddha realms.

Rechungpa, the disciple of the great yogi Milarepa, had the fortune to meet the nirmanakaya and realize the nirmanakaya level of enlightenment (*sprul sku sangs rgyas*). He did not attain complete enlightenment, but did manifest one type of accomplishment of the rainbow body, known as "going to the celestial buddha fields" (*khechara; mkha' spyod*). When we speak of Rechungpa's accomplishment of the condition of the rainbow body, or of his going to the celestial buddha fields, it is not something that can be explained well in a brief manner. There needs to be a detailed explanation of what these celestial realms are and how they come about.

Whatever pure realms are displayed, they are similar to a rainbow's appearing in the sky. The appearance of a rainbow is based upon a variety of interdependent conditions. For example, for a rainbow to appear there needs to be sun and rain and so forth; depending on these conditions, a rainbow may be seen. In the ultimate sense, there is no sun, no rain, no earth, and no rainbow; the appearance of a rainbow depends upon many interdependent connections.

By purifying his ordinary body through the creation stage (*kyerim; bskyed rim*) and meditating on the completion stage (*dzogrim; rdzogs rim*), Rechungpa had the inner vision of traveling among the twenty-four sacred lands. This does not mean Rechungpa actually flew to some place called a pure realm. Having first given rise to pure perception in one's practice, and secondly due to the existence of Samantabhadra's emanations and wisdom blessings, one will have one's own experiences like the inner visionary experience (*nang nyam; snang nyams*) of the twenty-four sacred lands.

The "place" to which Rechungpa went was within, the internal buddha field. He was able to perceive it due to his own faith, diligent practice, and accomplishment. As taught in the anuttaratantras and in the Anuyoga teachings, these buddha fields are inside, within one's vajra body of psychic channels (*tsa; rtsa*), energies (*lung; rlung*), and essential drops (*thig le*). The internal buddha fields can be experienced on the basis of accomplishing the practices based on these.

Rechung Dorje Drakpa went to the pure realms through the purification of his internal obscurations, ego clinging, ignorance, afflictive emotions, and grasping to the body and its ordinary aggregates. He attained the siddhis, the spiritual accomplishments, and traveled on the path of the subtle channels and vital energies. Rechungpa accomplished the creation stage practice in accord with the four measures of clarity and the four measures of steadiness, which we will discuss later in regard to the creation stage of deity yoga. This was united with his accomplishment of the completion stage practices of the central channel, due to which the grasping to one's body is diminished. Through these practices, one's personal experience of one's body is transformed into the nature of luminosity (*'od gsal gyi rang bzhin*), into the nature of the deity. It is a magical, illusory appearance; an illusory body (*sgyu lus*), a phantom apparition, a body of rainbow light.

If one accomplishes the practice of the creation and completion stages, then one will have the same fortune as the dakas and dakinis who are blessed by Samantabhadra. With the accomplishment of this illusory body, one can then practice the path further and attain the supreme accomplishment, which is to realize the union of luminosity and illusory body.

In summary, the celestial pure realms are all internal. To say that the pure realms are external places is merely for the sake of convention, to conform to the understanding of ordinary beings. On the relative level, we do not say that the pure realms do not really exist; but on the ultimate level, the universes in other directions and the pure realms do not exist, just as this world doesn't actually exist. They are a dreamlike, illusory display.

Outwardly, we can say that Samantabhadra or Buddha Vajradhara taught the Chakrasamvara Tantra and that Rechungpa flew and landed somewhere. In reality, the prayers and aspirations of Samantabhadra or Vajradhara met with his diligent practice of Chakrasamvara, and the union of these two conditions allowed Rechungpa to attain pure vision of the realms of light. Ultimately, the final point here is that Samantabhadra, Vajradhara, Chakrasamvara, and Vajravarahi are our own natural state of mind (*sem kyi naylug; sems kyi gnas lugs*), which is the inseparability of expanse and awareness (*ying rig yermay; dbyings rig dber med*).

Guru Padmasambhava and the Copper-Colored Mountain

To consider another example, the nirmanakaya pure land of Guru Padmasambhava is known as the Copper-Colored Mountain (Zangdog Palri; Zangs mdog dpal ri). If a yogi following the Nyingma teachings wants to go to the Copper-Colored Mountain, on the conventional level it may once again sound like there is a physical, external location, somewhere "out there," to which he or she needs to go. However, on the extraordinary level of understanding, as we have said, there really is no outer place to go to. As proof of this, ordinary beings who have not practiced the creation stage and completion stage of Vajrayana meditation are not able to just "fly off" to the Copper-Colored Mountain.

Some discoverers of treasure teachings or "tertöns" went to the Copper-Colored Mountain, either in meditation or in actuality with their body as well. Those who have been in those realms did so by accomplishing the practices of creation stage and completion stage, so they are no longer ordinary beings. They appear to be ordinary, but in their own experience (*rang snang*), they do not have a normal fleshly body; rather, they have a pure illusory body (*dag pa'i sgyu lus*). However, this does not mean that they do not have a fleshly body in the perception of others.

If we wish to go to the Glorious Copper-Colored Mountain, there are two internal causes. First, internally, our own karma and obscurations, as well as the grasping to our ordinary body, must be purified through the blessings of the creation stage and the power of our own meditation. Second, we have the same ultimate nature of Guru Rinpoche, so to accomplish the pure realm, the inseparability of space and awareness that is within us must be awakened and actualized, through the practice of the completion stage and the Great Perfection.

Once again, we are speaking of "external" and "internal" only because at present there is no other way for us to communicate than by making use of the dualistic level of ordinary language. Guru Rinpoche is the "external" emanation of Buddha Amitabha, who is the same essence as the dharmakaya buddha Samantabhadra. Thus Guru Rinpoche is inseparable from Samantabhadra, and so both have the power of the realization of mind nature. If there were not someone with the power of having realized Samantabhadra, the nature of mind, there wouldn't be any being who could manifest as Guru Rinpoche and appear in this world.

So what is the purpose and intention of practicing Guru Rinpoche as a meditation deity? By the blessing of Samantabhadra, Guru Rinpoche manifested a pure realm at the summit of the island of Chamara to train beings. The general teachings say that at Chamara, to the southeast of India, is the Glorious Copper-Colored Mountain. Its outer manifestation, which is found "below" the light realm of Guru Padmasambhava, is also known as a land of raksha demons. When he left Tibet, Guru Rinpoche went there from this world to prevent the rakshas from overrunning our human world of Jambudvipa. Above that realm of raksha demons is Guru Rinpoche's luminous pure realm with all of its enlightened qualities, where we aspire to be reborn through practicing Guru Rinpoche as a meditation deity.

This is explained for the sake of ordinary beings, as ultimately there is no physical place that is Guru Rinpoche's pure realm, just as this world is not really here. From the ultimate perspective, the Copper-Colored Mountain is not a substantial place or thing, and so it is not a place our fleshly body can visit. It is a relative, dreamlike manifestation that does not ultimately truly exist but appears for the benefit of beings. When one internally purifies karma and obscurations through practice, then by the prayers and aspirations of Samantabhadra and through the blessings of Guru Rinpoche, one can arrive at the Glorious Copper-Colored Mountain and request and listen to teachings there.

All such explanations are for the benefit of ordinary beings and are explained in a manner that is easy for them to understand. For instance, if we wish to use the example of dreaming, these deities are all the phenomena of dreams. The buddhas and deities emanate into the realms of samsara in order to awaken sentient beings who are asleep and dreaming in samsara. We are all sleeping soundly, and Samantabhadra is the one who is actually awake.

If we are dreaming and someone wishes to awaken us from the dream, the person's voice or touch must enter into our dream state and rouse us from sleep. When someone wishes to awaken us from a bad dream, his or her voice must reach us in our dreaming state in order to awaken us. This is really how it occurs; the one who would awaken us does become part of our dream in that moment when he or she tries to wake us from sleep.

The analogy here is that we cannot be brought to self-existing awareness by someone simply calling out to us, unless his or her voice and message reaches us within our dream. Our awareness is so obscured that we cannot just be awakened right away to dharmata, the natural state. In order to relieve us from the suffering that we're experiencing in our dream of existence within samsara, the one wishing to awaken us needs to be able to enter into the deluded perception with which we are afflicted in our dream.

What this means is that the buddhas and those who are awake must appear to the dreamlike, deluded perception of suffering sentient beings in a form similar to theirs, in a manifestation that they can relate to. The awakened ones know that if the sleeping person does not apprehend that he is dreaming, he will not be able to recognize dharmata. The one who is awake first needs to tell the sleeping person that he is asleep and having a bad dream, saying "Whatever dangers, fearsome appearances, wild animals, and so forth, that you see, they don't really exist and cannot harm you. It is just that you are dreaming and have not yet understood and recognized the nature of your mind. You need to really make an effort to wake up."

The deluded person will not be able to wake up immediately, but perhaps he will at least begin to consider the different reasons why he might be asleep and dreaming. Eventually the person will accept to some degree that he is dreaming; but even then the dream will not disappear right away. The person may believe that he is seeing elephants and then think, "Oh, this is just a dream." Through this, ego clinging will diminish, his deluded perception will become less powerful, and gradually he will awaken from the dream. When the person awakens, there is no elephant, there is nothing at all that remains of the dream. Everything that was perceived in the dream was completely insubstantial and nonexistent.

The dream analogy is used to indicate that in relation to dharmakaya Samantabhadra's wisdom mind, we are completely asleep and immersed in ignorance. In contrast to our condition, Buddha Samantabhadra is completely awake. And so we need to make a connection with his awakened mind, in order that we ourselves can awaken. If we can't yet truly understand and realize that all appearances are illusions, like a dream, we will not be able to make that connection directly, and we won't awaken right away. In order to awaken a dreaming person, one who is awake can say to her in the dream, "You need to pray to the Buddha who resides in the western pure realm." Or he may say, "Proceeding in a celestial direction, there are enlightened ones, dakas and dakinis. You should have faith that this is so, and give rise to intense devotion toward them." This will be of real benefit to the dreamer.

The Nirmanakaya That Takes Birth in This World

As mentioned earlier, there are three types of nirmanakaya emanations: the first type is the nirmanakaya of the nature (rang bzhin sprul pa), the buddha fields known as the ten pure realms of the ten directions. These are all collectively included within the buddha fields of the five families and five directions that are manifested for the purpose of liberating beings. The second type is the nirmanakaya that guides beings, both the supreme nirmanakayas like Shakyamuni Buddha and also the secondary emanations such as bodhisattvas, rulers, and so on. And the third type is the diverse nirmanakaya that manifests in manifold forms, appearing in animate forms such as various beings as well as in a variety of inanimate forms.

Thus far, we have discussed the Buddha and the supreme nirmanakaya, which belong to the second category of nirmanakayas, those who guide beings. Following this, we have spoken of the various ways the nirmanakaya manifests as deities and pure lands, which is the first category of nirmanakaya, the nirmanakaya of the nature.

The nirmanakayas of the second category are those that take birth in the six realms of samsara and guide sentient beings. Among those that take birth in this world, they may be either the supreme nirmanakaya buddhas, or in a second group that includes any other kind that either manifests or takes birth in this world, whether in the form of human beings or in the form of animals and other beings.

It is even possible that wisdom beings who are actually from the nirmanakaya buddha fields of the ten directions and five families may emanate and appear in our world. Among these nirmanakayas, there are those of the nirmanakaya of the nature, such as the dakas and dakinis of the pure realms of the five families, who sometimes manifest in this world or may take birth in this world. As the dakinis are the guardians or protectors of the teaching, they sometimes manifest themselves in our world and elsewhere to check up and see how the Dzogchen teachings are being transmitted. This is because the Dzogchen teachings are under the protection of the dakinis. If one perverts the meaning of the teachings, these dakinis might sometimes punish and inflict illness and injury upon those who pervert the wisdom intent of Dzogpa Chenpo and lead others astray on the dharma path.

For example, there was a guru who was transmitting the Dzogchen instruction manual known as *Supreme Wisdom* (*Yeshe Lama; Ye shes bla ma*). Among his disciples was a yogin called Jangchub Dorje, who was receiving these instructions along with a few other yogis. They would listen to the teachings at night with only a single butter lamp burning, so the room was quite dark. After receiving teachings in the experiential manner over a period of one year, this yogi went off begging in order to gather funds for provisions. He came to one house where he met a woman who said, "Recently, you were receiving the teachings of the *Yeshe Lama* together with two or three yogis, and there was just one butter lamp burning. Are you reading the *Yeshe Lama* now?" The yogi was amazed. "Who told you?" he asked. The woman replied, "I came at night, transported upon the feather of a bird." It was definitely true that she had been there, and this story illustrates the magical powers of the dakinis.

The second category of nirmanakaya are those who guide sentient beings. If we consider specifically those that take birth in this world, we can also consider them as pure or impure emanations. First, there is the pure aspect of nirmanakaya emanations who take birth in this world in the form of teachers. Second, there is the impure aspect of the nirmanakaya, among which are those who assume the forms of ordinary human beings, such as beggars, prostitutes, any possible type of human being. According to the capacity and fortune of the many varieties of beings, there are also buddhas and bodhisattvas who manifest in varied animal forms to show those species the path. There are limitless emanations of such nirmanakayas, and buddhas can even manifest as insects in order to show them the path.

According to the capacity and fortune of the great variety of sentient beings, buddhas can manifest wherever sentient beings are found to show them the path of dharma. So, whether we are speaking about manifestations of teachers or of other kinds of beings, there are an endless assortment of nirmanakayas who may be found in this world. There are an endless assortment of nirmanakayas who manifest in the six realms of samsara. In all the realms of the hells, hungry ghosts and spirits, animals, and so forth, there are the emanations of the nirmanakaya that do appear there for the benefit of those beings. They manifest as male or female, in any situation whatsoever, according to the capacity and fortune of the beings in those places and times.

To give an example, there was a Kagyu lama who, thousands of lives previously, had taken birth as the king of the ants. He remembered that in that lifetime he was able to teach the ants rules and guidelines so that they could behave in a positive way, and so he was able to actually establish them all on the path to enlightenment. In one monastery there was a scroll on the wall describing the previous lives of the lama, in which this account is found. Similarly, the great siddha Thangtong Gyalpo remembered when he had taken birth as a dog and also as a goat.

The Diverse Nirmanakaya

The third of the three categories of nirmanakaya is the diverse nirmanakaya (*sna tshogs sprul pa*). This is the nirmanakaya that manifests in endless ways and manifold possible forms according to sentient beings' fortune and capacity. There are an inestimable number of emanations that appear in the impure worlds to train beings. They can either be animate, taking the form of various kinds of beings, or they may be inanimate, appearing as any form that benefits beings, such as taking the form of nirmanakaya pure lands or manifesting in beneficial forms within the six realms of samsara. In fact, whatever brings benefit to sentient beings is seen as a nirmanakaya emanation of the buddhas. These various emanations don't have the face and form of a buddha but are objects that represent the manifold activity of the buddhas. All of these beneficial objects manifest in accordance with the merit of sentient beings, based on the fact that the Buddha has appeared in this world.

The enlightened activity of a buddha is what brings temporary happiness and ultimate peace and bliss to sentient beings. Based on their positive karma and merit, sentient beings experience happiness such as enjoying the rays of sunshine, water for drinking and for animals to live in, and any of the other conditions that beings can enjoy and benefit from. In some texts, it mentions that the buddhas manifest as boats and bridges. Some people may think that in such cases, we would actually be walking on a buddha, but the boats or bridges are not the buddhas themselves. Rather, it is their manifestation that appears, due to the all-pervasive capacity (*thugs rje kun khyab*) of the Buddha. These objects are an aspect of the buddha activity, manifold emanations that appear in accordance with beings' merit or positive karma.

Similar to the nirmanakaya that guides beings, the diverse nirmanakaya can take the form of any kind of sentient being to lead beings to liberation. As for speculating as to who is actually enlightened and may be a nirmanakaya, those like ourselves cannot say with any certainty. There are so many beings who are the emanations of the enlightened ones.

It is important to understand that these diverse nirmanakayas are all known to be phenomena that have the nature of illusion. For example, when a magician, illusionist, or an artist creates an image, it can appear in inconceivable ways; there are not really any limits on how it can appear. In the same way, the display of the nirmanakaya is beyond the limits of our conventional mind in terms of how they can show themselves, as they can assume any form. It really is beyond what we can conceptualize. It is inconceivable.

When the teachings speak of "the great illusory nature of samsara and nirvana" (*'khor 'das sgyu ma chen po'i rang bzhin*), one is introduced to the fact that buddhas and bodhisattvas are beings who have mastered illusory appearances. Phenomena display themselves like phantom apparitions, empty yet appearing. Understanding the manner in which the enlightened ones manifest helps us to understand the illusionary nature of all things within the worldly realms of samsara and the pure realms of nirvana.

DEITY YOGA: CREATION STAGE

At present we are practicing the meditation deity in the form of the dakini, from the terma treasure teachings of the second Dudjom Rinpoche, Jigdral Yeshe Dorje (1904–87). It is a teaching that has been revealed specifically for the benefit of beings in this dark age. This practice stems from the compassion of the three jewels and the blessings and aspirations of the buddhas and is an actual method to accomplish Guru Padmasambhava's consort Yeshe Tsogyal. The dakini Yeshe Tsogyal is the nirmanakaya emanation of dharmadhatu Samantabhadri, the consort of the dharmakaya buddha Samantabhadra, who is the female aspect of the ultimate deity (*don gyi lha*).

In order to help us realize this state for ourselves, through the power, blessings, and aspirations of Buddha Samantabhadra and consort, the dakini Yeshe Tsogyal arises as their actual manifestation and is born into this world. Yeshe Tsogyal was blessed and taught by Guru Padmasambhava and as part of her various enlightened activities, she wrote down and transmitted a method to follow her and accomplish the essence of her awareness wisdom (*rig pa'i ye shes kyi ngo bo*). Thus we have the practice of Yeshe Tsogyal as a yidam or meditation deity.

How are we to understand the real nature of meditation deities in their female aspect? The key point we should remember here is that internally, the true nature of our mind is the inseparability of expanse (*ying; byings*) and wisdom (*yeshe; ye shes*). When we speak of the expanse, this refers to the emptiness of dharmadhatu, which is also known as Prajnaparamita, the Great Mother of the Perfection of Wisdom (*prajnaparamita; shes rab pha rol tu phyin pa*). The wisdom spoken of here is Samantabhadri, the ultimate dakini of dharmata. She appears in the nirmanakaya realms as the dakini Yeshe Tsogyal.

The essence of our mind is pointed out by the guru as naked awareness (*rig pa rjen pa*), which actually refers to the unimpeded open transparency of the wisdom mind *(zang thal dgongs pa)*. While naked awareness is the nature of our own minds, just having this nature is not enough; we need to actualize it for ourselves, within our own experience. It is for this purpose that we engage in the practice of deity yoga.

There are two types of deities, the ultimate deity of dharmata (*chos nyid don gi lha*) and the conditional, symbolic deity (*chos can rtags kyi lha*). Samantabhadra's awareness wisdom is the ultimate deity, meaning the one who has realized the ultimate nature of mind as the inseparability of the expanse of space and primordial wisdom. When we say that Samantabhadra is the inseparability of expanse and wisdom, or the inseparability of expanse and awareness, this is symbolically represented by Samantabhadra in union with his consort.

Normally, the dharma teachings speak of male and female as the two aspects of skillful means and wisdom, respectively. Skillful means is the male aspect, and wisdom is the female aspect. However, when we speak of wisdom itself, which is the ultimate deity of dharmata, then our wisdom nature also has a male and female aspect. In this case, Samantabhadra is the male aspect of the ultimate deity, which is awareness (*rigpa*). His consort Samantabhadri symbolizes the female aspect of the ultimate deity, which is the expanse of space (*ying; dbyings*).

In brief, when we speak of empty awareness (*rig stong*), Samantabhadri is the emptiness aspect. The aspect of emptiness (*stong cha*) is the female, the expanse of space (*dbyings*), and the aspect of clarity (*gsal cha*) is the male, with "clarity" in this case referring to primordial wisdom (*ye shes*) or awareness (*rig pa*). Thus the teachings speak of wisdom as female and male, as emptiness and clarity, as expanse and wisdom, or as expanse and awareness.

The Great Mother of Wisdom, Prajnaparamita, as well as Yeshe Tsogyal, Vajrayogini, and all possible female deities are each symbolic forms of the ultimate deity. They originate from, and are manifested by, the ultimate deity. The conditional, symbolized deity refers to two categories of deities, the sambhogakaya deities and the nirmanakaya deities. These two are known as the rupakaya or "body of enlightened form" of the Buddha. The rupakaya refers to both the sambhogakaya rainbow bodies of the buddhas and deities, as well as the nirmanakaya forms that manifest within the three realms of samsara.

Among the various female deities of the sambhogakaya, there are Vajrayogini and the five female buddhas of the five families such as Pandaravasini and Buddha Lochana, as well as all of the female buddhas and deities beyond number. Among the female nirmanakaya deities, there are Guru Padmasambhava's consorts Yeshe Tsogyal and Mandavara, along with all of the place-born (*zhing kye; zhing skye*) dakinis of the twenty-four sacred lands, and all possible female forms. All of them are the forms of the conditional, symbolized deity, symbolizing the female aspect of buddhahood. As the tantras say, "Upon a single dust mote, there are innumerable buddhas."

The emanations of Buddha Samantabhadra's consort Samantabhadri are the female deities Vajravarahi, Vajrayogini, Yeshe Tsogyal, and all the other female meditation deities. Each of us has within our nature Samantabhadri, Vajrayogini, and all the female deities and enlightened ones. They are aspects of our buddha nature, our enlightened essence. In order to realize emptiness, shunyata, it is said to be particularly effective to depend on the female aspect of enlightenment symbolized by the mother deities (*yum*).

This is why completion stage practice is especially important in Anu-yoga and in the mother tantras, since completion stage is a special means to help one to experience and realize emptiness. According to the teachings of the anuttaratantras, practicing female deities together with the completion stage practices are key supports for realizing emptiness. Ultimately, when we realize the inseparability of space and awareness, then we attain the same level as, and become equal in fortune to, these female deities.

One of the key reasons for practicing deities is that it is through making an interdependent connection (*tendrel; rten 'brel*) with those who have realized the nature of mind that we gain the possibility of realizing our own mind nature. It is for this purpose that we practice sadhanas of the various deities. If there were no beings such as Samantabhadra who have realized the natural state of mind, then even though we all share the same essence, the inseparability of expanse and wisdom, we would never be able to actualize this essence for ourselves. This is why it is so crucial that we practice guru yoga and may engage in the practice of meditation deities.

We are at present concerned with the two stages of Secret Mantra meditation, the creation stage and the completion stage. If we wish to "go to the pure realms" and actually experience the pure appearances of buddha fields, then according to general tantric teachings, we need to complete the path of accumulation (*tshog lam*) through meditation on the creation stage. The path of accumulation is the first of the five stages or five paths that result in the attainment of complete enlightenment, and it is rapidly completed by training in the practice of the creation stage. Without the various creation stage practices, it will be very difficult and will take an incalculably long period of time to gain the necessary merit to complete the path of accumulation and enter further stages of the path. On the basis of creation stage practice, we are then able to engage in the second of the five paths, the path of joining (*jor lam; sbyor lam*), by meditating on the completion stage practices of the six yogas (*naljor druk rnal byor drug*).

When we wish to apply ourselves to the creation stage practice of deity yoga, we need to understand buddhas and deities in a new way. We need to understand them in relation to the creation and completion stage meditation methods of the path of skillful means (*thabs*). These methods of skillful means are still a conceptual approach. They are practices of the accumulation of merit with concepts, which enable one to approach the accumulation of wisdom beyond concepts. However, although the creation stage of deity yoga is a conceptual approach, in order to accomplish it, we do not need to enter into a lot of analyses, nor must we create a proliferation of thoughts and make excessive intellectual efforts.

This does not mean that one does not need to apply any effort at all in order to practice the path of skillful means; one does need to apply effort. As dharmata, the true nature of phenomena, is beyond thoughts and concepts, intellectual efforts are not the main point here. Rather, one's efforts are to be diligent in the practice of deity yoga, according to the two stages of Secret Mantra. We begin with the meditations of the creation stage, visualizing the body of the buddhas and deities. With our speech, we recite their mantras, and at the same time rest our mind in one-pointed samadhi, learning to recognize the true nature of mind.

For example, when we do the visualization practices of the preliminaries (*ngondro; sngon 'gro*) and those of the creation stage, we usually visualize the dharmakaya above, the sambhogakaya in the middle, and the nirmanakaya below. We imagine the pure realms of the three kayas as a three-story building, with the dharmakaya on the top level; this is very valuable, but is still a dualistic way of thinking. The visualizations are only described in this way so that our dualistic mind can gain a provisional understanding of what is being represented in the visualizations.

Even when thinking in this dualistic way, if we pray with faith and devotion while imagining the three kayas, it can still be very beneficial. This benefit comes about through prayer and aspirations, which will create positive, virtuous tendencies in our mind and form interdependent connections with the enlightened ones represented by the deities. We are taught these methods due to the skillful activity of the buddhas. These practices are not yet the natural state of Atiyoga, the Great Perfection (*dzogpa chenpo; rdzogs pa chen po*). They do not yet reveal the understanding of the secret, inconceivable nature. But if we have faith and devotion and imagine the three kayas in the dualistic way, it will still be very helpful.

In what way will it be helpful? The skillful means practices of the two stages are still within the spectrum of the dualistic mind. When we speak of what is within the range of dualistic thinking, it refers to whatever can be encompassed by conceptual thought. On the other hand, the inconceivable nature that the practices are intended to introduce is free from the normal thinking patterns that we resort to on the basis of our emotional and cognitive obscurations. If we understand only through dualistic concepts alone, there will be no way for us to realize the inconceivable nature that is beyond the scope of dualistic thinking. True understanding is not possible within our dualistic way of knowing and perceiving, since the way things truly are is the secret nature beyond concepts.

Why is this so? Our dualistic mind has the obscurations of afflictive emotions and the conceptual obscurations. When these are present, our view is impaired and we cannot see clearly. In order to purify these obscurations, we practice the two stages of creation and completion.

To accomplish the creation stage meditation of deity yoga, we need to accomplish the eight measures of clarity and steadiness (*sal ten shay gyay; gsal brtan tshad brgyad*); these are the four measures of clarity and the four measures of steadiness. The four measures of clarity are that one's visualization of the deity is distinct in all its details, it is alive, it is vibrant, and it is vivid. The four measures of steadiness are that one's visualization is unmoving, that it remains unchanging, that it is utterly unchangeable, and yet is totally flexible and pliant.[11]

Due to the existence of Samantabhadra's emanations, the multitude of deities appear, and we can meet them through our faith, devotion, and meditation practice. For this, we need to perfect these eight measures of meditation through the practice of deity yoga. We can meditate on ourselves as Chakrasamvara, Vajrayogini, Yeshe Tsogyal, and as other deities; and by accomplishing these eight measures, we can begin to gain some accomplishment of the attributes and qualities of the deity. For example, by meditating on ourselves as Vajrayogini and accomplishing the eight measures, our ordinary body is purified and begins to become ripened as the deity. Through this, externally, our ordinary, dualistic concepts decrease, and internally, our unawareness (*ma rig pa*) and habitual tendencies are diminished.

When we have accomplished calm abiding meditation (*shamatha; zhi gnas*) by training in the creation stage in this way, there are no thoughts arising in our meditation, and the mind rests in stillness. On this basis, we visualize and pray to buddhas and deities and assume their forms, giving rise to faith (*depa; dad pa*), devotion (*mogu; mos gus*), and pure vision (*dag nang; dag snang*).

We are to give rise to intense devotion and receive great blessings. Externally, through the aspirations of the buddhas, internally, through our own faith and devotion, and secretly, due to the fact that we have the natural state of mind, we can accomplish the pure realms and realize dharmata, based on all these factors. From the viewpoint of the creation stage, we realize this by gathering together all of these above-mentioned causes and conditions, on the basis of the interdependent connections between them all.

DEITY YOGA: COMPLETION STAGE

We have briefly discussed buddha fields and emanations mainly according to the key points of the creation stage (*kyerim; bskyed rim*) practices of the path. Now we need to understand how one approaches buddhas and deities from the point of view of the practice of the completion stage (*dzogrim; rdzogs rim*), the second of the two stages of meditation according to the Vajrayana tradition of Secret Mantra.

During the creation stage, we visualize buddhas and deities and imagine pure realms as a means of giving rise to pure vision and awakening to the true nature of mind. We use our imagination to begin to transform our dreamlike perception of the impure phenomena of samsara into the perception of pure appearances (*dag snang; dag snang*), the vision of pure realms, buddhas, and deities. Of the two stages of tantric meditation, creation stage relates more to the aspect of merit and completion stage relates more to the aspect of primordial wisdom. During the practice of the creation stage, the completion stage is practiced simply, by dissolving our visualization of the deity into empty luminosity (*stong gsal*), the nature of mind. After this stage, when one wishes to practice the aspect of primordial wisdom, the path of awakening from delusion, it is necessary to enter into the more detailed trainings of the completion stage such as the six yogas.

The completion stage practices of the path of skillful means are connected with the path of joining, the second of the five paths or stages to enlightenment. The completion stage practices are referred to as the "path of skillful means" (*thabs lam*), in contrast to Mahamudra or Dzogchen meditation, which is known as the "path of liberation" (*drol lam; grol lam*). These two paths of means and wisdom reflect the two principles of all Mahayana Buddhist meditation practice. According to the anuttaratantras such as Chakrasamvara, Hevajra, and Guhyasamaja, we are required to practice the path of skillful means in order to complete the first two paths of accumulation and joining, enabling us to realize the path of seeing, the third of the five paths.

The anuttaratantras teach the two stages of deity yoga. In these tantras we must first practice the path of skillful means in order to realize awareness wisdom; this is the means or method presented in these tantras. They teach that we must apply the path of skillful means practices together with a physical daka or dakini consort, or alternately with a visualized consort, in order to realize the wisdom of the path of seeing (*tong lam; mthong lam*), the third of the five paths. When the mandalas of the central channel of one's vajra body are actualized by means of the two stages, the truth of the path of seeing will be realized. This is how the results of practice are accomplished according to the anuttaratantras of the Secret Mantrayana. However, this is not how the path is taught according to the Dzogchen tantras, where the path of seeing does not depend on the skillful means practices of the central channel.

We have been meditating on the creation stage of the female deity Yeshe Tsogyal, the consort of Guru Padmasambhava. As we have not perfected the eight measures of clarity and stability of the creation stage, we have not been able to meet the face of the deity; however we have created some good tendencies through our interest in the practice. After we have practiced these very well, we will be able to meet the face of the deity.

Now it is time to work with the completion stage of the path of skillful means. At the end of one's creation stage practice, the completion stage is applied by dissolving one's visualized deity into empty luminosity (*tong sal; stong gsal*). But to really practice the completion stage of the path of skillful means, the samadhi or meditative absorption of the completion stage must be developed. The meditative absorption of the completion stage is variously understood as the samadhi of bliss, clarity, and nonthought, or as the unity of clarity and emptiness, the unity of bliss and emptiness, the recognition of mind nature, and so on. The way it is accomplished is through training in the practice of the vase breathing (*lung bumpa chen; rlung bum pa can*) and of the channels, vital energies, and essential drops (*tsa lung thigle; rtsa rlung thig le*).

In order to develop the samadhi of the completion stage, we do the meditations on the channels and energies (*tsa lung; rtsa rlung*), psychic heat (*tummo; gtum mo*), and so forth. These are also known collectively as the "practices of the central channel." Even though we meditate a little bit on our channels and vital energies in the practice of inner heat and related practices, in fact through this small amount of meditation, we won't be able to complete the path of joining, the second of the five paths. However, we will create very good tendencies through our interest and devoted commitment to the practice. We will also begin to develop the samadhi of the completion stage.

For what purpose are we to develop the samadhi of the completion stage? If we did not have the nature of space and wisdom (*ying rig; dbyings rig*) within our own mind, then even if there were an external Samantabhadra, we would not be able to realize his level. For example, if we have a piece of stone, no matter how hard we work to try to refine and process it, if there is no gold inside the stone, we will never be able to extract gold from it. To get gold, there must be gold within. If there is gold contained within the stone, we will be able to make it manifest.

Like the example of gold, as we already have the nature of Samantabhadri or Yeshe Tsogyal in our minds, we are able to recognize that nature. If we did not have the inseparability of space and wisdom within our minds, we would never be able to recognize it. To extract gold, one needs the correct instruments or tools, which for us are the instructions of the creation and completion stages. Also we need someone to instruct us as to where and how to find the gold. For example, if we rely on some fool who tells us that there is gold inside a piece of coal or iron, then all of our efforts to produce gold will be futile. However if we rely on someone who knows how to find gold, then we will actually be able to extract it.

Samantabhadra has realized the natural state of his own mind, the wisdom mind of dharmata. He dwells in the equality of the three times, remaining in dharmata, just as it is. From his realization, Samantabhadra acts for the benefit of countless beings, manifesting the teachers and imparting all the teachings that ultimately enable us to realize the inseparability of expanse and wisdom (*ying rig yermay; dbying rig dbyer med*).

MEETING THE DEITY

If we actually perfect and accomplish the development and completion stages of Yeshe Tsogyal, we will meet Yeshe Tsogyal. Likewise, according to the Chakrasamvara practice, we can meet Vajravarahi, who is the same as Yeshe Tsogyal. If one accomplishes the eight measures of clarity and steadiness of the creation stage, one's impure perception and obscurations, one's ignorance, attachment and aggression, and ego clinging will all be greatly diminished. Through the perfection of the four measures of clarity and the four measures of steadiness, then finally, after one no longer has dualistic grasping and fixation upon appearances, the pure appearance of Yeshe Tsogyal will manifest. At that time, through having gradually purified the impure perception of one's coarse body of flesh and blood, one will no longer have the perception of the body of flesh. One will actually come to meet Yeshe Tsogyal.

For example, each day can be divided into meditation sessions and the postmeditation period when one has arisen from one's meditation sessions. If one is always meditating on Yeshe Tsogyal, then even in postmeditation, the appearance of the deity will continue to arise in one's experience. For such a practitioner, at the time of resting in the natural state of dharmata, the appearance of Yeshe Tsogyal will continue. These yogis have realized that at all times, including during postmeditation activities, the mind itself has the nature of the deity. We however have not accomplished this yet. We are practicing only through the power of our faith, devotion, and aspirations.

If we meet Yeshe Tsogyal in our own experience, she will be able to take us under her care and bring us to the Copper-Colored Mountain of Guru Padmasambhava. If it is Vajravarahi, she will take us to the cities of the dakas and dakinis. These cities are not external places, but are experienced internally through perfecting the creation and completion stage practices. In particular, they are experienced through the blessings of the guru and lineage, through one's accomplishment of pure vision, and by the blessings of the completion stage meditations of the path of joining.

From the point of view of the completion stage, there is no longer some "place" somewhere else to which one must go. There is no longer an eastern or western pure realm, no buddha fields, no twenty-four sacred lands. They were explained as external places in the sutras and general teachings on the creation stage solely for the benefit of ordinary beings. These manifestations only seem to exist in the outer world on a relative level, but in fact they are illusory, like dreams. They do not truly exist but are manifested by the enlightened ones so that they seem to exist, for the sake of those beings to be trained and liberated.

The completion stage is practiced in order to be able to actually recognize the true nature of one's mind. Based on this, together with factors such as the purification and refinement of one's channels, vital energies, and essential drops, one's inner perceptions and experiences (*nang gi snang ba*) will manifest in a pure manner, as pure vision. It is not that one will have to imagine this, as in the creation stage. Rather, by practicing the completion stage, pure vision will actually manifest out of one's own experience of the nature of mind. The pure realms and buddha fields will arise as personal experience or self-appearance (*rang gi snang ba*).

Ultimately, according to the extraordinary level of understanding of the Great Perfection, which teaches the most profound meaning of completion stage practice, everything has the nature of awareness wisdom. Other than seeing awareness, the natural state, there is nothing else to see and nowhere else to go. When we awaken from the sleep of ignorance, then not only do other universes not exist, but even this world is in fact completely illusory.

If we meditate well on the creation and completion stages, the inseparability of expanse and wisdom that is within us will manifest. Through this, on the internal level, we will gradually traverse the five paths and the spiritual levels (*bhumi; sa*). When we practice Yeshe Tsogyal and come to realize within ourselves the expanse of space (*ying; dbyings*), which is the female aspect of emptiness or wisdom, then we will actually meet the ultimate dakini of empty awareness appearing as Yeshe Tsogyal. This is because Yeshe Tsogyal is none other than the ultimate Samantabhadri of dharmata (*chos nyid don gyi kun tu bzang mo*), the inseparability of expanse and awareness, manifest in the form of Yeshe Tsogyal for the benefit of sentient beings.

ADVICE FOR RETREATANTS

The ultimate meaning and intent of all dharma practices is to recognize and realize the nature of mind. So during meditation on the completion stage, please meditate well on the channels and vital energies as a basis for experiencing mind nature for yourself. To recognize and realize the nature of mind, we need to have trust and confidence. It doesn't depend on whether or not we are very intellectual, physically strong, or what kind of personality we have. It depends on our particular karma, on our faith, prayers and aspirations, and on our degree of endeavor and diligence. Based on these, in conjunction with Samantabhadra's prayers and aspirations and the blessings of our gurus, it is possible for us to recognize and realize the true nature of mind.

When we gather all of the primary causes, conditions, and interdependent connections, then we can awaken the buddha nature within us. This is similar to the way a rainbow appears in the sky, through the meeting of all the necessary conditions such as moisture and sunlight. If any one of these causes or conditions is missing, the rainbow cannot appear. It is the same when practicing dharma in order to realize the nature of mind. We gather all of the causes and conditions, such as all the aspirations and activities of Samantabhadra and the entire lineage of awareness-holding vidyadhara gurus, together with the blessings and compassion of our gurus, and these are combined with our own faith and devotion and diligent practice. In the presence of these factors, the occasion for realization of our practice has arrived. In this we must have great trust and confidence.

The pinnacle of all the teachings is the natural state of the Great Perfection. When we speak of the natural Great Perfection (*rangzhin dzogpa chenpo; rang bzhin rdzogs pa chenpo*), it implies that one needs a great mind endowed with great devotion and great faith in order to realize it. A small, narrow mind with many thoughts and concepts won't be able to realize it. What is it that must be realized? It is that whatever exists among all the things of samsara, nirvana, and the path is never separate from the vast sphere of dharmadhatu Samantabhadri (*chos dbyings kun tu bzang mo'i klong*), the natural state of the Great Perfection.

If we are to understand dharmata, the true condition of all phenomena, we should continue to reflect on the teaching that our world, our body and sense fields, our aggregates and elements, day and night, all of these are our very own deluded personal perceptions. For example, one who has bile disease may see white things as yellow, but this is just deluded perception due to the person's health. Likewise, we see all these nonexistent, empty reflections of phenomena as being real and actually existing. Yet, this belief is only delusion, nothing else.

Our fleshly body, this world, and everything that exists really does have a dreamlike nature! We think of everything as truly existing because of our dualistic perception. We grasp at all the worlds in all the different directions as though they were real. This dreamlike nature isn't just mere words. We can experience it for ourselves through seeing that phenomena have no inherent existence, seeing the true nature of things as they are.

From the viewpoint of the undeluded natural state (*naylug; gnas lugs*) of Samantabhadra, the natural state of the innate Great Perfection (*gnas lugs rang bzhin rdzogs pa chen po*), our perceptions and concepts are something very strange and really quite funny. On the other hand, it's something very tragic that should cause us to weep in sorrow. There is tremendous sadness in seeing sentient beings clinging desperately to nonexistent, empty images as though they were really existing (*bden grub*) and as possessing an identity (*bdag tu bzung ba*). Thinking that these are genuine perceptions, believing that something that does not in fact exist is real and significant, causes sentient beings so much continual suffering; it is very sad indeed.

Based upon these fictitious beliefs, beings develop pride and a solidified notion that they themselves exist as a separate entity. This is an aspect of what is known in the Dzogchen teachings as "conceptual ignorance" (*kuntag marigpa; kun brtags ma rig pa*), the second of the three types of ignorance. Out of this basic ignorance, based on the notion that we exist as a separate entity, the whole play of attachment and aversion springs forth. From this in turn comes the accumulation of karma and the endless creation of our existence within samsara. From time without beginning we have never found satisfaction in this cycle of existence, and we never will.

When we think of this state of affairs in which we and all sentient beings find ourselves, it is something that really ought to make us feel anguished. Thinking of the endlessness of suffering, we have to cry. But even though we have cried, still we find neither relief nor satisfaction. All things of samsara are empty, and yet sentient beings keep clinging to them as though they were real. Based on all of these empty appearances, beings experience distraction, suffering, laziness and indolence, and so on.

In reality, it is just like the illusion of a jewel created by a magical illusionist. The audience believes it to be a true jewel, even though it is really just something that momentarily appears and there is no jewel. It is the same as thinking a rainbow is actually a solid jewel. Sentient beings take this illusory jewel to be real, yet somehow this is hilarious! When the Dzogchen teachings speak of the humorousness of the situation, they refer to the fact that sentient beings regard relative things to be of ultimate value. Someone such as Buddha Samantabhadra, who has the ultimate realization of Dzogchen and sees the natural state of Dzogchen, sees all these endless phenomena as a comedic illusion.

Understanding everything within samsara and nirvana to be like magical illusions, we need to make the effort to realize the natural state of mind; this is the essence of practice. Ultimately, from the point of view of the natural state of the Great Perfection, all things are the continuous state of equality (*mnyam nyid ngang*) within Samantabhadra's vast expanse (*klong yangs*). It is the inseparability of space and primordial wisdom, unchanging throughout the three times and perfect in the ground free from transitions and transformations (*'gyur 'pho med pa'i gzhi*).

If a person of the highest capacity does not have this realization and is introduced to it by one who does, just by the guru's simply saying a single phrase of introduction, the superior type of person may gain realization. However, for almost all beings, direct realization is possible only through practice and applying oneself in meditation. If the person is not of superior capacity and the same phrase is uttered to them, he or she will not attain realization. Even if the realized one points their finger directly at the meaning, as though pointing out the moon to a child, the person listening may look off somewhere else in the sky and fail to see the moon.

In other words, if at the time of pointing out awareness (*rigpa ngotro; rig pa ngo sprod*), the guru says "This is the Great Perfection" and the disciple keeps saying "Uuhhh, what was the Great Perfection?" then in such cases what was pointed out was not recognized and there is no introduction (*ngotro; ngo 'phrod*). So don't be like that, and have complete faith and confidence in the guru's pointing-out instructions.

The wisdom mind of dharmata is unchanging in the three times. It is the inseparability of space and awareness that never fluctuates, never moves or changes, and is always present. This is Samantabhadra's realization, and it is the same realization as that of Amitabha, Chakrasamvara, Padmasambhava, Yeshe Tsogyal, and all wisdom deities. Samantabhadra has never moved from this state of ultimate realization. In the three times without beginning or end, his realization is called the "equality of dharmata." To actualize this state, all of our dualistic delusions must be purified; but of course the ultimate nature of dharmata itself does not need to be purified.

When we say that dharmata is like the example of the sky or space, we need to remember that physical space and dharmata are not the same. The sky and the outer, physical space are just a blank emptiness, as they are not endowed with knowing or awareness. Thus our awareness wisdom (*rigpai yeshe; rig pa'i ye shes*), the inseparability of expanse and wisdom (*ying dang yeshe yermay; dbyings dang ye shes dbyer med*), is not the same as the analogy of the physical sky. Dharmata is similar to the sky or space. Like space, the ultimate nature is pure and unchanging. It has no limits, nor can it be divided. It is the essential nature and true condition of everything, and this is what we must realize.

Please remember what I have said in these teachings, and practice well. The purpose of staying in retreat is to make prayers and aspirations and to practice constantly for the benefit of all sentient beings.

7. Introduction to Longchenpa's
Resting at Ease in Illusion

———————

When we speak of the buddha's teachings found in both the sutras as well as in the tantras of Secret Mantra, these must always be taught with the five perfections (*phun sum tshogs pa lnga*) of the perfect teacher, retinue, place, teaching, and time.

Resting at Ease in Illusion (*Gyuma Ngalso; Sgyu ma ngal gso*) was written by Longchen Rabjam, who was like the sun in his ability to illuminate the teachings of Dzogchen, the Great Perfection. In Longchenpa's writings there are both the vast treatises and the profound oral instructions, and many of his writings are of both categories. The vast approach of the pandita or learned scholar presents the stages of the path containing all the teachings of the Buddha. A treatise (*shastra; bstan bcos*) represents the vast type of written work and is written in the manner of the commentaries on the Buddha's teachings composed by the Indian masters. The profound type of written work refers to texts containing the oral instructions (*men ngak; man ngag*) needed for the practice of view and meditation.

The introduction to a treatise traditionally has five sections: the author, the subject of the text, the category of the text, the purpose for which the text was written, and the place in which the text was composed. *Resting at Ease in Illusion* is a treatise of oral instructions, meaning that it possesses the qualities of a treatise and at the same time contains the oral instructions necessary for putting the teachings into practice.

To summarize the five sections of the introduction to Longchenpa's *Resting at Ease in Illusion,* the third volume in his Trilogy of Resting at Ease (Ngalso Kor Sum; Ngal gso skor gsum):

The author of this text is Gyalwa Longchen Rabjam (1308–63), one of the greatest Buddhist masters in the history of Tibet.

The subject of this text is the nature of emptiness (*stong pa nyid kyi rang bzhin*), which is the essential meaning of all the teachings of sutra and tantra. The natural state of all phenomena is dharmata, and dharmata is illustrated here through the eight examples of illusion.

Regarding the category of the text, *Resting at Ease in Illusion* belongs to the category of the gradual path (*lam rim*) teaching cycles. Since the complete teachings of the Buddha from those of the first turning of the wheel of dharma up to the Great Perfection are expressed in this text, it is thus said to be of the gradual path category.

The purpose for which the text was written was for Longchenpa's disciples. It was also written for future beings who would live hundreds and even thousands of years after, right up until the time when the teachings of the Buddha will disappear from this world.

Finally, the place where the text was composed is the retreat place of Longchenpa called "Gangri Tokar" or "White Skull Snow Mountain." Gangri Tokar is known as the Tibetan Five-Peaked Mountain, after the famed Five-Peaked Sacred Mountain of Wutaishan in China. Mount Wutaishan is the very abode of the bodhisattva Manjushri in this world. As Longchenpa was an emanation of Manjushri, Gangri Tokar naturally became an earthly buddha field of Manjushri, just like Wutaishan in China.

Resting at Ease in Illusion is the third volume of Longchenpa's Trilogy of Resting at Ease. The first volume of the trilogy is called *Resting at Ease in the Nature of Mind* (*Semnyid Ngalso; Sems nyid ngal gso*). This volume is both vast and profound, as it is a vast treatise that also contains the profound oral instructions. The manner in which one is to meditate on the teachings given in the first volume of the trilogy, *Resting at Ease in the Nature of Mind,* is explained in the second volume, *Resting at Ease in Meditation* (*Samten Ngalso; Bsam gtan ngal gso*). This second volume is an instruction in three chapters, which cover the places suitable for meditation; the types of meditation practitioners; and the methods of concentration and meditation, within which are three sections relating to the three meditation experiences of bliss (*daywa; bde ba*), clarity (*salwa; gsal ba*), and nonthought (*mitogpa; mi rtog pa*).

The first volume of the trilogy, *Resting at Ease in the Nature of Mind,* is in thirteen chapters, covering all the stages of the path and fruition, from taking refuge all the way through to Dzogchen, the pinnacle of the Buddhist teachings. The ninth chapter of this book explains the meaning of the creation stage and the completion stage of Vajrayana meditation. The tenth and eleventh chapters concern calm abiding meditation (*shamatha; zhi gnas*) and insight (*vipasyana; lhag mthong*), respectively.

Arising especially from the tenth and eleventh chapters of this first volume, we have the third volume of the trilogy, *Resting at Ease in Illusion* (*Gyuma Ngalso; Sgyu ma ngal gso*), which explains the transcendent intelligence (*prajna; shes rab*) that apprehends emptiness. In this text, the meaning of emptiness is demonstrated through the famed eight examples of illusion, a traditional way of establishing the view of emptiness through eight analogies or metaphors.

Resting at Ease in Illusion teaches the empty nature of all conditioned things as taught by the Buddha—demonstrating that all the phenomena that we experience have, in essence, no intrinsic and true existence. In the entirety of the Buddha's teachings, throughout each of the different vehicles right up to, and including, Dzogchen, the essential truth of all things is the teaching of emptiness (*shunyata; stong pa nyid*). The teachings on emptiness show us how to let go of grasping and fixating on the apparent reality of the world and how to view all that we perceive as illusory, as empty appearances.

In general, it is very important that whenever we listen to teachings on emptiness, we should not focus our attention outwardly. The emptiness indicated by the Buddha is not something we can see with the naked eye. Instead, from the very first we need to look within and establish with confidence the emptiness of our own mind. The intention of all the wisdom teachings of the buddhadharma is that they enable one to understand and recognize the true nature of our mind, the unity of clarity and emptiness.

As we begin to develop our own experience of emptiness, our clinging to a sense of "self," together with the habits of grasping at experience as real and substantial, will start to diminish. Once we have established this basis by understanding the nature of our own mind, we will be able to prove to ourselves that outer objective phenomena don't exist intrinsically, within mind's nature. We will discover within our own experience that from the point of view of our mind's true nature, all that we perceive around us are empty appearances, phantasmal and insubstantial.

Thus what is most important is that we actually gain direct experience of emptiness within our own mind. Otherwise, if our attention is just directed outwardly and we learn and train in dharma with that kind of focus, it will be like the story of a traveling geshe who came to see Geshe Potawa. The Kadampa teacher Geshe Potawa was a disciple of Dromtonpa, who was the principal disciple of the Indian master Atisha; he was an eminent teacher who had attracted many followers. One day when Geshe Potawa was teaching his students, another traveling geshe came to see him, in hopes of debating Geshe Potawa. The visiting geshe stated that he wanted to question Geshe Potawa about emptiness and attempted to debate with Geshe Potawa on whether a rock was empty or not. In the traditional manner of debating using logical proofs, the visiting geshe climbed up on a rock and exclaimed, "Does this rock not inherently exist?"

Now Geshe Potawa was a very learned Kadampa master who had also developed great experience through meditation. He quickly tired of the debate and said, "If we both don't diminish our ego clinging and our habits of grasping at experience as something substantial and real, then what is there to discuss? Whether or not this rock is empty isn't what we should be asking ourselves." Geshe Potawa ended the conversation, saying, "Kindly excuse me, but this discussion would just be a waste of time," and went on his way.

What Geshe Potawa meant to teach the visiting geshe was that if we discuss emptiness by directing our mind outward and, in effect, trying to decide whether rocks and trees are empty, this really isn't the intent of the Buddha's teachings. If we aspire to gain genuine experience and realization, we need to practice in accordance with the meaning and intent of the buddhadharma. If we remain focused outwardly and enthralled with intellectualizing the view, this is exactly what is meant when the Great Perfection speaks of being "spoiled by concepts and fabrication." If we direct our mind outwardly while learning teachings on the view, this is exactly what will happen. But if we look within, into our own mind, we will certainly gain actual experience through the oral instructions of our teachers. We will practice in accordance with the buddhadharma and gain true experience and realization.

The essence of all the teachings of the common and extraordinary vehicles is concerned with the ultimate condition. Establishing the natural emptiness of all phenomena is the quintessence of the teachings, the essence of the essence. The manner in which all the vehicles of the buddhadharma establish this view is through the eight examples of illusion.

Longchen Rabjam's text *The Great Perfection: Resting at Ease in Illusion* (*Dzogpa Chenpo Gyuma Ngalso; Rdzogs pa chen po sgyu ma ngal gso*) demonstrates the empty nature, the ultimate teaching of all vehicles, through these same eight metaphors of illusion. The eight or twelve examples of illusion have been taught by the Buddha in scriptures such as the *King of Samadhi Sutra* (*Samadhiraja Sutra; Ting 'dzin rgyal po'i mdo*), and these examples are found throughout the Mahayana Buddhist sutras. Illustrious Indian masters such as Nagarjuna and Aryadeva set forth the philosophy of emptiness by writing treatises and explaining the teachings of the Buddha found in the sutras. The view of emptiness was established by the Indian masters through logic, reasoning, and analogies, and they made use of these eight metaphors to demonstrate the empty nature of all things from a variety of perspectives. In his *Resting at Ease in Illusion,* Longchen Rabjam also gives the profound meaning of these examples from the Dzogchen point of view.

The eight metaphors of the illusory nature of the world demonstrate that things appear but lack any true, intrinsic existence. They are the subject of the eight chapters of Longchenpa's *Resting at Ease in Illusion,* where each chapter is devoted to one of the eight examples. These eight metaphors are dream (*rmi lam*); magical illusion (*sgyu ma*); optical illusion (*mig yor*); mirage (*smig rgyu*); reflection of the moon in water (*chu zla gzugs brnyan gyi snang ba*); echo (*brag cha*); illusory heavenly abodes, the "city of the gandharvas" (*dri za'i grong khyer*); and phantom apparitions (*sprul pa*).

When we explain the nature of emptiness, we say that things appear but their nature is empty. Although everything appears to us, nothing that appears is actually real, concrete, and tangible. For example, to help us understand this through our own experience, one of the eight metaphors is the example of our nighttime dreams. This metaphor can be easily understood and communicated since anyone can contemplate and gain insights from the example of dreams. At night we dream, and we seem to experience everything as though it were really happening, but it is quite clear upon waking that the dream had no actuality and was just our imagination. Similarly, everything we perceive through our five senses is no more real than what we perceive in a dream; waking appearances are unreal and appear due to deluded perception. This is what is meant when it is said that whatever we perceive is just empty appearances.

The second example is that of a magical illusion. Nowadays, the examples of television, films, and illusionists' performances are similar to ancient magical shows and are comparable analogies that can be contemplated to gain the same insights. In former times in India, there were magicians who would create magical illusions through the interdependence of mantras, spells and incantations, props such as sticks and stones, herbal substances, and other things. By these means they were able to create illusory appearances of elephants and various beings that would seem completely real to whole crowds of people.

There were many such magicians who could manifest all kinds of interdependent appearances of illusory phenomena, and people would be convinced that these were real objects even though nothing was actually there. Since so many people in those times had either seen or heard of this kind of magic show, it was a convenient example to illustrate the empty illusoriness of all interdependent phenomena. All conditioned things are just temporary, and they are manifest due to the presence of many causes and conditions.

The third of the eight examples is that of a mirage. When we see mirages, they are once again produced by a variety of interdependent factors like the heat and light rays of the sun, an open area of flat land, the temperature of the air, and so forth. A mirage will appear in the distance, and human beings and even animals will see pools of water and will go toward them to drink. But when we pursue a mirage and arrive at the place where the water should be located, we find nothing there but empty space and barren ground. Similarly, all we perceive are merely temporary and adventitious phenomena, which disappear into space when any of their interdependent causes are not present. Thus the metaphor of a mirage is another excellent example of empty appearances that anyone can contemplate to gain insight into emptiness.

There is also the example of reflections, like the reflection of the moon in water or reflections in a mirror. We ponder this example so that when we see all the things that surround us, we begin to understand that they are relative, superficial phenomena, just like reflections in water. And like reflections, none of the phenomena of the world can ever be found to actually exist, either outside in the world, or inside within the mind, or anywhere in between. They are adventitious occurrences like reflections in water, which we can temporarily see or hear when the right causes are present; but in reality they are not inherently real, since upon investigation they are found to be mere surface appearances.

Another of the eight examples is that of an echo. When we hear an echo, if we investigate it, we find that the sound cannot be located anywhere in particular, neither inside nor outside, in front or behind, or anywhere in between. It is just like hearing the sound of a guitar or a flute; we can hear it, but the sound is not visible as an object and has no essential core that can somehow be pinpointed. If we examine the sound, it cannot be found to be some "thing" located "somewhere." It does not really exist objectively, being merely a temporary manifestation without form or substance. Of course, if we don't contemplate the actual nature of sound, we will fixate on sounds. Then we have the impression that sound is something that seems to exist objectively somewhere outside of us, rather than arising in our mind. But in fact sounds arise through the interdependence of many factors coming together to create perception, rather than being any kind of objective entity (*dngos po*). We can perceive sounds, but they cannot be pinpointed. Sounds are found to be empty perceptions pervading space.

In addition to the classical examples of illusion, the Dzogchen teachings have special key points on the nature of illusion that are important for understanding the deeper meanings of Longchenpa's *Resting at Ease in Illusion.* These unique, crucial points of the Dzogchen teachings introduce dharmata, the true nature of phenomena, as primordial emptiness (*ye tong; ye stong*). The viewpoint of the Dzogchen teachings is that all phenomena are primordially empty.

From the beginning of the first chapter of Longchenpa's *Resting at Ease in Illusion,* the chapter on the example of dream:

> The ground expanse (*gzhi dbyings*) is unchanging,
> The nature of mind is the immense space.
> It is empty luminosity, free of elaborations.
>
> From this, the phenomena of the victorious ones,
> Immaculate like the sun, moon, and constellations,
> Are naturally present as the three kayas and the primordial
> wisdoms;
> Indivisible, beyond formation and disintegration.
>
> The luminosity is spontaneously replete with all qualities.
> This is the innate, original natural state.
> It is known as "the illusion of the true ground" (*yang dag gzhi yi sgyu ma*).
>
> Within this are the adventitious clouds of delusion.
>
> The co-emergent ignorance
> Is the creator of dreams, having the nature of sleep.

The conceptual ignorance
Is the defiled mind that reifies the nondual into being dual.

The deluded perceptions of the beings of the six realms
Are like dreams, apparent yet nonexistent.
They experience each of their joys and sorrows
According to each one's personal experience.
After a long duration of this comes all of the habituation to
Their dwelling places, bodies, possessions, and so forth.

Arising from virtue and nonvirtue come joy and sorrow,
A multitude of forms like painted pictures.
From a single delusion, the many manifest;
From grasping at the many comes a continual stream of deluded
    phenomena.

The self-existing nature of mind is the single essence.
From the sleep of unawareness comes the deluded phenomena
Of the mind that grasps at subject and object.

This profusion of multifarious dream appearances
Is nothing other than one's own mind.
This is the "illusion of mistaken understanding," as the victors
    have taught.

Someone intoxicated by datura sees all kinds of visions,
Yet they come from a single delusion.
Likewise the experience of the deluded minds of beings of the
    six realms
Arises from the intoxication of the sleep of ignorance.
This is known as "the unreal" (*bden med*),
So realize this today!

In brief, there is the illusion of the innately present ground (*gnas pa
    gzhi gyuma*),
And there is the illusion of mistaken understanding (*log rtog sgyu ma*).
From not realizing the true nature of the ground (*gzhi*), the two
    kinds of ignorance manifest.

These are the co-emergent ignorance (*lhenkye marigpa; lhan cig
skyes pa'i ma rig pa*)
And the conceptual ignorance (*kuntag marigpa; kun tu brtags
pa'i ma rig pa*).
From this comes the illusion of deluded perceptions (*'khrul snang
gyi sgyu ma*).
If we become liberated from this illusion, we will reach the ultimate
fruition,
Which is the illusion of the kayas and primordial wisdoms (*ku dang
yeshe gyuma; sku dang ye shes sgyu ma*).

All the Buddhist teachings, including Dzogpa Chenpo, speak of the way
things appear (*snang tshul*) and the way things actually are (*gnas tshul*). The
way things appear is multifarious and diverse, and all appearances are like
illusions. But what is the way things actually are? According to the view of
dharmata, the ultimate nature "as it is," from the very beginning all appearances have never arisen or come into being; in the interim, all things have
never existed and have never abided anywhere; and in the end, whatever
has appeared and existed has never gone away nor ceased to be. Dharmata
is birthless and deathless, free of the arising, abiding, and ceasing of mind
and phenomena.

Just as our perceptions in a dream are temporary and have no foundation
and no core of existence, in the same way, there has never been any substantial basis upon which all appearances are founded. For example, the appar-
ently material phenomena of this world, all the infinite universes, planets,
stars, and so forth, seem to exist within infinite space. And yet, space is not
something substantial that serves as a support and basis for the universe. The
actual foundation for all appearances is the empty space of dharmadhatu.

As an example of this fact, some teachings give twelve examples of illusion rather than eight, one of which is the metaphor of a rainbow. If we
have the various connecting factors like sunlight, rain, water vapor, and the
mind observing the rainbow, and the right conditions coincide, rainbows
appear through the interdependent relationship between all their compo-
nents. And yet like everything else that appears and exists, they are mere
composite phenomena without any essential core.

We can check and try to see where the rainbow came from, where it actually abides, and finally where it vanishes to. But, we will never find any place
where it came from nor any place where it went to, other than empty space.

The appearance of a rainbow is without any basis or root from which it originates. It simply appears, remains, and disappears within space. A rainbow is empty, but this does not mean some kind of nihilistic emptiness where everything is absent (*med pa*), since phenomena do appear within space. A rainbow appears but is primordially empty, without foundation or root, empty yet appearing.

In brief, based on the eight examples of illusion as taught by Longchenpa, we establish the view that all our present perceptions are not what they seem to be, but are intrinsically without true existence. Thus the Dzogchen teachings speak of primordial emptiness (*ye stong*). To begin to establish the true condition of all things, we reflect on analogies in order to understand that the way things appear (*snang tshul*) is like an illusion, that everything is like a dream. Then we meditate on the meaning of this together with the introduction to the nature of mind that we receive from our teachers. Through this approach, we come to experience and realize the way things actually are (*gnas tshul*), which is that everything has always been empty from the very beginning. This is the understanding of the Dzogchen teachings.

Nowadays people sometimes speak of emptiness in a nihilistic manner, and there is certainly the danger of misunderstanding emptiness in a variety of ways. Some may read or hear Dzogchen teachings and mistakenly think that in the Dzogchen view, there is no karma, that there is neither virtue nor nonvirtue. If people think that this is so, they are confusing nihilistic voidness with primordial emptiness. Through intellectual assumptions, some people might arrive at a kind of blank emptiness where they think there are no positive or negative actions, that there is no such thing as either meritorious karma or negative karma. There is a vast difference between the primordial emptiness of everything and the mistaken nihilistic view of emptiness that ignores the reality of karma, the certainty of cause and effect.

Longchenpa tells us that he has practiced and has realized through his own experience the emptiness taught by the Buddha in the sutras and tantras through the eight examples of illusion. Thus Longchenpa's teachings in *Resting at Ease in Illusion* are not like the words of someone who has just gained information from reading a lot of books. Longchenpa realized the meaning of the primordial emptiness of all things. It was not something he had to think about and then render into some sort of intellectual composition. Longchenpa spontaneously wrote *Resting at Ease in Illusion* from out of his realization of primordial emptiness. In fact, Longchenpa's state of enlightened realization was so great that the Dzogchen protector deities actually acted as his scribes and wrote down his teachings themselves, for the benefit of present and future disciples.

At that time he wrote *Resting at Ease in Illusion,* Longchenpa was staying in a very small cave at Gangri Thokar, the "White Skull Snow Mountain." Longchenpa established his hermitage at Gangri Thokar and named it "Oddiyana Fortress" (Urgyen Dzong). I have not personally seen Longchenpa's cave there, but many people have said that it is very small, so Longchenpa must have been quite short. When Longchenpa was staying there, he realized the illusory nature of all of samsara and nirvana. Knowing the truth of the illusoriness of all conditioned things, the words of *Resting at Ease in Illusion* arose spontaneously in Longchenpa's mind from the greatness of his realization.

All these treatises of Longchenpa such as *Resting at Ease in Illusion* are composed through gathering and condensing a great realization and understanding of the Buddha's teaching into each text. There really is no difference in the qualities of Longchenpa and those of other enlightened buddhas. He was the emanation of Samantabhadra, and thus he possessed the wisdom mind of the dharmakaya buddha. He is also considered an emanation of Manjushri, the bodhisattva of wisdom. If we were able to read Longchenpa's *Treasury of Dharmadhatu* (*Choying Dzod*; *Chos dbyings mdzod*) and compare it to other texts by different authors, we would see a great difference in the way that other authors' writings are composed, in comparison to Longchenpa's writings. His works sprang spontaneously from the enlightened intent of his wisdom mind. They are spontaneous wisdom songs, treasuries of *dohas* like the spiritual songs sung by the mahasiddhas of India.

In summary, *Resting at Ease in Illusion* demonstrates the primordial emptiness of the ground (*zhi; gzhi*), the path (*lam*), and the result or fruition (*draybu; 'bras bu*). Longchenpa explains the eight examples of illusion and establishes through them how all the phenomena of the ground are illusory and do not inherently exist. This is what he refers to as the illusion of the innately present ground, the natural state (*naylug; gnas lugs*). Furthermore, he also establishes through the eight examples of illusion that all phenomena of the path have an illusionary nature and do not inherently exist. Finally, it reveals that all phenomena of the fruition are the totally pure illusion of the enlightened bodies (*kaya; sku*) and primordial wisdoms (*jnana; ye shes*). In the beginning, one understands the illusory nature of the ground;

in between, one practices liberating the illusion of deluded misconceptions while on the path; and finally the pure, authentic wisdom illusion arises as the result.

The renowned Patrul Rinpoche spent an entire year teaching the Trilogy of Resting at Ease, including the third volume of the trilogy, *Resting at Ease in Illusion*. The teachings were given to Patrul Rinpoche's main disciple Nyoshul Lungtok Tenpai Nyima and others. Nyoshul Lungtok came from the Derge kingdom in eastern Tibet, which is also where I am from. The amazing accounts of his life and teachings are still well known in that region down to this day. Nyoshul Lungtok was the teacher of Khenpo Ngawang Palzang (1879–1941), also known as Khenpo Ngakchung or as Khenpo Ngaga. Khenpo Ngaga was the root guru of my root guru Nyoshul Shedrub Tenpai Nyima (b. 1920). In addition to Patrul Rinpoche's writings, we also have works written by his students that describe how they practiced and how they developed their experience and realization.

Patrul Rinpoche had spent the major part of his life practicing, accomplishing, and transmitting the teachings of Longchen Rabjam. His disciple Nyoshul Lungtok Tenpai Nyima received all of Longchenpa's teachings from Patrul Rinpoche. There is a place in the Do region of Golok called Arik, near the area of Dodrupchen monastery. Patrul Rinpoche offered the teaching *Resting at Ease in Illusion* in a forest at Arik, and Nyoshul Lungtok was among the disciples. Patrul Rinpoche would give the instructions and then his students would practice until they gained authentic experience.

At this time, while Nyoshul Lungtok was practicing the teachings of Longchenpa's *Resting at Ease in Illusion,* through the blessings ensuing from his heartfelt prayers to Longchenpa as he was supplicating with fervent devotion, his wisdom realization (*gongpa; dgongs pa*) blazed forth, and he suddenly and spontaneously attained profound realization. His belief in the true existence of appearances completely collapsed, and all the phenomena of samsara and nirvana arose as the nature of illusion in a vast illusory display.

Later when Nyoshul Lungtok would teach the eight examples of illusion from Longchenpa's *Resting at Ease in Illusion,* he used to recall this experience. He would recount to his students how he had spontaneously realized the self-originating awareness (*rangjung rigpa; rang byung rig pa*) of the Great Perfection, free of all grasping and fixation. Nyoshul Lungtok explained that in his realization all appearances were automatically freed by themselves and that everything was just an unimpeded open transparency (*zang thal*). The apparent materiality of the world and beings was revealed to him to be an illusory display, unreal and insubstantial.

What was the nature of Lungtok Tenpai Nyima's realization? Right now, this building seems completely solid to us, and we cannot see through the walls to the outside. But when Nyoshul Lungtok was practicing, he was able to see whatever was within the walls of his dwelling as well as whatever was on the other side of the walls. It was not that he was seeing with the ordinary eye consciousness, which had suddenly somehow become able to see through walls. Rather, Nyoshul Lungtok had realized the illusory, insubstantial nature of all things, and so the expanse of his realization pervaded space, encompassing and penetrating everything.

Right now things are not transparent for us, due to our strong habit of self-grasping (*bdag 'dzin*) and subject-object fixation (*gzung 'dzin*). Our mind and body obscure perception, and so we do not recognize the way things actually are (*nay tsul; gnas tshul*) within the nature of dharmata. On the other hand, when the apprehending mind and the objects it perceives both simultaneously collapse, then all the constraints that come from fixating on the phenomena of samsara and nirvana are spontaneously eliminated. When subject-object grasping truly collapses, one's perception of the outer world and beings as substantially existing will be completely annihilated, and one will be liberated from dualism in an instant. For Nyoshul Lungtok, the universe and all beings simultaneously arose as the play of illusion. This is how he explained his experience.

When we first hear of this kind of wisdom realization, we probably think that Nyoshul Lungtok's experience was similar to looking outside through a window; but this is not how we should understand it. Rather, for someone who has experienced and gained some realization of the open transparency of awareness (*rig pa'i zang thal*), then even his or her body, eyes and senses, speech, mind, and indeed all apparent phenomena are experienced as empty and insubstantial. There is nothing to be found anywhere that intrinsically exists, since his or her own being and all the objects of perception are discovered to be illusory and immaterial. All that remains of his or her experience of the phenomenal world is just an unimpeded objectless transparency (*yul med zang thal*).

While receiving teachings such as Longchenpa's *Resting at Ease in Illusion,* we would do well to follow the example of the great lineage masters, to follow in the footsteps of Patrul Rinpoche's disciples such as Nyoshul Lungtok Tenpai Nyima. We should receive and study the teachings with faith and devotion and then gain actual experience of the instructions through putting them into practice. Then we will know for ourselves the truth of Longchenpa's writings.

8. THE IMPORTANCE OF MINDFULNESS

Mindfulness: The Mirror of Mind

Homage to the sovereign of self-occurring mindfulness!
I am the mirror of mindfulness,
Clearly reflecting your conscientious mindfulness.
Look, vajra friends! When you behold me, be mindful.
Seeing one's guru and Guru Rinpoche as inseparable,
Pray to the three jewels.
Look without distraction at the very essence of your mind!

Mindfulness (*dran pa*) is the root of dharma.
Mindfulness is the main part of the practice.
Mindfulness is the stronghold of your mind.
Mindfulness is the companion of self-knowing wisdom.
Mindfulness is the support of Mahamudra, Maha Ati, and Madhyamaka.
Mindlessness (*dran med*) will allow negative forces to overpower you.

With mindlessness you will be swept away by laziness.
Mindlessness creates all faults.
With a mindless lack of attention, you will accomplish nothing.
Mindlessness is like a heap of excrement.
Mindlessness is like fishing in a dry river bed.
Without mindfulness one is like a heartless corpse.
Beloved dharma friends, be mindful!

By the aspiration of the holy gurus,
With mindfulness, may you recognize your own essence.

This request to remember mindfulness was offered by the fallen monk, the foolish bucktoothed ox known as Jamyang Dorje, to his vajra friends possessing the dharma eye.

May all be auspicious!

ALL DHARMA TEACHINGS have a single purpose, which is to cultivate and develop our mind. Buddha Shakyamuni said, "To thoroughly cultivate one's own mind—that is my teaching."

As we approach the teachings on the true nature of mind, let's remember the positive mental attitudes that enable us to listen to, receive, and learn dharma teachings. At the beginning of listening to teachings, we need to turn our attention within and examine our own mind. Check whether your thoughts are positive, negative, or neutral. If you have negative thoughts, abandon them and let them go, and neutral thoughts should be transformed into positive ones.

For example, strong thoughts of anger will prevent you from listening to the dharma as well as hinder your practice of meditation. With such powerful thoughts occupying the mind, your attention will not be free to listen to the teachings. On the other hand, if your mind is not caught up with the three mental poisons of anger, attachment, and ignorance, then it has the freedom and leisure to practice the dharma. We need to become free of ignorance, which means that we need to cultivate and develop understanding, intelligence, and wisdom.

As I have been asked to say a few words about my song *Mindfulness: The Mirror of Mind,* it will help if we are able to understand what is meant here by "mindfulness" (*dran pa*). It is first of all important to know that a great variety of different approaches and methods are used in the buddhadharma to gain knowledge and insight, and these approaches give rise to the different dharma vehicles by which one traverses the path. The various schools of buddhadharma know ultimate truth by different names, such as "free from elaborations," "the wisdom realizing selflessness," "the nature of mind," "awareness," and so many others. The key point is that if you understand awareness (*rig pa*), you will understand the meaning of ultimate truth as well as understand the nature of everything that can be known.

One who knows perfectly both the true nature and the relative condition of all things is a buddha, an enlightened one. Sentient beings are those who do not see and understand the true nature and condition of all things, those who are deluded or mistaken. What is meant by delusion? For example, a young child may mistake a colorful painting of a tiger on a wall for a real tiger and become fearful, thinking that the tiger can harm him. But an adult knows that it is just a painting, sees it for what it is, and is neither deluded by it nor mistaken in his understanding of what it is.

If a painting can produce such fear in a child, then how much delusion, fear, and terror must be experienced by sentient beings who do not know the true nature of all things, and thus misunderstand the actual condition of all things? The root of all things is the mind. If you are mistaken regarding the nature of mind, how much more difficulty will you face in dealing with the whole range of confusing phenomena? So give up ignorance, discover your own awareness-wisdom (*rang rig pa'i ye shes*), and rely on it.

In order to discover awareness, it is necessary to make our mind peaceful and calm. A turbulent mind has no clarity. Clear water can reflect the moon with clarity, whereas if water is muddied, its clarity is obscured and it will not reflect the moon well. For water to be clear, it needs to be unstirred and undisturbed, left free of movement and agitation, then the image of the moon will appear with clarity. Likewise the mind (*sems*) needs to become still and peaceful, which in the practice of meditation is known as the aspect of calm abiding (*shamatha; zhi gnas*). This is how we are able to discover awareness (*rig pa*), which is the aspect of insight (*vipasyana; lhag mthong*), within meditation practice.

There are two major obstacles to the mind's being calm or still. The first of these is our attachment to outer objects, causing us to be preoccupied with food, clothing, wealth, and so on. The second obstacle is the inner defiled thoughts, which disturb the clarity of our mind and prevent us from gaining true insight. In the beginning of the path, we have no control over our mind. Merely hearing a sound causes our attention to stray, and we are equally distracted whenever we catch sight of an object. This is how the mind is always distracted and unable to come to rest and abide in itself. Through the calm abiding practice of stilling the mind through one-pointed meditation, we gain mastery of our mind (*sems la rang dbang thob pa*).

Here we see that the terms "calm abiding," "one-pointedness," and "mastery of the mind" are different ways of speaking of the same aspect of meditation. These mean that we need to remain focused, whatever meditation practice we are doing. Whether it is the recitations of Tara or Avalokiteshvara, or the accumulation of the preliminary practices (*ngondro; sngon 'gro*) such as performing prostrations, single-minded mastery of our mind is what is important. In fact the practice of concentration, of focusing the mind, is not only found in the buddhadharma but is taught in many other traditions as well. No tradition of meditation teaches us to be distracted; they teach stilling the mind and one-pointed concentration.

In buddhadharma, the principle of meditation is that based on the stillness of mind gained through calm abiding meditation (*shamatha; zhi gnas*), we can gain profound levels of insight (*vipasyana; lhag mthong*) into the true nature of mind and phenomena. Different schools have different levels of teachings on insight, depending on the capacity of the students. These different teachings will give rise to a variety of degrees of insight, some of which are more profound than others. On the basis of meditation, we are able to gain many insights into the truth of the dharma.

But in order for genuine insight to arise, the key point of all of the schools and approaches is to give up unawareness (*ma rigpa*) and to accomplish knowing or awareness (*rigpa*). In the use of the term common to the general vehicles, "rigpa" means "knowing," the opposite of "not knowing." Cultivating and developing this quality of knowing is the common aim of all the teachings of buddhadharma. In summary, ignorance or "unawareness" is the fundamental cause of samsara, and it means to be ignorant of the true nature of one's mind and phenomena. In order to be free of ignorance, it's important to begin to develop mindfulness by practicing calm abiding meditation.

No actual gap or real distance exists between buddhas and beings, between cyclic existence in samsara and liberation in nirvana, between unawareness and knowing. It is all within the mind. It is like the back and front of your hand—one side is unawareness (*ma rigpa*) and ignorance, and the other side is knowing and awareness. The Indian mahasiddha Naropa and the Tibetan master Gampopa often used the example of the hand. The term for their teaching on the ultimate view is "Mahamudra" (*chag gya chenpo; phyag rgya chen po*). It can be literally understood to mean "the vast hand" of samsara and nirvana. Samsara and nirvana should not be thought of as being somewhere apart from one another; they are like the two sides of your hand. They are both aspects of the mind, found within the mind itself. This is true for the minds of all beings

Regardless of whether we appear to be in the state of ignorance, or instead have presence of mind and know what is taking place, both of these are aspects of our own mind. For example, we have the word "mindfulness" (*drenpa; dran pa*), referring to the capacity to be present, and "noticing" or "attentiveness" (*shayzhin; shes bzhin*), referring to the ability to notice everything that is transpiring. These are combined in the term *drenshay* (*dran shes*), which means "attentive mindfulness," which is a way of describing the key point of calm abiding meditation.

All beings intrinsically possess this capacity for knowing. Hence it is so important to have the vast intention to establish all beings in "knowing," in the realization of transcendent intelligence (*prajna; shes rab*). In the Vajrayana teachings of Secret Mantra and especially in Dzogchen, this refers to primordial wisdom (*jnana; ye she*) and to "awareness," the special meaning of the term "rigpa" as understood in Dzogchen. In order to be able to help others to recognize their awareness, one must first recognize and stabilize one's own self-knowing awareness (*rang rig*). So we need to practice and meditate and to rely upon mindfulness and awareness.

Mindfulness is thus the essence of the buddhadharma—to be mindful at all times, while walking, sitting, eating, resting, and so on. Whether one is Buddhist or not, in this world we all need mindfulness. We need mindfulness to be able to accomplish our work and our various projects and to keep in focus the objects of our intention. While cooking, for example, we must practice mindfulness and attentiveness, or otherwise we will burn the food; we might even forget to cook a meal at all. We need to remember when it is necessary to go to the toilet. If we don't, we will soil ourselves and end up making a mess. If mindfulness is needed for even these small things, how much more necessary is mindfulness for meditation practice? Without mindfulness and knowing, we will not even remember to study the dharma or practice meditation.

We need to really train well in mindfulness, in order to become accustomed to it. Why is this so important? Our habits are like a piece of paper that has been rolled up. We unroll it, but it goes back to its original shape as soon as we let go of it. In the same way, we meditate for one minute, then we have completely forgotten our mindfulness in the very next minute and return to unawareness. We may meditate for an hour, and after that we completely forget what we are doing! This shows a lack of development of the capacity of mindfulness. We find that we meditate this morning, but by the afternoon it's all gone. We have forgotten our meditation by failing to maintain mindfulness throughout the day.

If we don't practice mindfulness, there is no real point of staying in retreat. Even if we stay for years in retreat, there will be no significant benefits. Whereas if we have very stable mindfulness, we can be liberated by hearing even a single word of instruction. Focusing on a single object, such as the deity Tara, can bring the accomplishment of the deity and mantra, as well as the accomplishment of both calm abiding and insight as a unity. Through such one-pointed practice alone, the nature of mind can be recognized and the entire path can be accomplished. So it is important that we always practice mindfulness in everything that we do.

The reason practitioners don't accomplish the path of dharma is because they have not developed stable mindfulness. There are two general reasons for not accomplishing dharma. The first reason is that one does not understand the method, the way to practice. The second is that although the practitioner knows the way to practice, he or she lacks the mindfulness to maintain and accomplish the practice.

For example, there is the case of someone like Jesus and his disciples. Jesus is said to have passed away and been resurrected. If this did occur, it seems that he did not teach the way to accomplish it to his disciples. No one who came after him is known to have gained the same accomplishment.

Another example is that of the master Garab Dorje, who came into this world shortly after the Buddha passed into parinirvana, and who taught Dzogchen, the Great Perfection. After Garab Dorje's passing, some of his followers such as Manjushrimita also attained the rainbow body. By many generations later, there were thousands who had attained the rainbow body in his lineage; so clearly, the way to accomplish the practice was taught by Garab Dorje. But at the same time, there were thousands who did not accomplish it. Even though they had received the same instructions, they did not gain the accomplishments (*siddhi; dngos grub*) because they did not maintain mindfulness and constant remembrance of the practice.

The attainment of the rainbow body is not just something that happened in the distant past. Even in these recent times, during the period of my lifetime when I was living in the East, seven people from my area of eastern Tibet have been confirmed to have attained the rainbow body. And even more recently, within the last several years that I have been in the West, another two yogis in eastern Tibet have accomplished the rainbow body. They achieved this accomplishment based on mindfulness and awareness. If we practice with mindfulness and awareness, we can also accomplish the rainbow body, so we should train in mindfulness and awareness.

9. *The Lion's Roar That Vanquishes the Diversions and Errors of Hermits Who Meditate upon the Heart Essence* BY JIGME LINGPA

In the innate natural continuity,
I bow to the Great Perfection,
Beyond meditation, modification, and change,
Without distraction or fixation,
Endowed with a core of awareness,
And transcending the conceptual mind that deliberately accepts
    and rejects.

This is the vital essence of the tantras of the luminous Great Perfection,
The heart essence of Padma, the heart blood of the dakinis.
It is the ultimate meaning that transcends the gradual approach of the
    nine vehicles.
It can be expressed only through the power of the wisdom mind
    transmission.
For the sake of those yogi meditators
Who are single-mindedly dedicated to the supreme essential meaning,
I have composed this text,
Not through restrictive conceptual analysis,
But from the treasury of the vast expanse of the wisdom mind.

Here, one's pure aspirations made in past lifetimes
Are joined with meeting a fully qualified holy guru
Who holds the ultimate lineage of realization.

Then, if you know how to supplicate,
Through surrendering to such a teacher with complete trust,

And with fervent, single-minded yearning faith,
Your devotion will serve as the contributing condition,
And the guru's realization will be transferred to the disciple.

This nature, free from conceptual elaborations,
Is the natural state of the Great Perfection,
Which cannot be shown by words or examples.

It is an unimpeded manifestation, without limitations,
And it does not fall into extreme views.
It is the immediate awareness of Directly Cutting Through,
Which never sheds its coat nor changes color.

As meditation has fully become just this,
You have purified the attachment to meditating.
Released from the chains of view and meditation,
Certainty is born from within.
The "thinker" is gone without a trace.

You are no longer benefited by good thoughts, harmed by bad
    thoughts,
Or misled by thoughts of an indeterminate nature.

Expanse and awareness have become all-pervasive.
And so the spiritual qualities, which are the signs of the path, have
    been actualized.
Even the names of so-called errors, diversions, and ways of straying
    do not exist.

However, although this teaching is the pinnacle of all vehicles,
There are individuals of the superior, middling, and lesser categories.
Since it is difficult to find those [disciples] of the most superior acumen,
There might be misunderstandings between guru and disciple.
In that case, even if the disciple meditates,
Due to this shortcoming, he or she will find it difficult to develop
    good qualities,
And will go astray.

In relation to this, from the viewpoint of
The personal meditation practice of those who follow a gradual path,
There are the three stages:
Intellectual understanding, actual experience, and realization.

[Interlinear note (*yig chung*) within the root text:
Relating these to the stages of the path of the general vehicle:
On the path of accumulation, one acquires intellectual understanding.
On the path of joining, one gains actual experience.
And on the path of seeing, one gains realization.
These words of the learned and accomplished ones appear to be
    very true.]

These days it seems there are many who consider
Their mere intellectual understanding to be genuine meditation.
And so, there are many who go astray by attaching conceptual labels
    [to experience].

To explain how this occurs:
At times consciousness is clear and empty,
Your meditative equipoise is without any thoughts at all,
And you are in a relaxed and comfortable mood.
When this happens, it simply indicates that the meditation experience
    of bliss is predominant.

[You may think,] "My meditation is exactly it! No one knows any better
    than me. My realization is just like this!" and you will feel proud.
However, if at this point you do not rely upon an authentic teacher, then
    as it says in the Dzogchen teachings,
"Intellectual understanding is like a patch, it wears off."

As this illustrates, there are many who, when they meet with good
    or bad circumstances, [separate from their practice] like water
    separates from milk.

Furthermore, bad circumstances are somewhat easier to successfully
    bring to the path,

But bringing good circumstances to the path is very difficult.
Thus there are those who arrogantly presume that they have high
    realization, yet strive for the glories of this life. They are distracted,
    filled solely with attachment to the "mara demon of the 'child of
    the gods.'"
This is due to not having understood the key point of the self-liberation
    of the six sense fields.

These days there are many who speak of these [kinds of views and
    meditation] as if they were amazing signs of accomplishment . . .
    although those who point this out are just [regarded as] "white
    ravens."

However, for those of you who practice the sacred dharma from your
    hearts, such a fixated conceptual view will not help your practice of
    meditation.

In the four sessions of daily practice, you should focus on guru yoga,
Receiving the four empowerments.
Then, within the state of merging your mind with the guru's mind,
Let awareness be free and unbound.
Persevere thus from the depths of your heart,
Until the essence of this experience
Has become unsupported and free of any reference point.

Likewise, for meditation experiences:
When calm abiding meditation predominates, there will be experiences
    of emptiness.
When insight predominates, there will be experiences of clarity and
    so forth.

In brief, knowing the vital point of discursive thoughts,
The power of discriminating intelligence blazes forth.

And although you know how to bring both stillness and movement
    into meditation,
Yet the essence of the "knower" is under the tight grip of ego fixation,
And you stray into a pattern of analytical examination and so forth.
These are highly undetectable and dangerous conceptual obscurations.

Therefore, as these are present, it is premature to label thoughts as
"dharmakaya."

Do not bind this immediate awareness, which is unimpaired and
uncorrupted,
With the meditators' "remedies,"
Or with attachment to your view.

You should solely take as the path
This free and unbound,
Unimpeded open transparency.

Moreover, if you fall under the influence of speculation
Based on your ideas about meditation and postmeditation,
Then you will [enter] the dangerous passage of diversions, errors,
and strayings on the path.
If you do not know how to identify these, then you will be unable
to distinguish whether or not [your meditation] is correct.

Therefore, the hidden flaws of these are explained here:

What is "emptiness"?
It is that which is empty and without a self-entity from primordial
beginning.
It is free from the four and the eight extreme views.
This immediate awareness, which is free and unbound and beyond
concepts,
Is known as "rigpa."

This may not be understood.
For example, in the lower vehicles, there is conceptual analysis to
affirm nonexistence and to negate existence. And following this,
you arrive at an empty, blank nothingness.
Or, as in the lower tantric classes with the svabhava mantra and so
forth, through meditative concentration, you purify everything into
emptiness, [asserting] a mere "clarity and emptiness."
Or, if you experience an [imputed] view that [everything] is like
an illusion,
These are errors.

Likewise, for "calm abiding meditation":
The coarse and subtle thoughts are naturally pacified in and of themselves.
The nature of mind, free of the waves of discursive thoughts,
Has an abiding aspect that is vividly clear and wakeful,
Self-illuminating self-awareness.

Misunderstanding this, thinking that calm abiding is a mindless vacant
state, is an error.

Regarding "insight":
It is the recognition that both stillness and movement
Are the natural reflection
Of the essence of your awareness.
It is clear and aware without grasping—that's it!
Otherwise if you do not understand this and investigate stillness and
movement,
It is an error.

There are a variety of ways of explaining
What are known as "meditative equipoise" and "postmeditation."

However, according Dzogchen's own terminology,
"Meditative equipoise" is to abide
While embracing the essence of whatever arises with mindfulness.

Then, while being attentive to that [practice],
The aspect of movement, that which transforms and changes,
Is known as "postmeditation."

Misunderstanding this, [you think that] to one-pointedly keep in mind an
empty viewpoint is "meditative equipoise."
And following this, you superimpose an illusion-like emptiness upon
whatever arises and call this "postmeditation."
This is an error.

What is meant by "nondistraction"?
It means that you do not stray into the subtle undercurrents of
deluded thinking.

And, you do not enter into a state of vague oblivion.
This is known as genuine, innate mindfulness.

If you are anxious about being distracted,
And if you are bound by deliberate, restricted mindfulness,
Then these are errors.

What is "ordinary mind"?
It is said to be immediate awareness,
Which is untainted by either faults or good qualities,
Left as it naturally is.
It is sustaining the continuous flow of awareness.

Misunderstanding this, to identify it as your ordinary, autonomous
mundane thinking is an error.

What is "nonmeditation"?
Entering the womb of the natural state,
The attachment to meditating or not meditating is purified.
Without any artificial modification or any reference point whatsoever,
You establish the citadel of all-pervasive mindfulness.

If you are in a state of careless indifference, remaining in your ordinary
manner,
Or if you are daydreaming in an indeterminate, vague oblivion,
These are errors.

What does "sustaining whatever arises" refer to?
Whatever thought arises, look directly at it,
Neither blocking it, nor examining it, nor following after it.
Release the thinker itself within awareness,
And sustain the unimpeded open transparency of stillness and movement.

Misunderstanding this, to carelessly follow after whatever thoughts arise
and analyze them is an error.

Similarly, there are three diversions:
If you are attached to bliss, you will be born as a god in the desire realms.

If you are attached to clarity, you will be born as a god in the
    form realms.
And if you are attached to nonthought, you will be born as a god in
    the formless realms.
These are known as points of diversion.

I will explain how to identify them and their errors:
That which is known as "bliss" is untainted by the three major root
    sufferings.
It is like, for example, when you cannot bear to separate from
[Abiding] within the natural state.
It is said to be the arising of the experience of joyful bliss.

This is not like the bliss of defiled, outflowing desire.
Nor is it said to be like the arising of thoughts of happiness and delight.
Nor is it being delighted with changing objective circumstances.

What is known as "clarity" is that which is not tainted by the obstructing
    forces of drowsiness and fogginess.
It is the unobstructed shining forth
Of rigpa's aspect of potency,
Or of [rigpa's] avenues of expression.

It is not the avenues of perception endowed with the characteristics
    of apparent objects such as shapes, colors, and so forth,
Which are the natural forms of deluded perception.

Moreover, in regard to "nonthought":
It is free from thinking all kinds of thoughts
And from being disturbed by the deluded thinking that reifies things
    as being real.
It is said to be thought-free, like space.

It is not like fainting and losing consciousness.
Nor is it a black darkness like deep sleep.
Nor is it like when the senses withdraw and you feel nothing.

In brief, these three types of experiences are merely the manner in which
    signs of the path manifest, and they naturally and spontaneously occur.

However, if you do not realize this and meditate deliberately hoping
   for them,
And when they do occur, if you embrace them as though they were
   genuine meditation and become attached to them,
Then this will cause you to be diverted into the three realms of
   existence.

Likewise, there are the four ways of straying (in regard to emptiness):
Straying into emptiness's having the character of a knowable object,
Straying into taking emptiness as a path,
Straying into taking emptiness as a remedy, and
Straying into superimposing emptiness.

Each of these four is said to have an original straying point
And a temporary straying point.

However, if we briefly summarize them:
The essence of ultimate emptiness is primordially pure.
It is free from the fetters of being a compounded phenomenon
And of being a mental construct.
This present awareness is immense, boundless, primordial purity.

Misunderstanding this key point, if you regard emptiness as something
   separate,
Like stamping emptiness onto appearances,
This is straying into [emptiness's] having the character of a knowable
   object.

Likewise, you may not be convinced that it is ordinary mind or
   self-knowing awareness (rang rig) that you take as the path.
You may not understand that cause and result are by nature inseparable
And are from the very beginning spontaneously present and already
   complete.

Then by meditating on emptiness as a path, you exert yourself
   with the hope that the result of the dharmakaya will arrive from
   somewhere else.
By this, your meditation is mentally constructed.
This is the straying point of taking emptiness as a path.

Once again, whatever thoughts and emotions arise,
Their essence is none other than emptiness from the very beginning.

As there is nothing beyond that,
There is no need for these two things:
The afflictive emotion that is to be abandoned
And emptiness as a remedy [for it].

When your awareness identifies the "object to be abandoned,"
At that very moment, like a snake naturally unknotting itself,
It is self-liberated.

Misunderstanding this vital point,
If you need to meditate by applying an additional remedy of "emptiness"
Onto the thought or emotion that is to be abandoned,
This is straying into [taking emptiness as] a remedy.

Concerning the straying of superimposing emptiness:
Whether the [practice] is elaborate or unelaborate,
Within the primordial, vast sphere,
The spacious expanse of Samantabhadri,
Clarity and emptiness are spontaneously present as a great unity.

By not understanding this,
Then the reified meditator
And the conceptual way of dissolving [all phenomena] into emptiness
Are not unified,
And thereby skillful means and wisdom are divorced.
And thus, you are not sustaining the continuity
Of "ordinary awareness" beyond concepts,
Through the nonreferential "watcher."

And keeping your previous intellectual theories in mind,
You think:
"There is nothing to meditate upon and no meditator."
"Everything is emptiness."
"All is dharmakaya."
"Karma and its results do not really exist."

"This is mind."
"These are thoughts."
"Nothing at all can be found to exist."

This is what is known as superimposing [an intellectually] resolved
    view of emptiness.
Nowadays there are a great many who do this.

In brief, while meditation has been placed in your hand,
On the journey to the level "endowed with the excellence of all aspects,"
There are the concealed places and narrow, treacherous pathways
Of errors, diversions, and points of straying.

If you do not carefully discern these experiences,
Even if you are a clever talker and a shrewd writer,
As it says in the Dzogchen teachings,
"Meditation experiences are like mist, they will fade away."

As it is explained, even trifling positive and negative circumstances
Can deceive a "great meditator."
This is due to his becoming completely confounded in the face of
    circumstances.

Therefore, if you don't embrace [your practice] by means of
This extraordinary vital point for removing obstacles and bringing
    enhancement,
Then staying in a strict retreat away from all human contact,
You will bemoan the ascetic hardships of your concentration practices.
You will bind yourself tightly in meditation postures,
Meditating on deities and reciting mantras,
Cultivating the practices of the channels and vital energies, and so forth.
But how will you attain liberation and enlightenment,
Merely through the difficulty of searching for and buying such goods?

As it says in the *Condensed Perfection of Wisdom Sutra,*
"Though one may remain for countless years
In a mountain valley filled with snakes,
Five hundred miles from anywhere,

Yet such a bodhisattva, who does not understand [the true meaning of]
    solitude,
Will only develop further pride and will remain in samsara."

Therefore, through understanding this vital point of taking whatever arises
    as the path,
Then in the hermitage of the body,
There is the practitioner, the mind,
Accomplishing the practice of remaining in solitude.
There is no path more effective than this.

Thus, don't hope to make much of your months and years spent in retreat,
But just count your whole lifetime as the measure [of your retreat].
Place your efforts into sustaining the continuity of the uncontrived
    natural state.

Whatever good or bad thoughts may arise,
Do not apply the "patch" of just directly apprehending it,
Noticing, "Oh, here is a thought."
Nor should you apply a remedy, as though it were a "moxibustion"
    treatment,
Onto the thought to be abandoned.
Doing nothing whatsoever, be unconcerned,
Like an old man watching children play.

By passing day and night without interruption
Within the state free from conceptual elaborations,
Thereby, you will perfect the mastery of thought-free insight.

Whether there is stillness, movement, or mindful awareness,
Whatever arises, [whether] good or bad thoughts,
By achieving stability within the expanse of empty awareness,
The Great Perfection beyond concepts,
Then as it says in Dzogchen,
"Realization is like space, unchanging."

So it is said that although the yogin's body may appear ordinary,
Since his mind remains in the wisdom realization of

The dharmakaya, free of effort and activity,
All that appears and exists is the mandala of the guru.
Whatever arises is all-pervading primordial wisdom,
And apparent objects are [experienced as] symbols and scriptures.

The [yogin's] wisdom mind, naturally at ease,
Is beyond the activities of the levels and paths.
And from the primordially liberated vast expanse of samsara and nirvana,
In the interim [until all beings are enlightened],
He will effortlessly and spontaneously
Accomplish the benefit of the teachings and living beings.

Then at the same time as the enclosure of your physical body dissolves,
Just as when a vessel breaks
And the space within it merges inseparably as one with the space outside,
[The realized yogin] will manifest true enlightenment
Within the youthful vase body,
The primordial ground expanse of inner luminosity,
Free from the investigating mind.
This is the final, ultimate accomplishment!

In summary:
Relative deluded appearances, the great falsehood,
Have dissolved into the vast expanse
Of the essential nature of awareness.
Thus the mind play of discursive thoughts, like a child's dance,
Has subsided within the continuity of mindfulness beyond concepts.

As I am not intoxicated by stuporous sleep
From imbibing the beer of good thoughts that pursue a high view
And bad thoughts that shackle in doubt,
I remain at ease in naked ordinary awareness.

These profound and pithy vajra verses
Of the wisdom mind transmission
Will overpower, one hundred times over,
The exaggerated claims of those who spout their theoretical
   understanding,

As well as the piercing torment of the treacherous passage
Of stillness and movement.

Due to the auspicious connection of my previous accumulation [of merit]
And pure aspirations,
Together with the kindness of the profound path of the vajra yoga,
The knots of my central channel were released.
And as a testimony of this, I wrote these oral instructions on the vital
    points,
Based on my own experience.

When the roar of the summer thunder-drum resounds,
It splits asunder the mouse-like hearts of pretentious learned ones.
And as profound experience and realization have overflowed from within,
I was unable to conceal these words that spontaneously burst forth.

By this virtue,
Through sustaining the natural flow of mindfulness,
All of the nonvirtue accrued from straying into erroneous, restricted
    mindfulness
Is spontaneously purified within the innate continuity.

May all realize the Great Perfection!

The Lions Roar That Vanquishes Diversions and Errors was insistently requested
many times by my attendant Dampa Longdrol Ying Rig, who is rich in the wealth
of faith, generosity, and learning, while constantly maintaining the practice of the
luminous Great Perfection due to his past karmic connection; and also by Kusum
Ying Rig, whose mind abides in the three solitudes, and remaining in closed retreat,
is focused on the practice of the Luminous Vajra Heart. Based on these requests, I,
the Kusulu yogin, Padma Wangchen Yeshe Palgyi Rol Tso (Powerful Lotus Wisdom Glorious Lake of Enjoyment), who consider myself familiar with the direct
experience of the natural state (*mngon sum gyi gnas*) of the luminous Great Perfection, wrote this text during my retreat in the Great Secret Flower Cave of Ogmin
Khadro Tshok Khang, "Feast Hall of the Akanishtha Dakinis," which is at the navel
of Samye Chimpu. Do not show this text to those who have not received these
instructions, or to those who, even if they have received them, hold wrong views;

being intoxicated with the poisonous waters of pride, they thus lack the fortune to apply these vital points of the path. All those of you who are dedicated to practice, read this text again and again!

All those who have certainty may be given the reading transmission of it.

It is entrusted to the care of the sacred Nyingthig Protectors.

SAMAYA GYA GYA GYA

10. COMMENTARY OF ORAL INSTRUCTIONS ON JIGME LINGPA'S *The Lion's Roar*

INTRODUCTION TO *THE LION'S ROAR*

WHEN [...] Dzogchen practices such as those within the [...] *ma,* there will be errors and misconceptions a[...] There will likewise be mistakes with regard to [...] the way in which one continues in and sustain[...] *Lion's Roar* was written by Jigme Lingpa to el[...] errors, the faults that occur in the practice of view [...] which there are three types, known as "errors," "diversio[...] nts of going astray." In *The Lion's Roar,* Jigme Lingpa teaches the [...] errors, the three diversions, and the four points of going astray.

The first of these three types of faults or mistakes in view and meditation is known by the general term "errors," or *nor sa* in Tibetan. The second type is called "diversions," or *gol sa* in Tibetan. Diversions refer to a point in the practice of meditation where one can become sidetracked or diverted. One is diverted away from the correct path, deviating into modes of meditation that will not lead to the intended result.

The third of these is known by the term "points of going astray" or *shor sa* in Tibetan; *shor sa* is similar in meaning to *gol sa*. In *The Lion's Roar* teaching, *shor sa* or "points of going astray" refer to points at which one can stray from the correct view of emptiness as it is understood in the Dzogchen teachings. It also refers to the manner in which one actually strays, starting from those initial points of departure; thus *shor sa* can also be understood as "ways of straying." In the points of going astray, one falls prey to the pitfalls that come from an inaccurate understanding, and mistaken application, of the view of emptiness.

When they enter into the practice of Directly Cutting Through to

Primordial Purity (*ka dag khregs chod*), the meditation of those of superior capacity is like someone's discovering a golden land; their view and meditation are simultaneously perfected. For those of middling capacity, if they are able to successfully unite calm abiding and insight, they will not fall into diversions and the ways of straying. Those who are unable to stably unite calm abiding and insight will definitely succumb to errors in their practice.

Those of lesser capacity, who make up the vast majority of practitioners, will certainly need the teachings of *The Lion's Roar*. Most practitioners have not yet successfully united calm abiding and insight and still experience these two aspects separately in their meditation practice. Because of this, they will lapse into fixated states of calm abiding meditation. Also, it is likely that at times they will stray in their practice of insight into the nature of dharmata.

As a result of such errors in view and meditation, ordinary practitioners will fall into diversions and ways of straying. And even if they are able to unite calm abiding and insight to some degree, they will not yet have gained much stability in their practice of the recognition of the nature of mind. Until they gain stability, there will continue to be mistakes in their practice, and these are the diversions and ways of straying.

In the natural state (*naylug; gnas lugs*) of Dzogpa Chenpo itself, there are no diversions nor any points of straying. True Dzogchen practice is the province of those of the highest capacity. When we speak of the "highest capacity," there are five qualities that if well developed, give one greater capacity for accomplishing dharma. These are the capacity of faith (*depa; dad pa*), the capacity of transcendent intelligence (*prajna; shes rab*), the capacity of meditative absorption (*samadhi; ting nge 'dzin*), the capacity of mindfulness (*dran pa*), and the capacity of diligence (*tsondru; brtson 'grus*). For example, when human beings have their five sense organs intact, they are able to function at full capacity. Similarly, to fully enter into realization of the teachings of the Buddha, these five capacities are needed.

If an individual is endowed with the full development of these five qualities, he or she is said to be a practitioner of superior capacity. Among these five, the two most essential are to have supreme faith and to have transcendent intelligence. To be able to realize Dzogchen, the Great Perfection, it is necessary to possess this quality of intelligence. Also, it is especially important to have great faith and devotion to, a deep interest in, and a karmic connection (*tendrel; rten 'brel*) with the Dzogchen teachings. In Dzogchen, it is essential to have within oneself a wellspring of interest, faith, trust, and devotion toward the enlightened mind (*gongpa; dgongs pa*). In particular, one needs to have faith and devotion toward the view and realization of the lineage masters, those who uphold the transmission and actualization of the ultimate meaning (*nges don*), Dzogpa Chenpo.

Through the power of intelligence, we can eradicate all of our doubts and misconceptions regarding dharmata and arrive at a genuine understanding and experience of the view. The Dzogchen teachings are said to require the aptitude and acuity of individuals of the highest capacity, and it is for such persons that the Dzogchen teachings exist. Those who lack the development of the five qualities of practitioners of the highest capacity must first enter into the general teachings in order to cultivate extraordinary capacity if they wish to realize Dzogpa Chenpo.

Individuals with the highest development of superior capacity do not make any errors in view and meditation, and so do not fall under the influence of diversions and points of straying. When those of the utmost capacity realize the meaning of Dzogchen, there will be no mistakes and faults, and they will not descend into confusion again.

By merely hearing the meaning of the Dzogchen teachings, they experience liberation simultaneous with understanding. This is traditionally likened to someone suddenly arriving in a golden land where there are no ordinary stones and all is gold. They have realized the ultimate view of the natural state, and their view and meditation have at this time been simultaneously perfected. Like a person arriving in land of gold where one is unable to find ordinary rocks and stones, all phenomena are the display of wisdom.

For example, in East Tibet there lived a shepherd who was incredibly devoted to the fifth Dzogchen Rinpoche, Thubten Chokyi Dorje. One day Thubten Chokyi Dorje and a group of twenty monks were traveling through a region frequented by shepherds, and camped there overnight. A shepherd inquired as to who was residing in the party's tents, and when he heard that it was Dzogchen Rinpoche, he was filled with joy. Traditionally, villagers in Tibet did not use the term "Dzogchen," but would ask for a "mind teaching" (*sem tri; sems khrid*) or an "introduction to the nature of mind" (*sem ngo; sems ngo*). And so the shepherd thought to himself, "Well, I have never received any introduction to the nature of mind. Now I really have to ask this amazing lama for such a holy instruction."

The shepherd went to the lama and offered three prostrations. The lama inquired of him what it was he wished to ask, and the shepherd replied that he would like an introduction to the nature of mind. Immediately

Dzogchen Rinpoche uttered just a single word, and thereby the shepherd directly recognized the nature of his mind, understood the true sense and meaning of Dzogchen, and was liberated. For beings of supreme capacity like this shepherd, simply hearing with faith one word from a realized master can liberate them, and they directly stabilize the recognition of mind nature. Renowned masters such as Garab Dorje, Shri Singha, and Guru Rinpoche are among those known to have been of the supreme capacity, but there have been many others.

One of my root teachers was Jigme Namgyal, who in his previous lifetime was a lama named Jigme Dongak Tenzin, who lived for eighty-two years. Jigme Dongak Tenzin received the Dzogchen pointing-out instructions from the great master Dzatrul Kunzang Namgyal, of Kathok monastery in East Tibet. Jigme Dongak Tenzin said that from the moment he was introduced to awareness wisdom (*rigpai yeshe; rig pa'i ye shes*), he never again wavered from that state, not even for an instant.

Individuals who possess such superior capacity do not err in their realization of view and meditation, and so they never fall under the power of the diversions and the ways of straying. Amazingly, those of the very highest spiritual capacity attain liberation the instant they understand the meaning of Dzogpa Chenpo. At that time, all ordinary phenomenal perception is transformed for them into pure vision; like a person discovering a golden land, only pure phenomena remain. This kind of individual does not require the teachings found in *The Lion's Roar*.

However, such persons are very rare. This being so, practitioners of middling capacity and those of lesser capacity need teachings like *The Lion's Roar* of Jigme Lingpa. This is because when they apply the teachings of view and meditation, faults will occur. The teachings on the three main topics of *The Lion's Roar*, those of the errors, diversions, and points of straying, are indispensable for all such yogins wishing to follow the path of Dzogchen.

Why do we need these teachings? If we wish to actually experience and realize the teachings, simply knowing many details of the dharma in an intellectual way will be of no use, unless that knowledge becomes a part of our living experience. There are three stages of dharma: the stage of intellectual understanding (*go-wa; go ba*), experience (*nyongwa; myong ba*), and realization (*togpa; rtogs pa*).

It is said in the buddhadharma teachings that it is better to be aware of a single fault than to know a hundred things. If we are unaware of our faults and mistakes, then eventually they will creep up on us and destroy our practice, like bandits lying in wait to attack. In general, we are always babbling on and on about "the essence," mumbling this and that about "awareness," about "Dzogchen," about so many things. There is no end to what we can talk about; there really isn't any limit. But if we remain unaware of our faults and mistakes, they will come back to haunt us. They will wait patiently, and one day we will discover errors and diversions in our practice.

For those yogins of middling and lesser capacity, meditation is what is most necessary in order to develop wisdom. In Longchenpa's work *Resting at Ease in the Nature of Mind (Sems nyid ngal gso)*, he explains the importance of practicing meditation in solitude. Longchenpa teaches that it is necessary for our mind to be tamed through cultivating the three positive mental attitudes of faith, renunciation, and bodhicitta, as these encompass the meaning and intention of the foundational practices (*ngondro; sngon 'gro*). Then we can engage in the main practice of meditation.

When we begin to practice meditation, there are five basic kinds of hindrances that will arise and can impede our progress. The five obscurations or hindrances (*dribpa nga; sgrib ba lnga*) are sensory craving (*'dod pa la 'dun pa*); ill will and malice (*gnod sems*); lethargy and sluggishness (*rmugs pa dang gnyid*); restless agitation and regretfulness (*rgod pa dang 'gyod pa*); and doubt and indecision (*the tshom*). As we learn meditation, we will find that a wide variety of these hindrances seem to constantly arise as soon as we engage in practice. Even if we intend to meditate well for one hour, there is no way that we will not begin to experience the five hindrances after a few minutes have passed.

For example, first of all we know well about our craving for sense pleasures and gratification through the enjoyment of the senses. When meditating, we may find ourselves hankering after enjoyable activities and longing for something to distract us; this is the first of the five hindrances.

Second, thoughts of ill will and malice toward others are also a great hindrance. It is helpful to remember that if we find ourselves wishing anything other than liberation and enlightenment for anyone, we have already begun to damage our bodhisattva vow to free all beings from suffering and establish them in the state of buddhahood.

Third, the hindrance of lethargy and sluggishness is a state where the mind sinks into dullness; we lack clarity and have no presence of attentive mindfulness (*dren shay; dran shes*). As dullness intensifies, it becomes heavier, and we feel drowsy and sleepy. These are the signs of the hindrance of lethargy and sluggishness.

Fourth, the hindrance of restless agitation means that we experience an unruly and scattered mind. When we have a profusion of thoughts, thinking about our family, house, relationships, and everything else, it is impossible for the mind to be still. We find ourselves restless and agitated because of the presence of our habitual tendencies (*bag chags*). Our habitual tendencies are deeply related to our afflictive emotions (*klesha; nyon mongs*), the three principal afflictive emotions being the mental poisons of attachment, aversion and delusion.

Another aspect of the fourth hindrance is regretfulness. When we experience the hindrance of regretfulness, we reflect on things of the past, mulling over whether they seem to have been good, or were perhaps not so good. For example, in the past we may have sold a house, and now we find ourselves thinking that it may not have been such a good thing to have done. We will revisit again and again all kinds of different things that we did or did not do, actions that might have been right or might have been wrong for us to do at the time. We end up going round in circles in our mind, thinking about all kinds of past experiences and having many regrets.

And fifth, at times we will also have a great variety of doubts, indecision, and uncertainty about what we are doing with our life, about our meditation practice, our relationships, about all of our many concerns. The hindrance of doubt creates many obstacles for the practices of calm abiding and insight, and for the recognition of mind nature. Another aspect of the fifth hindrance is the hindrance of indecision, where we find ourselves thinking "Is this right or not? Maybe I should do this, or perhaps I should not do this but should move in another direction instead. I am really not sure what is best for me right now. I'm not sure what I should do." The hindrance of indecision will once again generate an abundance of thoughts and can make it difficult for us to proceed along the path.

The best way to liberate all of these hindrances is through the power of the view. Individuals of superior capacity can recognize whatever hindrances arise and liberate them within the space of awareness (*rigpa*), the "sole sufficient king" (*chig chod gyalpo; chig chod rgyal po*). Awareness is like a king, and the recognition of awareness has the power to enable us to master all circumstances and overcome all hindrances. As is said, "Knowing one liberates all."

The middling way of dealing with the five hindrances is to transform them through visualization and meditative absorption, focusing the mind one-pointedly in various ways as antidotes to the hindrances. For example, for the hindrance of restless agitation, we can use the remedy of lowering our gaze and looking into space along the angle of the tip of the nose. For the hindrance of lethargy and sluggishness, we can raise our gaze, looking into space along the direction of the point between the eyebrows. In the middling approach, where we transform hindrances, it is important that we not be overpowered by the five hindrances. When hindrances arise, we immediately apply the appropriate remedies, focusing the mind through one-pointed absorption (*ting 'dzin rtse gcig*), attentive mindfulness (*dren-shay; dran shes*), visualization, recitation practices, and so on.

The inferior way to deal with hindrances is to transform them through physical activity. For instance, we may be practicing and find that we feel lethargic and sluggish and are overcome by heavy dullness. If the first two remedies of liberating the hindrance through the view and transforming the hindrance through meditation have not been successful, we can try to get some fresh air. We might open the window, walk about, exercise our body, and use similar physical means. For those who are not of superior capacity, if they practice a range of such methods to clear away the hindrances, they will be able to refresh and continue to improve their practice of view and meditation.

The author of our present text, *The Lion's Roar* (*Senge Ngaro; Seng ge'i nga ro*), is the awareness-holder (*vidyadhara; rig 'dzin*) Jigme Lingpa. Rigdzin Jigme Lingpa was born in 1730, 366 years after the passing of the omniscient Longchenpa in 1364. At the time of Jigme Lingpa, the essential teachings of Dzogchen, the Great Perfection, were in danger of degeneration. The experiential transmission (*nyong gyu; myong brgyud*) of the practice lineage (*drubgyu; sgrub brgyud*) was disappearing from this world.

What is meant when it is said that the experiential transmission was disappearing? It is traditionally explained that the buddhadharma, including the Dzogchen teachings, can never be destroyed from the outside. Even when the armies of the Chinese Communists came and slaughtered many hundreds of thousands of Tibetans, the Dzogchen teachings survived. Similarly, in the past when Islamic invaders entered India, destroying the Buddhist temples, universities, and dharma libraries of India, the buddha-dharma and Dzogchen teachings survived.

How then can Dzogchen teachings be extinguished in this world? The tradition can be destroyed only from within, by those who follow or claim to follow the teachings. This occurs when the understanding of Dzogchen becomes corrupted, jumbled together with all kinds of concepts and intellectualized. If practitioners start to intellectualize Dzogchen, they will end up with a muddle of ideas about it, thinking "Dzogchen is really like this . . . although, it is also like that. The Dzogchen teachings are pure and perfect . . . and yet sometimes certain aspects don't seem quite so pure and perfect. At times the meaning seems very clear . . . and sometimes the meaning isn't explained clearly. Maybe the teachings need something extra, to make the meaning clearer . . ." and so on. Through entertaining all manner of doubts and engaging in intellectual speculation, one will not reach the level of the Great Perfection. One will fail to discover and genuinely experience the essence of their own self-knowing awareness (*rang rig pa'i ngo bo*).

Since it is a general rule that people like to analyze everything, the masters advise that it is better to keep the teachings of Dzogchen out of the public arena. It is not that the Dzogchen teachings must be kept completely secret so that no one can find them. Rather, what is meant is that it is possible that some people will not understand and appreciate the value and blessings of the Dzogchen teachings and lineage. Lacking pure vision, faith, and appreciation for the teachings and the lineage, such persons' connection with the teachings can be damaged and their understanding and experience will be obscured.

This can lead to having erroneous and even negative attitudes toward the Dzogchen teachings, and these may remain as obstacles on the path for many lifetimes. It is like giving something extraordinarily valuable to a young child to play with. Not understanding its value, after a while the child will become bored with that precious object and look for other things to play with. For this reason, an authentic teacher will know when the student is ripe to be introduced to Dzogchen.

Another factor that leads to the decline of the Dzogchen teachings is for people to have misconceptions about them. For students who are not sufficiently ripened and spiritually mature, when teachers explain Dzogchen it will not be understood as it would be by those who have the fortune and capacity to be vessels for the teachings. The student who is not really ready for Dzogchen will have all kinds of concepts about it, thinking "This could be something new, but maybe it's not and is just like certain other teachings. It is probably referring to emptiness . . . but maybe it is not really speaking about emptiness, but about something else, like consciousness, or . . ." They will have all kinds of thoughts and become swept up in discursive conjecture, occupied with trying to reinterpret the teachings.

For such individuals, speculation of this sort can become a serious obstacle to receiving Dzogchen's experiential, direct introduction to the nature of mind. They will assume that they already know what it means, not suspecting that their understanding is flawed. This is because spiritually immature persons may have many preconceived ideas about mind nature and might simply wish to confirm and defend their previous understanding. One might have presumptions and come to intellectual conclusions about the meaning of Dzogchen, rather than seeing the meaning of the teaching "as it is" (*jitawa; ji lta ba*) and thus understanding what the teachings are meant to indicate.

Then, when individuals with such dispositions are unable to realize the unique meaning of Dzogchen through their own experience, they will feel that perhaps the Great Perfection is not so great or so unique. They will look for some other teaching that they think is better than, or the same as, Dzogchen, and then confuse and muddle the meanings together with Dzogchen. Due to these kinds of errors and misconceptions, their connection with the Dzogchen teachings will be spoiled.

This can create further obstacles for them, and the effects of these obstacles can enter into any other spiritual practice they undertake. Having developed a wrong view through misunderstanding the Dzogchen teachings, they have created the potential for being diverted on the path, and even deviating toward inferior rebirths. While it is certainly possible that problems such as these can be purified and corrected under the guidance of one's teachers, it is much better if such obstacles never arise in the first place, before the damage is done.

When we speak about realizing the wisdom mind, it is important to know where the line of demarcation between understanding and not understanding is found. The Dzogchen teachings speak of "mixing with intellectual speculation" (*yid dpyod dang 'dres pa*), where "yid cho" (*yid dpyod*) means "intellectual speculation" or "intellectual assumption" or "speculative conjecture." It refers to the tendency to assume one understands Dzogchen based on theoretical understanding rather than actually encountering the depth of the teachings based on actual direct experience.

The term "mixing with intellectual speculation" calls our attention to the possibility that the direct experience of the Dzogchen view can be hindered by too much analysis and thinking. We assume that we know the meaning without having experienced it. One is engaging the dualistic mind (*sems*) rather than discovering the uncontrived nature of mind (*ma bcos sems kyi rang bzhin*). It is due to exactly these tendencies that the

Dzogchen teachings will decline and degenerate at different times and in certain eras.

Through excessive theorizing, making assumptions, and coming to conclusions, we obscure our inconceivable and ineffable essence of dharmata. We might then begin to talk a lot and even write a lot about the view of Dzogchen, offering self-assured pronouncements that "Dzogchen is like this, and Dzogchen is like that" until gradually, any connection to the meaning of Dzogchen is completely lost to us. Those who practice correctly, gaining direct experience and true realization, are eventually able pass this experience on to others. On the other hand, those who claim to teach Dzogchen without any true basis and deep understanding will be of no real enduring benefit to others, and may in fact harm them on the path.

The uncontrived essence of dharmata (*ma bcos chos nyid kyi ngo bo*) is said to be "naked" (*jenpa; rjen pa*), meaning that it is divested of the coverings of concepts. It is said to be "without artificial modification" or "uncontrived" (*cho may; bcos med*), meaning that it is to be left free from being manipulated and altered (*choma; bcos ma*), free from all grasping and fixation (*'dzin ba*). For this reason, it is known as "naked awareness" (*rigpa rjen pa*), and this is exactly what is spoiled through analysis and speculative meditation.

Rather than being something that is arrived at intellectually, the ultimate wisdom mind (*mthar thug gyi dgongs pa*) of Dzogpa Chenpo is introduced to us by our teacher, and then we begin to experience the meaning through our own practice.

There are four main reasons why the wisdom mind of one's teacher may not be realized through one's own practice of the experiential instructions (*nyong tri; myong khrid*). It may be that the disciple lacks pure vision (*dag nang; dag snang*), that the disciple lacks faith (*depa; dad pa*) and devotion (*mogu; mos gus*), that the disciple has an insufficient accumulation of merit (*sonam*), or that the disciple has not received the complete oral instructions (*man ngag*) of the lineage.

In summary, some people will receive the teachings and arrive at genuine faith, progressing through the stages of intellectual understanding, experience, and realization of Dzogchen. Others will have wrong views and mistaken attitudes in regard to the teachings, lineage, and tradition. Some who encounter the teachings won't be able to genuinely enter the path of Dzogchen at all, since they lack the necessary foundation and spiritual maturity.

Or, if they do enter into the Dzogchen teachings, they will not correctly understand the meaning of Dzogchen and will fail to gain genuine experience and realization. Their many concepts will lead to conjecture and assumption, and this will serve only to obscure their own essential nature. As the tendency among students to encounter the buddhadharma in this fashion increases, thereby the essence teachings (*nyingpoi cho; snying po'i chos*) of the Buddha, including Dzogchen, will begin to decline. In order to help avoid such consequences, teachings like *The Lion's Roar* of Jigme Lingpa will be very beneficial for practitioners to take to heart.

THE LION'S ROAR BY JIGME LINGPA

> In the innate natural continuity,
> I bow to the Great Perfection,
> Beyond meditation, modification, and change,
> Without distraction or fixation,
> Endowed with a core of awareness,
> And transcending the conceptual mind that deliberately
>   accepts and rejects.

Dharmata, the "true nature of phenomena," is our buddha nature (*sugatagarbha; bde gshegs snying po*). Dzogpa Chenpo, the Great Perfection, is the most supreme yoga that cannot be objectified or made into something to meditate upon. The buddha nature never changes, and thus does not improve when it manifests as a buddha, or deteriorate when manifesting as a sentient being. It is neither altered nor affected by causes and conditions.

Remain without distraction in this uncontrived essence (*ma bcos pa'i ngo bo*); dharmata is naturally free of distraction. This uncontrived essence, the Great Perfection, is not an object that can be held or grasped with mindfulness (*dran pas ma bzung*), yet it is endowed with a core of awareness (*rig pa'i snying po can*). It is the natural Great Perfection, beyond the range of the conceptual mind's deliberate fixations on something that needs to be accepted or rejected. Within the innate, natural continuity of recognizing his own essence (*rang ngo shes pa'i rang babs gnyug ma'i rgyun*) Rigdzin Jigme Lingpa pays homage.

> This is the vital essence of the tantras of the luminous Great
>   Perfection,
> The heart essence of Padma, the heart blood of the dakinis.

It is the ultimate meaning that transcends the gradual approach
of the nine vehicles.
It can be expressed only through the power of the wisdom mind
transmission.
For the sake of those yogi meditators
Who are single-mindedly dedicated to the supreme essential
meaning,
I have composed this text,
Not through restrictive conceptual analysis,
But from the treasury of the vast expanse of the wisdom mind.

Jigme Lingpa tells us that this is the vital essence (*bcud*) of the tantras
of the luminous Dzogpa Chenpo, the heart essence (*thugs thig*) of Guru
Padmasambhava and the lifeblood of all the wisdom dakinis. This is the
ninth vehicle of Atiyoga, which is beyond the other eight vehicles. This ultimate meaning of the Most Secret Unexcelled (*yang gsang bla med*) teachings of the Nyingthig can be expressed only through the power (*mthu*) and
blessings of the wisdom mind transmission, and never through concepts
put into mere words.

These teachings can be explained only through the blessings (*jinlab;
byin rlabs*) of an authentic teacher who possesses the "enlightened realization" or "wisdom mind." The blessings of the teacher enter into the disciple
who possesses openhearted devotion (*mos gus*). The true meaning cannot
be expressed through just studying some books and then writing something
down. Those who explain or write about the Great Perfection must have
received and been genuinely ripened by the blessings of the wisdom mind
transmission (*dgongs brgyud*) within their own heart; only then will it be
possible to transmit the meaning of the Great Perfection.

In brief, whoever writes about or teaches Dzogchen must have fully
received the blessings of the teacher and the lineage within his or her heart.
If this has truly taken place, that disciple's mind has become inseparable
from the teacher's enlightened realization, and so he or she has realized the
teacher's wisdom mind. To accomplish this intellectually is simply impossible. However, for the sake of his disciples, future beings, and great meditators who live in the mountains solely practicing the supreme essential
meaning of the Great Perfection, Jigme Lingpa composed this teaching,
The Lion's Roar. He did not write it through the power of his intellect; it
naturally arose and spontaneously manifested (*rang byung rang byon*) from
the vast expanse of his enlightened realization.

Here, one's pure aspirations made in past lifetimes
Are joined with meeting a fully qualified holy guru
Who holds the ultimate lineage of realization.

Then, if you know how to supplicate,
Through surrendering to such a teacher with complete trust,
And with fervent, single-minded yearning faith,
Your devotion will serve as the contributing condition,
And the guru's realization will be transferred to the disciple.

We need to have excellent karma and a very great accumulation of merit to even hear the name of Dzogchen, the Great Perfection. To have the opportunity to receive oral instructions and advice is extremely fortunate and is a sign of our great merit accumulated in the past. If we consider the number of beings in the world, then how many of them have ever heard of the teachings of Dzogpa Chenpo? There are millions and billions who have never heard of Dzogchen. Among all of the billions of people in the world, there may be only a few hundred thousand who have heard of Dzogchen. Within that number, there are probably only a few thousand who have received teachings and been able to gain some decisive understanding. Among those who were able to gain a decisive understanding of the meaning of Dzogchen, there remain only a very few who are dedicated to actually practicing Dzogchen throughout the day and night.

This nature, free from conceptual elaborations,
Is the natural state of the Great Perfection,
Which cannot be shown by words or examples.

It is an unimpeded manifestation, without limitations,
And it does not fall into extreme views.
It is the immediate awareness of Directly Cutting Through,
Which never sheds its coat nor changes color.

As meditation has fully become just this,
You have purified the attachment to meditating.
Released from the chains of view and meditation,
Certainty is born from within.
The "thinker" is gone without a trace.

> You are no longer benefited by good thoughts, harmed by bad
> thoughts,
> Or misled by thoughts of an indeterminate nature.
>
> Expanse and awareness have become all-pervasive.
> And so the spiritual qualities, which are the signs of the path,
> have been actualized.
> Even the names of so-called errors, diversions, and ways of
> straying do not exist.

When we speak of the natural state (*gnas lugs*) of Dzogchen, it is beyond verbalization, analysis, and concepts. It cannot be shown or expressed through words, examples or analogies. It does not fall into the extremes of existence and nonexistence, surpasses the bounds of samsara and nirvana, and is not delimited by the extreme positions of eternalism and nihilism. The natural state of awareness (*rig pa'i gnas lugs*) transcends all such limitations. "It does not fall into extreme views" means that one is to be free of the duality of subject and object.

Also here, Jigme Lingpa uses the term "unimpeded manifestation" (*go ma 'gags pa*). It means that the natural state of the Great Perfection is not just a completely blank, void state but rather, that all phenomena manifest as its natural expression (*chos thams cad rang rtsal du shar ba*).

Once those of superior capacity have been introduced to the Dzogchen view of Directly Cutting Through (*trekchod; khregs chod*), thoughts and thinking are cut through. They never stray from that present instant of awareness (*rig pa skad cig ma*) to which they have been introduced. This is the measure of realization for those of the most superior capacity (*dbang po yang rab*), those of the very highest acumen. Like the account of the shepherd mentioned earlier, and the case of the Dzogchen master Garab Dorje, this is the manner in which all those of the very highest aptitude become enlightened. They are freed from any necessity of maintaining attachment to meditation. Like someone's arriving at a golden land where there are no ordinary rocks and stones, their realization is replete with all the spiritual qualities of enlightenment.

Jigme Lingpa says that one is "released from the chains of view and meditation," because view, meditation, and conduct all are complete and perfected (*dzog; rdzogs*) within awareness (*rig pa*) itself. There is no longer any separate view, meditation, and conduct; they are all one in the present instant of awareness (*rig pa skad cig ma*). One is liberated, and thus transcends view, meditation, and conduct. Certitude is born from within. As is said:

> Practice by making this life, the bardo, and the next life a single
> unity;
> Practice by uniting view and meditation as one.

Jigme Lingpa also mentions here the "thinker" (*skye mkhan*), the one who gives rise to thoughts. The "thinker" cannot be grasped by the attention as an object of attention. This is because there is no subject. There isn't any "thinker."

One of the great masters of the Longchen Nyingthig was Nyoshul Lungtok Tenpai Nyima (1829–1901), the principal disciple of the renowned Dza Patrul Rinpoche (1808–87). As we read in the biography of Nyoshul Lungtok, at one time he was residing at a mountain retreat place called the "Small Grove at Dzogchen" (Rdzogs chen nags chung ma), a little wooded area above Dzogchen Monastery in eastern Tibet. It was here that Nyoshul Lungtok received direct introduction to the nature of his mind from Patrul Rinpoche. Up to this point in his life, Nyoshul Lungtok had received teachings on the *Way of the Bodhisattva* (*Bodhicaryavatara*) one hundred times, as well as receiving many Dzogchen teachings from other masters, including Gyalsey Shenpen Thaye (1800–55/70). However the teacher with whom he had the strongest karmic connection was Patrul Rinpoche.

For over twenty years, Nyoshul Lungtok had practiced the Hearing Lineage of Great Experiential Guidance (Nyengyu Nyongtri Chenmo; Snyan brgyud myong khrid chen mo), and so he was sufficiently ripened to receive the introduction to the final, ultimate Great Perfection (*rdzogs chen mthar thug pa*). This is the introduction to awareness, the true primordial wisdom (*rig pa don gyi ye shes*). At this time, the ultimate realization of Dzogchen was introduced to Nyoshul Lungtok's mind stream by Patrul Rinpoche.

One evening at the "Small Grove" mountain retreat, Patrul Rinpoche was outside, engaging in the sky practice of the threefold space. As Patrul Rinpoche gazed into the sky, he said to Nyoshul Lungtok, "Come sit here, near to me."

"Do you know what meditation is?" Patrul Rinpoche asked.

"Not exactly," Nyoshul Lungtok replied.

"Well, do you hear the dogs barking at Dzogchen monastery? Do you see the stars in the sky? Do you hear us talking now? This is Dzogpa Chenpo! This is awareness wisdom (*rig pa'i ye shes*)!"

As soon as Nyoshul Lungtok heard these words of Patrul Rinpoche, the realization of guru and disciple became one. All his doubts and misconceptions were completely cut through, and a deep confidence welled up from within. The chains of doubt in regard to view and meditation, of thinking "realization is like this" and "realization is not like that" were demolished. Lungtok Tenpai Nyima had realized the naked wisdom of empty awareness (*rig stong ye shes rjen pa*). From that moment, he never wavered from that state. This came about through the blessings of the guru and the openhearted devotion of the disciple.

Later Nyoshul Lungtok confided to his students that through the power of one's devotion and the blessings of a realized teacher, this can happen. As this was so, Nyoshul Lungtok counseled them that it is essential to practice guru yoga, to pray with fervent, heartfelt devotion (*mogu dragpo; mos gus drag po*), and then mingle their mind with the wisdom mind of the lama.

When we speak of such exemplary teachers, these are individuals of superior capacity, of the very highest acumen. For most beings, realization does not happen as it did in the case of Nyoshul Lungtok. The great majority must practice meditation and gradually they will progress through the five paths. They will progress from the path of accumulation to the path of joining, then enter the path of seeing and progress onward through the path of meditation, until gradually attaining enlightenment, the fifth path of "no more learning." This is why, from the time one is introduced to the view by one's gurus, it is necessary to be very diligent in meditation practice.

Once the great Patrul Rinpoche was camped in Minyak La'u Thang, a place that was known to be haunted by nonhuman spirits. As he was falling asleep, Patrul Rinpoche had a powerful experience of terrifying apparitions of gods and demons. He prayed fervently to his guru Gyalwai Nyugu (1765–1843). Through the power of his wholehearted supplications, Patrul Rinpoche was blessed with the realization of his teacher's wisdom mind, the ultimate enlightened realization of the Great Perfection (*rdzog pa chen po don gyi dgongs pa*). Afterward, Patrul Rinpoche related his experience to the mahasiddha Do Khyentse Yeshe Dorje, who told him it was a sign that he had subdued the four mara demons with a single blow and that he had become enlightened. In the case of Patrul Rinpoche, this occurred instantaneously through praying to his teacher. Patrul Rinpoche confided in his main disciple Nyoshul Lungtok that after this experience, he no longer had a proliferation of discursive thoughts arising.

The Victorious One, Longchen Rabjam, in many of his writings such as The Profound Innermost Essence (Zabmo Yangthig; Zab mo yang thig) and Innermost Essence of the Guru (Lama Yangthig; Bla ma yang thig), relates that by having prayed with great devotion to his gurus, a special state of meditative absorption arose in his mind and that henceforth he never separated from this realization. Longchenpa told his students that based on his own experience, it was vital to pray to one's gurus and to have faith. These are all examples of individuals who are endowed with the most superior aptitude. As Jigme Lingpa says, for those superior beings, even the words "errors" and "diversions" cannot be found.

> However, although this teaching is the pinnacle of all vehicles,
> There are individuals of the superior, middling, and lesser
>   categories.
> Since it is difficult to find those [disciples] of the most superior
>   acumen,
> There might be misunderstandings between guru and disciple.
> In that case, even if the disciple meditates,
> Due to this shortcoming, he or she will find it difficult to develop
>   good qualities,
> And will go astray.

There are many different kinds of individuals, and most do not possess the most superior capacity or highest acumen; some are of middling ability and some possess inferior faculties. Even though the teachings and practice of Dzogchen are of the most superior type, the great majority of disciples are of the middling and lesser type. For this reason *The Lion's Roar* states that some misunderstandings and misconceptions can arise between guru and disciple. This creates obstacles, so that even if the student meditates, his or her practice will not be fruitful. Obstacles that come about due to the student's capacity can make it difficult for spiritual qualities to arise.

This situation, which may occur for students of middling and lesser faculties, is in contrast to the situation of those of the highest acumen, who upon receiving direct introduction never waver from nor lose sight of the view of Dzogpa Chenpo. When such situations occur, the best means of remedying them is to supplicate the guru and receive the four empowerments again and again, merging one's mind with the wisdom mind of the teacher in the recognition of the view.

> In relation to this, from the viewpoint of
> The personal meditation practice of those who follow
>   a gradual path,
> There are the three stages:
> Intellectual understanding, actual experience, and realization.

> [Interlinear note (*yig chung*) within the root text:
> Relating these to the stages of the path of the general vehicle:
> On the path of accumulation, one acquires intellectual
>   understanding.
> On the path of joining, one gains actual experience.
> And on the path of seeing, one gains realization.
> These words of the learned and accomplished ones appear to
>   be very true.]

At the time of establishing the view, we go through the three levels of intellectual understanding (*gowa; go ba*), actual experience (*nyongwa; myong ba*), and finally, realization (*togpa; rtogs pa*). First, establish the view as it is explained in the guidance manual *Supreme Wisdom* (*Yeshe Lama*) and related or similar teachings. Then, the view has to be integrated with our mind (*sems dang 'dres*) through meditation, as we progress through the three levels of intellectual understanding, actual experience, and realization.

As Jigme Lingpa explains, those of the highest capacity never move from the awareness that they have been introduced to. They have direct realization and do not experience diversions and errors. However, those of middling and lesser faculties most certainly do pass through the stages of intellectual understanding and actual experience before entering the stages of realization. Such practitioners will probably have a variety of questions, doubts, or uncertainties regarding the pointing-out instructions, the intro-duction to awareness (*rig pa*) that they received from their teacher. This is especially true of those of lesser aptitude, as for some period of time, they will not have any real stability in their meditation practice, and this will cause doubts and obstacles to arise.

It is a fact that most beings have to go through the different stages of intellectual understanding, experience, and realization. In the gradual path teachings of the general vehicle that outline the Mahayana Buddhist trainings, as well as in the teachings of Secret Mantra, there are five paths or stages of enlightenment. The first of these is the path of accumulation (*tshogs lam*). According to the perspective of the Dzogchen teachings, at this stage, one develops theoretical, intellectual understanding of the view, while accumulating great merit. On the second of the five paths, the path of joining (*sbyor lam*), one gains some degree of actual experience of the view, through one's own practice of meditation.

Then on the third of the five paths, the path of seeing (*mthong lam*), one recognizes the view very directly for oneself. One begins to gain realization of the view, entering the first spiritual level (*bhumi; sa*) of a bodhisattva. From there, one emphasizes the practice of the view (*tawa; lta ba*), which is the recognition of awareness wisdom, gradually stabilizing the recognition and progressing through the spiritual levels of a bodhisattva until completing the five paths to buddhahood.

As one enters the third path, the path of seeing, one finally sees emptiness in actuality (*stong pa nyid mngon sum du mthong*), free of the four extreme views. In regard to actually seeing for oneself the view of emptiness, the Dzogchen teachings speak of seeing the truth of dharmata (*chos nyid kyi bden pa*), or the natural state of all phenomena (*chos thams cad kyi gnas lugs*), or the emptiness of self-nature (*rang bzhin stong pa nyid*), and many others. All of these refer to what is recognized on the path of seeing. For those of middling and lesser faculties, this may also be recognized in glimpses of emptiness that gradually become sustained and that are based on the direct introduction by one's gurus. In this case, the yogin has glimpses of the path of seeing but has not yet been stably established on it.

At this point, we may wish to understand the difference in the manner in which those of middling faculties and those of lesser faculties, meaning those who take the gradual approach, progress to the path of seeing. Individuals of medium ability are able to meditate on the union of calm abiding and insight. In their experience, calm abiding and insight are a unity, and so they progress relatively quickly through the first two paths of accumulation and joining. Those of lesser aptitude must first meditate on calm abiding and stabilize this, and then they begin to experience insight, to gradually enter into the actual experience of emptiness. This is an important key point.

According to the Dzogchen tradition, the reason why the Buddha

appeared in this world is to introduce dharmata, "the true nature of phenomena." The Buddha reveals the true nature of all that we see and hear, all
phenomenal appearances.

In brief, first there is the fundamental condition of the primordial ground
    (dod ma'i gzhi lugs).
The empty essence (ngo bo stong pa) is like the middle of the vastness
    of space.
Within the space of the empty essence, the unobstructed display (rolpa
    'gags med) of phenomena appears, like the stars and planets within
    space.
Awareness (rig pa) is like the still surface of the ocean, or like a clear
    pristine mirror, which can reflect all the stars and planets.
This is the nature (rang bzhin), the natural state of the ground (gzhi'i gnas
    lugs).
It is known as awareness, the natural state of mind (rig pa sems kyi gnas
    lugs),
Or as the natural state of all phenomena (chos thams cad kyi gnas lugs).
This is what is meant by the original ground (thog ma'i gzhi).

The dharmakaya buddha Samantabhadra has realized the natural state of
mind exactly as it is (sems kyi gnas lugs ji bzhin rtogs pa). The primordial buddha Samantabhadra was enlightened through six special qualities (khyad
chos drug), on the basis of recognizing the essence of primordial wisdom's
self-display (ye shes rang snang gi ngo bo). But for those beings yet to be
enlightened, there are the three types of capacities.

Those of the very highest acumen may be enlightened instantly through
receiving introduction. However, those of middling and lesser aptitude do
not recognize that all phenomena are their own "self-manifestation," their
own "self-appearances" (rang snang). They hold what is their own manifestation to be something outside and elsewhere (rang snang yin par gzhan du
bzung ba).

This is the key point. Because of this mistaken understanding (log rtog),
one's own manifestations arise as though they were something other, somewhere else (rang gi snang ba gzhan du shar ba), and from this, one succumbs
to mistaken understanding. Following on from this mistaken understanding, by holding one's own manifestations to be separate from oneself, there
is delusion (rang gi snang ba gzhan du bzungs nas 'khrul pa yod red). On the

other hand, to recognize phenomena as one's own self-created appearances is the cause of enlightenment.

What is meant when it is said that since those of lesser and middling faculties do not recognize all phenomena to be their own manifestation, they fall into mistaken understanding (*log par rtog pa*)? According to the Dzogchen teachings, it means that sentient beings are deluded within the three realms of cyclic existence on the basis of three kinds of ignorance. These are the ignorance of the single identity (*bdag nyid gcig pu'i ma rig*), the co-emergent ignorance (*lhan skyes ma rig*), and the conceptual ignorance (*kun btags ma rig*). In this state of having fallen under the power of the threefold ignorance (*ma rig pa gsum*), whatever manifests from oneself is regarded as external to, and separate from, oneself. This is what is meant by "mistaken understanding," and thereby one falls into delusion and bewilderment.

To better understand this, let's return to the example of sleep and dream. During sleep, one's consciousness and perceptions dissolve into the "all-ground" or "underlying basis of everything" (*kun gzhi*); at this time all of the dualistic thoughts that we normally experience dissolve into the all-ground. Following this, one briefly enters the luminosity of sleep (*gnyid kyi 'od gsal*), and this may be recognized and sustained by the yogin.

For individuals who do not recognize the luminosity of sleep, after dissolving into the all-ground, their mental consciousness will again become active; dualistic thinking will once again stir, creating all manner of dreams. There is also another very important aspect of sleep that may be experienced by the yogin, known as the "dream luminosity" (*milam osal; rmi lam 'od gsal*), which one can also recognize and rest in meditative equipoise within the dream luminosity. There are three points here: first, to know that one is dreaming; second, to recognize clear luminosity (*osal; 'od gsal*) within the dream; and third, to remain or continue in that.

For those who are able to recognize dreams as personal experience, rather than fixating on them as something objectively real, dreams are naturally liberated merely by recognizing them as such. Thus if yogins who have this accomplishment dream of a ferocious lion, they will know it is unreal, like a stuffed lion in a museum. They have no fear, understanding that it cannot possibly harm them. In contrast, those without the ability to know that they are dreaming will experience fear when dreaming of a wild lion.

As in the example of dreams, all things are dreamlike appearances without any truly existing foundation. All the phenomena of samsara and nirvana, whatever manifests, has no locatable place of origin or source, no place where they can be found to abide, and finally, no destination to which they depart. They are unborn, illusory phenomena like dreams. We need to be introduced by our gurus to this condition in which things have no true existence, known as dharmata, the "true nature of all phenomena."

Buddha Samantabhadra is the one who realized dharmata. We must be introduced to dharmata, and we need to have it clearly explained when the teachings of the Buddha are given. When dharmata is pointed out, then those of superior capacity, who are known as the instantaneous type (*chig charwa; cig car ba*), will immediately realize it. But there will be others who will not be able to understand what is being indicated. And even if they have some understanding, they will not gain any decisive conviction about dharmata or actual experience of it, so whatever they understand will not be genuine understanding. It is for this reason that the different levels of dharma teachings presented by the Buddha are gradually unfolded, as they correspond to the degree of understanding, experience, and realization of each individual practitioner.

In our present perception, everything we see seems to be solid, concrete, stable, and actually existing. From the viewpoint of Samantabhadra, all our perceptions of the six senses are as insubstantial as rainbows in the sky. A rainbow originates and appears when all the necessary conditions are present, and if one condition is missing, it will not appear. Then the rainbow seems to abide as something tangible, when in reality there is nothing there. A rainbow cannot be located or pinpointed either outside, inside, or anywhere in between. Finally, to where does a rainbow depart or disappear? The answer is: nowhere; a rainbow just naturally fades away when the causes and conditions that make it appear are no longer present.

In the same way, we say that thoughts are like rainbows. There is nowhere they arise from, like a rainbow; there is nowhere they abide, since like a rainbow, they have no substantial basis; and there is no destination or place to which they depart, like rainbows. Thoughts appear when all the conditions for their occurrence are present, and when any of these conditions are not present, thoughts naturally disappear, just as rainbows do.

In brief, in order to introduce our primordial nature, the various manifestations of Samantabhadra teach the dharma, showing us the path we must practice. When we undertake this path, we will go through the three stages of intellectual understanding, experience, and realization. Merely having intellectual understanding will certainly not destroy our delusion. Since we have been deluded since beginningless time, in the beginning, we will not gain confidence and certainty, as the power of our delusion (*'khrul pa*) is simply too strong. Even if we know and can recognize our primordial nature, if we cannot remain stably within this recognition, we will not be able to bring an end to our deluded perception of samsara.

As it says in the Dzogchen teachings, "If we don't practice meditation, we will not be enlightened." And as the Victorious One, Longchenpa, has said, "If we don't remain in the primordial nature, we will not be enlightened."

> These days it seems there are many who consider
> Their mere intellectual understanding to be genuine meditation.
> And so, there are many who go astray by attaching conceptual
>   labels [to experience].
>
> To explain how this occurs:
> At times consciousness is clear and empty,
> Your meditative equipoise is without any thoughts at all,
> And you are in a relaxed and comfortable mood.
> When this happens, it simply indicates that the meditation
>   experience of bliss is predominant.

These days there are many practitioners of lower and medium capacity who have only arrived at an intellectual understanding and have begun to have meditation experiences or moods, and then they consider this to be genuine meditation (*gom nalma; sgoms rnal ma*). They fall into the trap of attaching conceptual labels (*rgyas 'debs su shor ba*), of superimposing their understanding onto the experience of meditation.

Here, Jigme Lingpa is speaking to those who practice meditation and have gained some actual experience. Such individuals may have the ability to rest free of thought in meditative equipoise (*nyamzhag; mnyam gzhag*). Their consciousness (*shes pa*) is able to experience some degree of clarity and emptiness. Meditation becomes very relaxed and at ease, a meditation experience (*nyams*) in which feelings of well-being and bliss are dominant. But because they are still only at the stage of intellectual understanding, they fall into the trap of imposing concepts onto their meditation. This means that they may think that meditation experiences are genuine meditation and that they must now know very well what the Dzogchen teachings are introducing. They may even think that they have reached the ultimate realization of Dzogchen, and so on.

This cautionary note offered by Jigme Lingpa refers to the fact that it is not easy to become enlightened, since there are many unfavorable circumstances, obstacles, and experiences that can occur, such as the errors, diversions, and ways of straying. At the time of Jigme Lingpa, there were many practitioners who had exactly such meditation experiences and believed them to be authentic meditation. However, nowadays similar experiences are not so common among practitioners, as most people do not practice a great deal; certainly not like they did in Jigme Lingpa's time. When having such powerful experiences, you may feel:

> "My meditation is exactly it! No one knows any better than me.
>   My realization is just like this!" and you will feel proud.
> However, if at this point, you do not rely upon an authentic
>   teacher, then as it says in the Dzogchen teachings,
> "Intellectual understanding is like a patch, it wears off."
>
> As this illustrates, there are many who, when they meet with
>   good or bad circumstances, [separate from their practice]
>   like water separates from milk.[12]

For the practice of Dzogchen, if there is an authentic teacher and a student who wishes to learn, this is the starting point. But there might not be a pure spiritual bond between them, or the student may not possess true faith and devotion, or all the other outer, inner, and secret conditions may not be present. Then, no matter how much the student listens to teachings on emptiness, about how all things are like an illusion or dream, or about awareness, and so forth, after a few days the student's theoretical understanding of these teachings will begin to fade away. After a year or so his or her understanding will have completely disappeared, just like a patch on one's clothing. The "patch" of mere words will not remain very long and will certainly wear off sooner or later.

As Jigme Lingpa teaches in *The Lion's Roar*, when practitioners at this stage of mere intellectual understanding (*gowa; go ba*) practice meditation, experiences of bliss (*dewa; bde ba*), clarity (*salwa; gsal ba*), and nonthought (*mitogpa; mi rtog pa*) will arise. If they cling to these and think they have arrived at the ultimate Great Perfection, they will be bound and hindered by this partial, incomplete understanding of the meaning of the teachings. As they will have no idea how to actually sustain in practice that which is groundless and self-liberated (*gzhi med rang grol*), they will find themselves unable to integrate (*sre wa; bsre ba*) their meditation practice with the positive and negative situations of daily life.

In the Dzogchen teachings, what is paramount is for us to realize awareness wisdom (*rigpai yeshe; rig pa'i ye shes*). Without gaining actual experience and realizing awareness, intellectual understanding will be of no real enduring benefit. When we are at the stage of intellectual understanding, we have meditation experiences, but these are only temporary, like a patch sewn onto clothing. At some point, after a shorter or longer period of time, the patch will wear off. The meaning here is that if we don't meet a genuine teacher and identify and acknowledge our errors (*nor sa*) as they occur, we will end up being separated from real practice, like water that has been separated from milk. Our mind will become separated from the dharma, and our so-called "dharma practice" and "experience" will be lost when we encounter good and bad circumstances (*rkyen*).

> Furthermore, bad circumstances are somewhat easier to
>   successfully bring to the path,
> But bringing good circumstances to the path is very difficult.
> Thus there are those who arrogantly presume that they have
>   high realization, yet strive for the glories of this life. They are
>   distracted, filled solely with attachment to the "mara demon of
>   the 'child of the gods.'"
> This is due to not having understood the key point of the self-
>   liberation of the six sense fields.[13]

> These days there are many who speak of these [kinds of view
>   and meditation] as if they were amazing signs of accomplish-
>   ment . . . although those who point this out are
>   just [regarded as] "white ravens."

Now, Jigme Lingpa mentions positive and negative experiences and circumstances as they arise along the path. Negative circumstances can be of many varieties and take many forms. For example, as mentioned earlier, there are five types of hindrances in meditation. It is common, especially for those of lesser capacity, to fall under the power of the five hindrances, and these can cause many interruptions and obstacles in their meditation practice. When we fall under the power of the five hindrances, we will not be able to practice meditation correctly.

Similarly, we may have all kinds of distractions. Sometimes we may feel an overabundance of nervous energy (*lung; rlung*); sometimes we will be overwhelmed by thoughts; sometimes our mind and energy are very peaceful, sometimes very clear, sometimes dull; and sometimes wild and irrational thoughts may even erupt. When this happens, there will be no progress in our meditation practice unless we apply remedies to these hindrances. For example, when there is dullness, or when our mind becomes excited, if we are overcome by such hindrances and lose our mindfulness, it is important to take note of this and to remedy all such hindrances when they occur. It is the same with doubts and regrets. Do not let yourself be carried away by them, but engage in the practice of mindfulness and apply the appropriate remedies.

On the other hand, there is the question of so-called positive experiences. For some meditators, when practicing, they begin to have very pleasant and relaxing experiences and feel that they have now entered into genuine meditation. Here Jigme Lingpa is both cautioning and scolding the yogis. In these degenerate times, people think that to have mere intellectual knowledge and a few powerful meditation experiences is something wondrous. With these alone, they feel that they have now arrived at a very high level and have become quite significant personages. They become proud of their intellectual understanding and meditation experiences, feeling that they have reached an advanced stage of meditation or have even become highly realized.

Such individuals, after meditating according to the Dzogchen instructions only briefly or for a relatively brief period of time, come to think that their meditation must be something incredible. They think, "Now I am a great lama. I have had wondrous signs of meditation, astounding signs of accomplishment. I understand everything, and my meditation is highly advanced. Truly, I must have entered the ranks of the great ones." So they become inflated with pride, due to having a misplaced confidence in their understanding of the teachings. And yet they have had no deep, actual experience of the view at this stage, and certainly no genuine realization. The important point is that we should not be satisfied with these "positive" experiences in and of themselves or become attached to them along the path. To do so only leads to complacency and an increase in grasping and fixation, and will thus not benefit our meditation practice.

These days if someone points out these errors (*nor sa*), speaking frankly and honestly on the matter, then no one wants to listen to him or her. Such a person is perceived as something like a "white raven." Since all ravens are black, in Tibet a white raven is regarded as negative, as a bad omen or a freak of nature. No one wants to look at a white raven. No one will listen to him or her or pay any attention at all. With this example, Jigme Lingpa is speaking to all of these so-called meditators who are consumed by, and reveling in, what are actually distractions and errors on the path. Jigme Lingpa is also saying that those who point out these facts to yogis who cling to misguided meditation practice are very rare indeed, as rare as white ravens.

At the stage Jigme Lingpa is speaking of here, actual experience and realization of the Dzogchen view have not yet arisen to any degree. In spite of this, many practitioners at this stage may feel overly confident in their understanding and experiences. These days people are under the influence of distractions and are attached to what they know and what they experience in meditation. They consider anyone who attempts to show them their faults to be like a white raven, regarding them as one to be shunned and ignored.

> However, for those of you who practice the sacred dharma from
> your hearts, such a fixated conceptual view will not help your
> practice of meditation.
>
> In the four sessions of daily practice, you should focus on
> guru yoga,
> Receiving the four empowerments.
> Then, within the state of merging your mind with the
> guru's mind,
> Let awareness be free and unbound.
> Persevere thus from the depths of your heart,
> Until the essence of this experience
> Has become unsupported and free of any reference point.

In general when you meditate you will have three types of meditation experiences (*nyams*): those of bliss (*dewa; bde ba*), clarity (*salwa; gsal ba*), and nonthought (*mitogpa; mi rtog pa*). These three are also known as *shay nyam* (*shes nyams*), which means "mind experiences," or "meditation moods," or "altered states of consciousness." If you become attached to them, they will cause you to fall under the influence of errors (*nor sa*) and diversions (*gol sa*).

As Jigme Lingpa has said, we may have negative experiences of hindrances and so forth. Or we may have "positive" experiences such as those of bliss and think that this is genuine meditation and feel very pleased about it. Then there is the risk that we will thus become fixated on having meditation experiences and on maintaining and continuing to have these meditation experiences. However, in meditation practice it is important not to cling to experiences of happiness or sadness, to have neither hope for good experiences nor fear of bad experiences.

In brief, Jigme Lingpa is urging us not to simply be satisfied with intellectual understanding and having meditation experiences. If you find you have a conceptualized experience of meditation, what should you do? Don't just remain in this fixated conceptual view that is characteristic of the stage of intellectual understanding, as it will not serve your meditation practice.

If different kinds of "positive" experiences arise when you are practicing meditation, it is best not to consider them to be anything special. Instead, the instruction is to constantly and diligently endeavor in the practice of guru yoga, receiving the four empowerments and merging your mind inseparably with that of your teacher. In the four daily sessions of meditation practice, continue in devotional supplication, praying one-pointedly to the guru.

As Jigme Lingpa says in our text, "Merging your mind with the guru's mind, let awareness be free and unbound." Rest in meditative equipoise, completely relaxed and without holding on to anything or modifying anything. From the depth of your heart, it is important to persevere unremittingly in this (*snying la rdo rus gtug*), until your experience of meditation is utterly free of any fixation or reference point; until meditation experiences are destroyed (*nyams bshig*) without a trace.

The vital point here is that by doing so and repeatedly destroying the fixation on meditation experiences, again and again, and through allowing the experiences to collapse, your own naked awareness (*rang gi rig pa rjen pa*) will emerge. Keep practicing in this way until all clinging to the experience of meditation collapses (*zhig song*). Then, as attachment to experiences collapses, realization is born in your mind.

As it states in the *Three Words That Strike the Vital Point* (*Tsig Sum Nedek; Tshig gsum gnad brdegs*) of Patrul Rinpoche:

> The more the yogi destroys his meditation experiences,
> His meditation will improve accordingly,
> Just like water flowing down a steep mountain.[14]

It also says in Patrul Rinpoche's text that one may exclaim "PHAT!" (*pay; phat*) for this same purpose, and this has the same intention as what we are referring to here.

Whatever meditation experiences (*nyams*) of bliss, clarity, and non-thought arise in the mind, until, as Jigme Lingpa says, you are "free of any reference point" (*gtad med*), you must continue to practice according to the instructions. Until awareness is "unsupported" (*khungs med*), meaning there is no fixation present and no basis of support for awareness, you should endeavor diligently in the practice. All conceptual fixation on the experience of meditation has to be destroyed, through the power of praying to the guru with deep devotion and merging with the guru's wisdom mind. If you continue to practice in this way, over time you will pass through the stages of actual experience (*nyongwa; myong ba*) and realization (*togpa; rtogs pa*). If you want to genuinely experience and realize the teachings, it is important to pray to your guru constantly, throughout the day and night.

> Likewise, for meditation experiences:
> When calming abiding meditation predominates, there will
>   be experiences of emptiness.
> When insight predominates, there will be experiences of clarity
>   and so forth.
>
> In brief, knowing the vital point[15] of discursive thoughts,
> The power of discriminating intelligence blazes forth.
>
> And although you know how to bring both stillness and
>   movement into meditation,
> Yet the essence of the "knower" is under the tight grip of ego
>   fixation,
> And you stray into a pattern of analytical examination[16] and
>   so forth.
> These are highly undetectable and dangerous conceptual
>   obscurations.
> Therefore, as these are present, it is premature to label thoughts
>   as "dharmakaya"[17]

When you meditate a lot on calm abiding, you will have many experiences of emptiness in particular; and if you meditate on insight, there will be more experiences of clarity. If you meditate on both calm abiding and insight together, then the power of discriminating intelligence (*so sor rtog pa'i shes rab*) will blaze forth.

The "key point of discursive thoughts" is that the mind either abides in stillness or there is thought movement or there is the knowing (*rig*) of these two, and one of these three is always occurring. One must recognize the essence of the one that is abiding, or the one that is moving, or the one that knows stillness and movement. Until these three completely dissolve in their essence, you must continue to practice. If you have not reached to that level where you are free of the tight clinging to the "subject" or "knower" and free of the pattern of mental analysis and investigation, then it is too early to say thoughts are dharmakaya.

Whether experiences of bliss or clarity and so forth arise in the mind, or if the mind is still, or if there is movement or knowing, you should meditate until the essence of the "knower" (*shes mkhan kyi ngo bo*), the essence of the "one who abides" (*gnas mkhan*), and the essence of the "one who moves" (*'gyu mkhan*) are without any reference point or source (*gtad khung med*). To simply say that thoughts are the dharmakaya, and then to just ignore or drop whatever thoughts arise, will only cause your mind to be lost in delusion (*sems la 'khrul pa 'byams*). You are led away by a chain of thoughts (*sems gcig la gcig lu gu rgyud*), and delusion will arise. So don't fall under the influence of this kind of delusion.

The mind is either still, moving, or knowing stillness and movement. When the mind is still, from that stillness a thought will arise, then again there will be stillness. There is always this alternation between stillness and thought movement. Then the third factor is the observer, the subject who is noticing this and observes the stillness and thought movement. The knower is the subject who knows whether there is movement or the absence of movement. But this is a dualistic process, as there is grasping to a subject and an object. Stillness and movement become knowable objects, they become objects of consciousness (*shes bya'i yul*), and the "knower" of stillness and movement becomes the subject. So you develop grasping and fixation (*'dzin pa*) and an analyzing mind that scrutinizes and thinks, "Now what is happening in the mind?"

Don't practice like this! Understand from the start that they are all already empty and are beyond requiring any remedies. You should bring them onto the path as being empty, and not differentiate stillness, thought movement, and the knowing of these as though they were three separate entities that you must attend to or remedy one by one. If you apply remedies to them instead of seeing their empty essence, then you will fall into error.

> Do not bind this immediate awareness, which is unimpaired and
>   uncorrupted,
> With the meditators' "remedies,"[18]
> Or with attachment to your view.
>
> You should solely take as the path
> This free and unbound,
> Unimpeded open transparency.
>
> Moreover, if you fall under the influence of speculation
> Based on your ideas about meditation and postmeditation,[19]
> Then you will [enter] the dangerous passage of diversions,
>   errors, and strayings on the path.
> If you do not know how to identify these, then you will be unable
>   to distinguish whether or not [your meditation] is correct.

When the Dzogchen teachings speak of "being attached to the remedy," this refers to fixating on stillness, or on thought movement, or on the knowing of these two. There is no clinging to or fixating on these three, none whatsoever. There is only the unimpeded open transparency of free and unbound awareness (*zang thal kha yan rig pa*).

> Therefore, the hidden flaws of these are explained here:
>
> What is "emptiness"?
> It is that which is empty and without a self-entity from
>   primordial beginning.
> It is free from the four and the eight extreme views.
> This immediate awareness, which is free and unbound
>   and beyond concepts,
> Is known as "rigpa."
>
> This may not be understood.
> For example, in the lower vehicles, there is conceptual
>   analysis to affirm nonexistence and to negate existence.

> And following this, you arrive at an empty, blank
> nothingness.
> Or, as in the lower tantric classes with the svabhava mantra
> and so forth, through meditative concentration, you purify
> everything into emptiness, [asserting] a mere "clarity and
> emptiness."
> Or, if you experience an [imputed] view that [everything] is
> like an illusion,
> These are errors.

As mentioned, in the practice of Dzogchen there are eight errors (*nor sa brgyad*), three diversions (*gol sa gsum*), and four ways of straying (*shor sa bzhi*), all of which are taught by Jigme Lingpa in *The Lion's Roar*. Now Jigme Lingpa begins by teaching us the eight errors (*nor sa*).

The first of the eight errors is erring in regard to emptiness:

What is "emptiness" (*shunyata; tongpa nyid; stong pa nyid*)?
It is primordially empty (*ye gdod ma nas stong pa*) and is without
    any self-entity (*bdag med*).
It is natural emptiness (*rang bzhin gyi stong pa*).
It is the essence of dharmata (*chos nyid kyi ngo bo*),
The immediate awareness (*da lta'i shes pa*), beyond the
    conceptual mind,
Free and unbound (*kha yan*).
This very one is known as *rigpa,* "awareness."

Primordial emptiness (*ye tong; ye stong*) is free of the two types of self-hood: the selfhood of persons and the selfhood of phenomena. It is free of the four extreme views: those of existence, nonexistence, both existence and nonexistence, and neither existence nor nonexistence. Similarly, it is free of the eight extreme views of arising and ceasing, permanence and nihil-ism, coming and going, and unity and diversity. Awareness is primordially empty; by not properly understanding this, we fall into error.

So how do we fall into diversion and error?

In the lower vehicles, they slip into an empty, blank nothingness (*ci yang med pai stong pa*), which is arrived at through intellectual affirmation and negation, where one logically affirms "nonexistence" and negates "existence." Through this process of conceptual analysis, they reach a kind of empty, blank nothingness, and this is known "analytical emptiness" (*dpyad pa'i stong pa*).

Also, in the approach of the lower tantras when reciting the mantra OM SVABHAVA SHUDDHA SARVA DHARMA SVABHAVA SHUDDHO HANG, everything is purified into emptiness through the power of meditative absorption. They further assert the view of things being empty appearances, "mere clarity and emptiness," stating that all things abide in the manner of illusions. But from the Dzogchen point of view, all of these views are mistaken in the sense that they are still only provisional ways of understanding (*drang don*); they are not the ultimate meaning (*nges don*) of emptiness.

According to the Dzogchen teachings, you must understand that emptiness is the natural, intrinsic emptiness, the essence of awareness, beyond the domain of the intellect. But in the lower vehicles, in accord with the Madhyamaka view, they posit an "emptiness" that is arrived at through an analytical process that establishes that all phenomena are empty. They prove the truth of emptiness through intellectual reasoning, but this is really not comparable to the primordial emptiness of Dzogchen.

Similarly, the tantras state that all things are pure in their nature, inherently pure (*rang bzhin gyi rnam par dag pa*). When the svabhava mantra is recited, all things of samsara and nirvana are said to be as empty. But in the view of the Dzogchen teachings, this also is not yet the correct understanding, as we need to establish the natural, intrinsic emptiness (*rang bzhin gyi stong pa*) of all the phenomena of samsara and nirvana. According to Dzogchen, it is a mistake if you simply adopt a conceptual view of mere clarity and emptiness, of mere appearance and emptiness, and then just conceive of the view as being like an illusion. These are the key points of the first error.

> Likewise, for "calm abiding meditation":
> The coarse and subtle thoughts are naturally pacified in and of
> themselves.
> The nature of mind, free of the waves of discursive thoughts,
> Has an abiding aspect that is vividly clear and wakeful,
> Self-illuminating self-awareness.
>
> Misunderstanding this, thinking that calm abiding is a mindless
> vacant state, is an error.

Now Jigme Lingpa explains the second of the eight errors. Calm abiding meditation (*shamatha; shinay; zhi gnas*) is viewed differently in Dzogchen than in the lower vehicles. In Dzogchen, when the coarse and subtle thoughts have naturally subsided, waves of thoughts no longer arise. This is the natural abiding aspect of mind (*sems rang bzhin kyi gnas cha*), also known as the "natural face" or "own essence" of awareness (*rig pa'i rang ngo*), or as the "inherent essence of dharmata" (*chos nyid kyi rang ngo*).

When the nature of mind is free from the waves of thinking and remains vividly clear and wakeful (*dvangs seng nge*), this is what is meant by "self-illuminating self-awareness" (*rang rig rang gsal*). According to the meaning of calm abiding in Dzogchen, calm abiding possesses the quality of being self-illuminating or self-cognizant (*rang gsal*). If this is misunderstood and one considers calm abiding to be a blank void, a mindless vacant state (*dran med had po*), or some kind of "unknowing" trance state, then this is an error (*nor sa*).

In the approach of the lower vehicles, in the practice of calm abiding meditation, one has the intention to make the mind free of disturbance or movement, so one makes an effort to pacify the mind. One selects a single object of concentration and tries to remain one-pointedly focused on that object, in order to pacify all the thoughts that normally arise in the mind. In Dzogchen, one does not practice this kind of one-pointed concentration (*rtse gcig ting nge 'dzin*). Rather, what is practiced is self-knowing awareness (*rang rig*), and the manner of practicing it is known as "natural meditation" (*rang babs kyi bsam gtan*). In Dzogchen, the quality of being naturally cognizant or self-cognizant (*rang gsal*) is a key aspect of calm abiding; so it is a mistake to regard calm abiding as a blank, unconscious, thought-free state. This is the second error.

> Regarding "insight":
> It is the recognition that both stillness and movement
> Are the natural reflection
> Of the essence of your awareness.[20]
> It is clear and aware without grasping—that's it!
>
> Otherwise, if you do not understand this and investigate
>   stillness and movement,
> It is an error.

What is meant by "insight" (*vipasyana; lhag mthong*), according to the Dzogchen teachings? This awareness that is free of grasping and fixation is what is understood as insight. Whether there is stillness or movement, their essence is naturally cognizant (*rang gsal*) and free of grasping and fixation ('*dzin med*). If you start to analyze, to scrutinize and mentally investigate stillness or thought movement, this is an error. Both stillness and movement are recognized as rigpa's own essence (*rang ngo rig pa*). They are the self-manifestation or natural reflection (*rang gdangs*) of rigpa. Not understanding this, if you investigate stillness and movement with the conceptual mind, this is an incorrect way to practice, the third error.

> There are a variety of ways of explaining
> What are known as "meditative equipoise" and "postmeditation."[21]
>
> However, according Dzogchen's own terminology,
> "Meditative equipoise" is to abide
> While embracing the essence of whatever arises with mindfulness.
>
> Then, while being attentive to that [practice],
> The aspect of movement, that which transforms and changes,
> Is known as "postmeditation."
>
> Misunderstanding this, [you think that] to one-pointedly keep
> in mind an empty viewpoint is "meditative equipoise."
> And following this, you superimpose an illusion-like emptiness
> upon whatever arises and call this "postmeditation."
> This is an error.

Now we come to the fourth error, which concerns meditative equipoise (*nyamzhag; mnyam bzhag*) and postmeditation (*jethob; rjes thob*). According to the tradition of Dzogchen, when your own awareness is seen (*rang gi rig pa'i mthong*), this is meditative equipoise.

Then when you arise with attentiveness (*shes bzhin*) from resting in meditative equipoise, this is the aspect of movement, the postmeditation. You stir from resting in equipoise in the essence of your awareness (*rig pai ngo bo gyos nas*), and you enter into all kinds of activities such as moving, sitting, and so on, whatever they may be. In the practice of Dzogchen, the key point of postmeditation is that you remain in "rigpa's own place of repose" (*rig pa'i mal*), and without forgetting the essence of awareness, you engage in all kinds of activities. This is the true postmeditation practice.

In brief, when you see the essence of awareness (*rig pa'i ngo bo mthong ba*), this is meditative equipoise. When you move from that state into different activities, if you remain in your own "seat of awareness" (*rig pa'i rang mal*) without forgetting this during all your activities, this is postmeditation.

All of the transformations and changes (*sprul bsgyur*) that occur in the mind are the aspect of movement (*'gyu ba'i cha*). Not understanding this, if you think that meditative equipoise is "to one-pointedly keep in mind an empty viewpoint (*lta stangs kyi stongpa*) and that postmeditation is just superimposing the idea that everything is dreamlike onto all your activities, these are errors (*nor sa*).

> What is meant by "nondistraction"?
> It means that you do not stray into the subtle undercurrents of
>   deluded thinking.
> And, you do not enter into a state of vague oblivion.
> This is known as genuine, innate mindfulness.
>
> If you are anxious about being distracted,
> And if you are bound by deliberate, restricted mindfulness,
> Then these are errors.

The fifth error is in regard to the understanding and practice of nondistraction (*g.yeng med*). Nondistraction is when you do not get lost in the undercurrent of thoughts (*'og 'gyu*) that create delusion; and neither do you fall into an indifferent state of vague oblivion (*lung ma bstan*). Sustaining the practice while remaining free of these is said to be genuine, innate mindfulness (*yang dag gnyug ma'i dran pa*).

However, if you are paranoid, tense, and anxious about being distracted, you may be always thinking "Now I am distracted "and "Now I am not distracted." You may feel it is not permissible to be distracted and that you must therefore bind your mind with the remedy of the tight fetters of deliberate, restricted mindfulness (*sdug btsir 'jur dran gyis bcings ba*), a kind of stringently forced mindfulness. If you think you are not allowed to be distracted and thus try to enforce mindfulness, or if you fall into a vague unconscious state, these are errors.

What is "ordinary mind"?[22]
It is said to be immediate awareness,
Which is untainted by either faults or good qualities,
Left as it naturally is.
It is sustaining the continuous flow of awareness.

Misunderstanding this, to identify it as one's ordinary,
   autonomous mundane thinking is an error.

The sixth error concerns the two ways in which to understand what is meant by "ordinary mind" (*tha mal gyi shes pa*). According to the meaning of the term in Dzogchen, it is what your teacher pointed out to you, self-originating primordial wisdom (*rangjung yeshe; rang byung ye shes*). If you think it is something other than that, such as if you identify your ordinary mind as simply being the normal, mundane thinking that goes on in your mind, that is an error. This mundane ordinary mind is completely different from the ordinary mind of Dzogpa Chenpo. This latter ordinary mind is Dzogchen's self-originating primordial wisdom, the immediate awareness (*da lta'i shes pa*) to which you have been introduced by your guru; this is what you must practice.

The present knowing (*da lta'i shes pa*) of the ordinary worldly mind is deluded by thinking, while the immediate awareness (*da lta'i shes pa*) that your teacher introduced is the awareness wisdom (*rig pa'i ye shes*) of the Great Perfection. It is necessary to differentiate between these two, and not to do so is an error.

What is "nonmeditation"?
Entering the womb of the natural state,
The attachment to meditating or not meditating is purified.
Without any artificial modification or any reference point
   whatsoever,
You establish the citadel of all-pervasive mindfulness.

If you are in a state of careless indifference, remaining in your
   ordinary manner,
Or if you are daydreaming in an indeterminate, vague oblivion,
These are errors.

The seventh error concerns the way in which "nonmeditation" is to be understood. If you are able to sustain the meditative equipoise taught to you by your guru for a long time, then it will become completely free of any reference point (*migmay; dmigs med*). If you sustain or remain within the continuity (*ngang skyong*) of this, it is known as the yoga of the natural river-like flow (*rang bzhin chu bo rgyun gi rnal 'byor*) that is naturally present and self-sustaining (*rang gnas*). Nonmeditation means to continue on in this.[23]

You should remain in the ordinary mind that your guru introduced you to. If you call anything else besides this "nonmeditation," such as just remaining like an ordinary person in a normal everyday condition, that is mistaken; that is just the worldly ordinary mind. Likewise, if you lapse into a state of daydreaming, oblivious to what is taking place, this is also an error.

> What does "sustaining whatever arises" refer to?
> Whatever thought arises, look directly at it,
> Neither blocking it, nor examining it, nor following after it.
> Release the thinker itself within awareness,
> And sustain the unimpeded open transparency of stillness and
> movement.

> Misunderstanding this, to carelessly follow after whatever
> thoughts arise and analyze them is an error.

Now we come to the eighth and final error (*nor sa*) taught by Jigme Lingpa in *The Lion's Roar*. What is meant by "sustaining whatever arises"? Here, Jigme Lingpa teaches us that whatever thought arises, by directly watching it with no effort to stop or block it, without analyzing the thought, checking whether it is positive or negative and so on, without following after the thought in any way, one simply recognizes the thought. That is, look directly at the thought and "release the thinker itself within awareness" (*shar mkhan kho rang gi rig thog tu klod*). Then simply sustain the unimpeded, open transparency of both stillness and thought movement (*gnas 'gyu zang thal du skyong ba*). Some practitioners do not understand this, and whatever arises, they just follow after the thought, analyze whether it is positive or negative, and so on. This is an error.

> Similarly, there are three diversions:
> If you are attached to bliss, you will be born as a god in the
> desire realms.

If you are attached to clarity, you will be born as a god in the
   form realms.
And if you are attached to nonthought, you will be born
   as a god in the formless realms.
These are known as points of diversion.

Having explained the eight errors, Jigme Lingpa will now teach the meaning of the three diversions (*gol sa sum; gol sa gsum*). If you become attached
to the meditation experiences of bliss, clarity, or nonthought, you may be
reborn in the god realms of the desire, form, or formless realms, respectively.
In relation to these three types of experiences, neither should you make an
effort to have them nor should you try to stop or block them. If they occur,
simply continue to practice without becoming attached to them.

The Dzogchen teachings speak of the ground (*gzhi*) of awareness as being endowed with the essence (*ngowo; ngo bo*), the nature (*rangzhin; rang
bzhin*), and the capacity (*thugje; thugs rje*), where the latter can also be understood as "compassion," "responsiveness," or "compassionate activity."

The meditation experience of nonthought (*mitogpai nyam; mi rtog pa'i
nyams*) is the natural reflection (*rang gdangs*) of the dharmakaya. Arising
as the natural reflection of the empty essence (*ngo bo stong pa*) of awareness, there is the wisdom of nonthought (*mi rtog pa'i ye shes*). Based on the
meditation experience of nonthought, the wisdom of nonthought will arise
in your mind.

The meditation experience of clarity (*sal nyam; gsal nyams*) is the natural
reflection, or the luminosity, of the sambhogakaya or rupakaya. Arising as
the natural reflection of the nature of clarity (*rang bzhin gsal ba*), there is the
wisdom of clarity (*gsal ba'i ye shes*). Based on the meditation experience of
clarity, the self-cognizant wisdom (*rang gsal ba'i ye shes*) will arise.

The meditation experience of bliss (*day nyam; bde nyams*) is the natural reflection of the nirmanakaya. Arising as the natural reflection of all-
pervasive capacity (*thugs rje kun khyab*), there is the wisdom of bliss (*bde ba'i
ye shes*). Based on the experience of bliss, the wisdom of bliss, or the wisdom
of all-pervading capacity (*thugs rje kun khyab pa'i ye shes*), will arise.

As you meditate, these meditation experiences will naturally arise, but the
key point is that you should not become attached to them. They are signs
on the path that automatically, spontaneously arise (*rang shugs su byung ba*).
They are actually qualities that arise from the practice of meditation, since
in general if you don't meditate, these experiences will not normally occur.

If you become attached to experiences, and hope to acquire them and have fear and apprehension of losing them once they occur, then it is the same as being attached to the three realms of worldly existence; and you will thus be planting the karmic seeds to be born in the three realms of samsara. But if you practice well and continue to sustain the view without being attached to experiences, then it is possible to see them as positive signs that you are practicing meditation well. In this case, they will be supports on your path as you continue to progress in meditation.

> I will explain how to identify them and their errors:
> That which is known as "bliss" is untainted by the three major
>   root sufferings.
> It is like, for example, when you cannot bear to separate from
> [Abiding] within the natural state.[24]
> It is said to be the arising of the experience of joyful bliss.
>
> This is not like the bliss of defiled, outflowing desire.
> Nor is it said to be like the arising of thoughts of happiness
>   and delight.
> Nor is it being delighted with changing objective circumstances.

The first of the three diversions is the meditation experience of bliss (*day nyam; bde nyams*). The three root sufferings are the suffering of suffering, the suffering of change, and the all-pervasive suffering of being conditioned. Here, Jigme Lingpa is not speaking of the impure bliss of desire and passion, or of sexual union, but of the pure bliss that arises from Dzogchen meditation practice. This experience of bliss is the bliss of dharmata (*chos nyid kyi bde ba*), the bliss that comes from resting in the continuity of the natural state (*gnas lugs de'i ngang*), and from which you may not wish or feel able to part. It does not mean simply having happy thoughts and feelings. It is not bliss created by the happiness that arises on the basis of outer circumstances and objects, nor is it the bliss that comes from joyful thoughts. If you become attached to this experience, this is the first diversion.

> What is known as "clarity" is that which is not tainted by the
>   obstructing forces of drowsiness and fogginess.
> It is the unobstructed shining forth
> Of rigpa's aspect of potency,
> Or of [rigpa's] avenues of expression.

> It is not the avenues of perception endowed with the
>   characteristics of apparent objects such as shapes, colors,
>   and so forth,
> Which are the natural forms of deluded perception.

Now Jigme Lingpa refers to the second diversion, which is the meditation experience of clarity (*sal nyam; gsal nyams*). The Dzogchen teachings speak of the nature of clarity (*rang bzhin gsal ba*), which is the clarity aspect (*gsal cha*). Here, "clarity" does not refer to anything that has a form, shape, or color, like, for example, seeing a rainbow or a vision. What is the meditation experience of clarity? It is untainted by obstructions like drowsiness and fogginess. It is the vivid potency of the clarity aspect of awareness, shining forth without obstruction. It is self-cognizant awareness (*rig pa'i rang gsal*). If you fixate on this clarity in your practice and become attached to it, this is the second diversion.

> Moreover, in regard to "nonthought":
> It is free from thinking all kinds of thoughts
> And from being disturbed by the deluded thinking that reifies
>   things as being real.
> It is said to be thought-free, like space.
>
> It is not like fainting and losing consciousness.
> Nor is it a black darkness like deep sleep.
> Nor is it like when the senses withdraw and you feel nothing.

The third diversion is the meditation experience of nonthought. When there are very few thoughts arising and you are able to see the essence of awareness, this is what is understood to be the experience of nonthought. It is not like when one has fainted or is unconscious. If you fixate on this experience of nonthought in your practice and become attached to it, this is the third diversion.

> In brief, these three types of experiences are merely the manner
>   in which signs of the path manifest, and they naturally and
>   spontaneously occur.
>
> However, if you do not realize this and meditate deliberately
>   hoping for them,

> And when they do occur, if you embrace them as though they
>   were genuine meditation and become attached to them,
> Then this will cause you to be diverted into the three realms
>   of existence.

These three types of meditation experiences are the manner in which signs of the path arise; they are self-occurring signs of the path (*rang byung gi lam rtags*). If you practice meditation well, there is no way that they will not occur. Bliss, clarity, and nonthought are the qualities of meditation experiences (*nyams*).

Misunderstanding this, you may desire to have these experiences, and then you may meditate while intentionally trying to create them, and then when they occur, you may hold on to them, become attached to them, and think that this is genuine meditation (*bsgom rnal ma*). If you fixate on and become attached to them, this will only create causes for you to be diverted into the three realms of existence.

The expression (*rtsal*) of the empty essence (*ngo bo stong pa*) is the wisdom of nonthought; the expression of the nature of clarity (*rang bzhin gsal ba*) is the wisdom of clarity; and the expression of all-pervading capacity (*thugs rje kun khyab*) is the wisdom of bliss. For this reason, everyone who meditates well will have these three experiences.

> Likewise, there are the four ways of straying (in regard to
>   emptiness):
> Straying into emptiness's having the character of a knowable
>   object,
> Straying into taking emptiness as a path,
> Straying into taking emptiness as a remedy, and
> Straying into superimposing emptiness.

> Each of these four is said to have an original straying point
> And a temporary straying point.

> However, if we briefly summarize them:
> The essence of ultimate emptiness is primordially pure.
> It is free from the fetters of being a compounded
>   phenomenon
> And of being a mental construct.
> This present awareness is immense, boundless, primordial purity.

> Misunderstanding this key point, if you regard emptiness as
>   something separate,
> Like stamping emptiness onto appearances,
> This is straying into [emptiness's] having the character of a
>   knowable object.

Now Jigme Lingpa teaches the four points of straying in regard to emptiness:

The straying point of emptiness's having the character of
   a knowable object.
The straying point of taking emptiness as the path.
The straying point of taking emptiness as a remedy.
The straying point of superimposing emptiness.

Let's briefly consider the first of the four points of straying (*shor sa bzhi*) taught by Jigme Lingpa in *The Lion's Roar*. In essence, "emptiness" refers to that which is utterly pure from the very beginning (*ye nas dag pa*). According to the Dzogchen teachings, all phenomena are primordially empty (*ye stong*). Other than this, if you think that there is another emptiness that is established through mental designations and constructs (*blos btags byas*) or by intellectual investigation (*dpyad pa*) using the reasoning of refutation and assertion to establish emptiness, then such emptiness is an artificial fabrication (*bzo bcos*).

Therefore, you will not be able to see the emptiness that is the ultimate natural state of all things (*dngos po'i gnas lugs*) through artificial fabrication. If you think, "This is, or this is not, emptiness," and "It exists; or, it does not exist," then that is what is meant by "mentally constructed" or "designated" emptiness. If you believe in "things" as being real entities (*dngos po*), or even if you believe them not to be real (*dngos med*), you need to drop all these mental constructs.

Present awareness is primordial purity, an immense boundlessness (*phyogs yan chen po*). You must understand that the essence of awareness is emptiness. Not realizing this, if you attempt to acquire emptiness from somewhere else and place this patch of emptiness onto the essence of awareness, which is empty, this is what is meant by the first straying point. One has made emptiness into an object of knowledge, and this is straying into emptiness's having the character of a knowable object (*stong pa nyid shes bya'i gshis la shor ba*), the first straying point.

Likewise, you may not be convinced that it is ordinary mind or
self-knowing awareness (*rang rig*) that you take as the path.
You may not understand that cause and result are by nature
inseparable,
And are from the very beginning spontaneously present and
already complete.

Then by meditating on emptiness as a path, you exert yourself
with the hope that the result of the dharmakaya will arrive from
somewhere else.
By this, your meditation is mentally constructed.
This is the straying point of taking emptiness as a path.

The second of Jigme Lingpa's four points of straying is in regard to
approaching emptiness as though it were the result of a path that one follows. On the path, we talk about the "ordinary mind," but if you don't
realize that the essence of awareness (*rig pa'i ngo bo*) is actually the path,
if you feel that now you are meditating on the essence of awareness and
sometime in the future the fruit of emptiness will come from somewhere
else (*gzhan nas*), this is called "emptiness straying into a path." If you don't
recognize that the very essence of your awareness is empty (*rang rig pa'i ngo
bo la stongpa ngo ma shes na*), then you will start to think that, through a
causal process, you will gain the fruit or result of emptiness later on from
somewhere else. This is called "the straying of taking emptiness as a path"
(*stong nyid lam du shor ba*), the second straying point.

Once again, whatever thoughts and emotions arise,
Their essence is none other than emptiness from the very
beginning.

As there is nothing beyond that,
There is no need for these two things:
The afflictive emotion that is to be abandoned
And emptiness as a remedy [for it.]

When your awareness identifies the "object to be abandoned,"
At that very moment, like a snake naturally unknotting itself,
It is self-liberated.

Misunderstanding this vital point,
If you need to meditate by applying an additional remedy of
    "emptiness"
Onto the thought or emotion that is to be abandoned,
This is straying into [taking emptiness as] a remedy.

The third point of straying Jigme Lingpa wishes us to understand concerns going astray by regarding emptiness as a remedy. If you "apply emptiness" to thoughts and afflictive emotions, as though it were a separate remedy, this is called the "straying of emptiness becoming a remedy." Whatever thoughts (*namtok; rnam rtog*) and defilements arise, their essence is already primordially empty. They have never been anything other than emptiness from the very beginning, and there is no further step beyond that. Hence it is not necessary to think in terms of the afflictive emotions (*nyon mongs*) as something to be abandoned and a separate remedy of "emptiness."

By awareness identifying (*ngos zin*) the afflictive emotions to be abandoned, at that very moment (*mnyam du*), they will vanish, like a snake unknotting itself. If you do not understand this vital point of the self-liberation of the defilements to be abandoned (*spang byai nyon mongs kyi rang grol*) and then think that you have to meditate by placing an additional "emptiness" on top of them, this is what is known as "straying into taking emptiness as a remedy."

What is it that you must understand? In the Dzogchen teachings, "emptiness" is understood to be the essence of your own awareness. When emptiness is meditated on as an additional remedy, it means that you have not recognized the essence of awareness as emptiness (*stong pa nyid rig pai ngo bo la ngo ma shes*). Thoughts and emotions are liberated in the essence like a snake unknotting itself, so there is no need to search for another remedy. If you search for emptiness somewhere else as a remedy, it means that you are taking awareness as something different from, or in opposition to (*rig pa logs su bzhag pa*), the thought to be abandoned. This is the third straying point, straying into taking emptiness as a remedy (*stong pa nyid gnyen por shor ba*).

Concerning the straying of superimposing emptiness:
Whether the [practice] is elaborate or unelaborate,
Within the primordial, vast sphere,
The spacious expanse of Samantabhadri,
Clarity and emptiness are spontaneously present as a great unity.

By not understanding this,
Then the reified meditator,[25]
And the conceptual way of dissolving [all phenomena]
    into emptiness
Are not unified,
And thereby skillful means and wisdom are divorced.
And thus, you are not sustaining the continuity
Of "ordinary awareness" beyond concepts,
Through the nonreferential "watcher."

And keeping your previous intellectual theories in mind,
You think:
"There is nothing to meditate upon and no meditator."
"Everything is emptiness."
"All is dharmakaya."
"Karma and its results do not really exist."
"This is mind."
"These are thoughts."
"Nothing at all can be found to exist."

This is what is known as superimposing [an intellectually]
    resolved view of emptiness.
Nowadays there are a great many who do this.

Now we come to the fourth of the four ways of straying taught by Jigme
Lingpa, the straying point of superimposing emptiness (*stong nyid rgyas
'debs su shor ba*). This term literally means straying into "sealing with emptiness" or "stamping with emptiness."

In brief, your teacher introduced you to your own awareness (*rang rig*),
which is primordially beyond cause and effect, beyond things to be adopted
and those to be abandoned. If you remain within awareness without waver-
ing (*rig thog nas ma gyos ba*), then in the great spontaneously present nature
(*rang bzhin lhun grub chen po*), there is no such thing as positive or negative
actions.

Awareness, the essence of one's own primordial wisdom (*rig pa rang gi
yeshe kyi ngo bo*) is what is meant by "emptiness" in the Dzogchen teachings.
Within rigpa's own essence (*rig pa rang gi ngo bo*), there is neither good nor
bad; there is nothing to adopt or reject; these dualities do not exist in the
essence of awareness (*rig pa'i ngo bo*).

For individuals of superior capacity, those who attain instantaneous realization (*cig car ba*), they will never be diverted from this realization and will not fall again into delusion. However individuals of middling and lesser acumen will not be able to remain within awareness (*rig thog tu gnas pa*), as different kinds of defilements will arise in their minds. These defilements are the afflictive emotions such as anger or desire, as well as all kinds of powerful thoughts, accepting and rejecting, and so on.

The nature of all these defilements is emptiness. If you just think everything is empty without actually applying the practice, you may say, "This is all empty. There is no path, no stages of the path, and no positive or negative karma." This attitude is known as superimposing the view of emptiness (*stong ltas rgyas 'debs*). But until you arrive in the immediate presence of awareness (*rig thog tu ma slebs bar*), there is no point in simply uttering such things.

Individuals who directly arrive in the immediacy of awareness are called the "instantaneous" type, and they are those of the very highest capacity. They are free of delusion, like someone who has reached a golden land where there are no ordinary stones. Individuals of middling and lesser faculties are either not able to directly recognize awareness, or are not able to remain within awareness (*rig thog tu gnas thub kyi ma red*). They may say there is no karma, no cause and effect, that there are no paths or spiritual levels (*sa med lam med*), that there is no good or bad, and so on. But by merely saying that there is nothing whatsoever, they are only falling into the extreme view of nihilism. They will simply be lost in delusion (*'khrul 'byams*).

If you don't recognize the essence of your own awareness (*rang rig pa'i ngo bo*) and merely think it is empty, you are only saying it is empty while remaining under the power of the ordinary state of delusion. This is nothing more than labeling things as empty, or superimposing the concept of emptiness. This will not only be of no benefit, but such persons will just fall further into delusion. Unfortunately, these days there are many who do exactly this.

In Tibet there were often misguided "practitioners" who would come to the village or town and drink beer, saying, "There is no good or bad, no negative or positive actions. It does not matter if we get drunk, as there is no dharma to practice, no karma of cause and effect to observe; everything is empty." Although they would say this, it actually does matter!

Within the vast sphere of the wisdom mind of dharmata (*chos nyid dgongs klong*), Samantabhadri, it doesn't matter or make any difference. However, we ourselves have not been able to attain the stability of remaining always in the vast expanse (*klong*) of the wisdom mind of dharmata. Until we attain stability (*tenpa tob; brtan pa thob*) and are able to actually remain within awareness (*rig thog tu*), then there most definitely is karma, cause and effect. There is good and bad, and there are things that are to be adopted (*blang*) and those that are to be abandoned (*spang*). These all still exist on the relative level, and so they will definitely either benefit or harm us. Just to say everything is empty and nothing exists is of no benefit to anyone! As Jigme Lingpa says, "These days there are a great many like this." This is the fourth way of straying.

> In brief, while meditation has been placed in your hand,
> On the journey to the level "endowed with the excellence of all
> aspects,"
> There are the concealed places and narrow, treacherous pathways
> Of errors, diversions, and points of straying.

Regarding the awareness our teacher introduced us to, our guru has said to us, "This is it!" In doing so, he has placed buddha in our hands by placing our own awareness (*rang rig pa*) in our hands, just like placing our own wealth in our own hands. He has given us the wealth of our own innate awareness (*rang rig pa'i nor*). Until we reach the level of buddhahood, the level that is "endowed with the excellence of all aspects" (*rnam kun mchog ldan*), there will be many types of errors, diversions, and straying points along the way.

For this reason, Jigme Lingpa has taught us the eight principal errors (*nor sa rgyad*) that occur when we try to sustain empty awareness (*rig stong*), as well as the three kinds of diversions (*gol sa sum*) that can befall us through the meditation experiences of bliss, clarity, and nonthought, and the four points of straying (*shor sa zhi*) in relation to emptiness, as we have explained thus far.

> If you do not carefully discern these experiences,
> Even if you are a clever talker and a shrewd writer,
> As it says in the Dzogchen teachings,
> "Meditation experiences are like mist, they will fade away."

If you don't become resolved (*gdar sha gcod pa*) regarding the nature of all these meditation experiences, then you may be clever at using words as a pretext for your conduct and may just repeat "It is all empty and there is no benefit in applying remedies." However, as it says in the Dzogchen teachings, "Meditation experiences are like mist, they will fade away." There is another saying in Tibet:

> There is no limit to the meditation experiences of the yogis,
> Just as there is no limit to the varieties of flowers that grow in
>   meadow plains in summer.

There are limitless varieties of flowers; we cannot say this will grow and this won't. Likewise the meditation experiences of the yogis are like flowers that appear only for a season. All these experiences will vanish like mist. And so it is said:

> Intellectual understanding is like a patch, it will wear off.
> Meditation experiences are like mist, they will fade away,
> Realization is like space, unchanging.

> **As it is explained, even trifling positive and negative
>   circumstances
> Can deceive a "great meditator."
> This is due to his becoming completely confounded in the face
>   of circumstances.**

> **Therefore, if you don't embrace [your practice] by means of
> This extraordinary vital point for removing obstacles and
>   bringing enhancement,
> Then staying in a strict retreat away from all human contact,
> You will bemoan the ascetic hardships of your concentration
>   practices.
> You will bind yourself tightly in meditation postures,
> Meditating on deities and reciting mantras,
> Cultivating the practices of the channels and vital energies,
>   and so forth.
> But how will you attain liberation and enlightenment,
> Merely through the difficulty of searching for and buying
>   such goods?**

> **As it says in the *Condensed Perfection of Wisdom Sutra*,
> "Though one may remain for countless years**

In a mountain valley filled with snakes,
Five hundred miles from anywhere,
Yet such a bodhisattva, who does not understand [the true
   meaning of] solitude,
Will only develop further pride and will remain in samsara."

If you decisively know the essence of your own awareness (*rang rig pa'i ngo bo yar thag chod shes*), and if you definitely practice the instructions of your teacher, then you will develop actual experience. But if you don't conduct yourself in this way, even if you stay in retreat for three years, or even one hundred years, it will not truly benefit you. Even if you meditate on hundreds of deities, recite great quantities of mantras, meditate extensively on the yogic practices of the channels and vital energies (*tsa lung; rtsa rlung*), all of this won't be of any ultimate benefit. You will never attain liberation or enlightenment just by putting yourself through ascetic hardships alone.

In the Kangyur, the collection of "translated words of the Buddha," we find an abridged sutra in eight chapters known as the *Condensed Perfection of Wisdom* (*Prajnaparamita Samcayagatha; Shes rab pha rol tu phyin pa'i mdo sdud pa*). This sutra condenses the essence of the Prajnaparamita or Perfection of Wisdom sutra teachings. The quote mentioned here by Jigme Lingpa describes the importance of relying upon solitude (*dben pa la bsten pa*). This quote from the sutra is quite something. The meaning it explains is that if you simply remain in an isolated place, five hundred miles from anywhere and full of wild animals and snakes, and even if you remain there for thousands of years, it will not be of ultimate benefit if you do not recognize the essence of awareness (*rig pa'i ngo ma shes na*). Not only that, you might actually develop pride from staying in an isolated retreat for so long. Already possessing ordinary pride, you further compound it with the additional pride in having stayed in retreat.

Though you may stay for many years in external isolation, in a place where no other human beings can be found, the vital point is that you must come to know the true inner solitude (*nang gi dben pa*). This is the awareness of dharmata (*chos nyid kyi rig pa*), your own self-awareness (*rang rig*). If you don't recognize the essence of your awareness, there will be no real benefit to remaining in such a place. You must come to know awareness wisdom (*rig pa'i ye shes*), which is solitude from afflictive emotions and indeterminate states of vague oblivion (*lung ma bstan dang nyon mongs las dben pa*). The place of solitude (*dben sa*) that is free from these is the wisdom of non-thought (*mi rtog pa'i ye shes*).

If you do not realize this, then your retreat will not have been particularly beneficial. You started off as a normal, everyday person. Now that you have stayed in retreat without realizing the real inner solitude (*nang gi dben pa*), the essence of awareness, you will just develop the extraordinary pride of having dwelt in isolation among wild animals. You will think, "I am a great mountain yogi," but you will still just be an ordinary person.

> Therefore, through understanding this vital point of taking
>   whatever arises as the path,
> Then in the hermitage of the body,
> There is the practitioner, the mind,
> Accomplishing the practice of remaining in solitude.
> There is no path more effective than this.

> Thus, don't hope to make much of your months and years spent in
>   retreat,
> But just count your whole lifetime as the measure [of your retreat].
> Place your efforts into sustaining the continuity of the
>   uncontrived natural state.

Therefore, the key point is to know how to apply the practice to whatever arises, as we have explained. Knowing this and understanding the analogy that the mind is the meditator, who practices in solitude in the hermitage of the body, there is no more effective path than this. Your body of this lifetime is the hermitage, and the mind is awareness wisdom, which is in the solitude (*dben pa*) of being free of all thoughts and afflictive emotions such as anger, ignorance, and so on.

If you rely on this solitary place of awareness wisdom (*rig pa ye shes kyi dben sa*), then you can keep practicing for your whole life, until your body is taken to the cemetery; it is not just a question of making efforts to practice for a few weeks, months, or years. From the time your teacher has pointed out your awareness, saying, "This is it!" you should meditate constantly, until your body is carried off to the cemetery. You must practice for your entire life!

In the practice of retreat it is important to remain free of hopes and expectations. Do not solely rely on the efforts of staying in retreat for months and years. Practice constantly throughout your whole life, and put your diligent endeavor into sustaining the continuous flow of the uncontrived natural state (*ma cho naylug gyun kyong; ma bcos gnas lugs rgyun skyong*). So it is important to apply yourself assiduously to practicing meditation according to this way of understanding the meaning of retreat.

Jigme Lingpa's teachings up to this point have explained how we can fall into errors, diversions, and ways of straying. Now this last section of the text is a summation of how to practice in a way that we will remain free of mistakes and errors.

> Whatever good or bad thoughts may arise,
> Do not apply the "patch" of just directly apprehending it,
> Noticing, "Oh, here is a thought."
> Nor should you apply a remedy, as though it were a "moxibustion"
> treatment,
> Onto the thought to be abandoned.
> Doing nothing whatsoever, be unconcerned,
> Like an old man watching children at play.
>
> By passing day and night without interruption
> Within the state free from conceptual elaborations,
> Thereby, you will perfect the mastery of thought-free insight.
>
> Whether there is stillness, movement, or mindful awareness,
> Whatever arises, [whether] good or bad thoughts,
> By achieving stability within the expanse of empty awareness,
> The Great Perfection beyond concepts,
> Then as it says in Dzogchen,
> "Realization is like space, unchanging."

Now, Jigme Lingpa unfolds the practice in more detail. As we have explained, the mind may be still, there may be thought movement, or there may be the noticing of stillness and movement. These are the only three things that can occur in the mind. Sometimes our mind is still for a while, and sometimes there will be the movements of thoughts such as desire or anger; there will be neutral, positive, or negative thoughts. At this time, the "knower" (*rig mkhan*) of stillness and movement is what is known as "mindfulness" (*dran pa*).

Jigme Lingpa tells us that whatever positive or negative thoughts arise, we should not be fixated on taking note of whether a thought is arising or not arising. He says that we should not apply this conceptual "patch" of another thought that apprehends the thought that arises; this means thinking about the arising thought or watching out for a thought to arise. Similarly, Jigme Lingpa teaches us that in the practice of Dzogchen, when a negative thought "to be abandoned" arises, we should not apply a positive thought on top of it. To do so would be like performing the medical treatment of "scarring moxibustion," placing a burning hot metal instrument onto an acupuncture point, just like Dr. Amchi Chodrak did on my head [Khenpo shows the scars] in several places. In this practice, we do not apply another thought, even a positive thought, as a remedy.

If we have a negative thought like anger or a problematic thought, whatever disturbing emotion may arise, there is no remedy superior to simply sustaining the continuous flow of awareness wisdom (*rig pa'i ye shes rgyun skyong ba*). Be just like an old man watching children at play. Whether the old man notices something good or bad happening in the children's game, he sees it all as part of their play. He doesn't entertain any thoughts or judgments about it, so he feels neither pleased nor upset by whatever happens in the game.

Similarly, whatever thoughts arise, you do not need to have any reaction of "ego clinging" or "self-grasping" (*dag dzin; bdag 'dzin*) toward them; nor do you need to have any fixated direct apprehension (*cer 'dzin*) of them. Rather, be in a state that is carefree and unconcerned (*snang med*) about whatever arises, without engaging with the thoughts and emotions that occur. You should pass day and night within this state of simplicity (*spros bral gyi ngang*), the continuity free of conceptual elaborations (*spros bral*) and mental constructs, remaining unconcerned with, and uninvested in (*snang med*), whatever arises. If you practice in this way, just sustaining this single vital point, then you will gradually gain mastery and reach the full maturation (*rtsal rdzogs*) of nonconceptual insight (*mi rtog pa'i lhag mthong*).

When Jigme Lingpa speaks about "empty awareness beyond concepts" (*rig stong blo 'das*), this is what your teacher introduced you to. It is the true nature of your mind (*sems nyid*), self-originating wisdom (*rang byung ye shes*), or simply "empty awareness" (*rig stong*). The unmistaken meaning of the natural Great Perfection is the wisdom realization (*thugs kyi dgongs pa*) of Garab Dorje and Samantabhadra. It is like the vital essence within the heart's blood of one hundred thousand wisdom dakinis and is known as "awareness beyond concepts" (*blo 'das kyi rig pa*).

Until, as Jigme Lingpa says, you achieve "stability within the expanse of empty awareness, the Great Perfection beyond concepts" (*rig stong blo 'das rdzogs pa chen po'i klong du btsan sa zin pa*), you must by all means definitely continue to practice meditation. Then, as it says in the Dzogchen teachings, "Realization is like space, unchanging."

> So it is said that although the yogin's body may appear ordinary,
> Since his mind remains in the wisdom realization of
> The dharmakaya, free of effort and activity,
> All that appears and exists is the mandala of the guru.
> Whatever arises is all-pervading primordial wisdom,
> And apparent objects are [experienced as] symbols and
>   scriptures.
>
> The [yogin's] wisdom mind, naturally at ease,
> Is beyond the activities of the levels and paths.
> And from the primordially liberated vast expanse of samsara
>   and nirvana,
> In the interim [until all beings are enlightened],
> He will effortlessly and spontaneously
> Accomplish the benefit of the teachings and living beings.
>
> Then at the same time as the enclosure of your physical body
>   dissolves,
> Just as when a vessel breaks
> And the space within it merges inseparably as one with the
>   space outside,
> [The realized yogin] will manifest true enlightenment
> Within the youthful vase body,
> The primordial ground expanse of inner luminosity,
> Free from the investigating mind.
> This is the final, ultimate accomplishment!

As Jigme Lingpa says that realization is unchanging like space, we should continue to practice until we reach this level. Though the realized yogin's body may appear ordinary, his mind remains stably in the wisdom mind of the dharmakaya, "free of all effort and activity" (*bya rtsol dang bral ba*). His body is still a body of flesh and bone, but his mind has attained the dharmakaya.

From the *All-Creating King* (*Kunje Gyalpo; Kun byed rgyal po'i rgyud*), a tantra of the Dzogchen Mind Series (*sems sde*):

> Although the body may appear in human or divine form,
> Yet for those who remain in the true condition of nonaction,
> Their mind is the actual sacred Buddha,
> Effortlessly and spontaneously benefiting others.

What Jigme Lingpa is telling us is that realized yogis appear to have an ordinary body but their mind (*dgongs pa*) is the actual Buddha. They have reached the level of dharmakaya Samantabhadra. They are inseparable from the Buddha, and remain so in the state of effortlessness.

When we say that realization is unchanging like space, you may think that once you have attained realization it will not fluctuate or change until complete buddhahood, that it will always be unchanging like space. You might understand this to mean that without passing through the different bodhisattva levels (*bhumi; sa*), one day you will suddenly be fully enlightened. I am not saying that it is not possible for some beings to have complete instantaneous realization. As we have explained, there are beings of the three degrees of capacity, and these can be further divided into three subcategories, so that there is the highest of the highest, middling of the highest, and the lesser of the highest; highest of the middling, middling of the middling, and lesser of the middling; and the highest of the lesser, middling of the lesser, and lesser of the lesser; nine in all. Beings may be of any of these degrees of aptitude.

For instance, according to the teachings of the general vehicle, there are ten stages or spiritual levels on the path to complete buddhahood. It sometimes happens that when certain persons are introduced to Dzogchen awareness (*rdzogs chen rig pa*) by their teacher, when they sit down, they are ordinary sentient beings. After receiving introduction, they arise from their seat having reached the eighth bodhisattva level, or having even become fully enlightened buddhas. Some beings, from the moment of introduction, never waver from the state of dharmakaya. Some people may reach the degree of stability in awareness equal to a bodhisattva on the third spiritual level at the time they receive the pointing-out instructions. There are also beings who, by hearing just a single word from their teacher, will reach the first spiritual level. But all of these cases are very rare.

With the exception of those who reach the eighth bodhisattva level directly, for everyone else, throughout all the stages up to the eighth level, there will be a deepening of the profundity of realization. So we cannot say that there is no change in the realization of beings passing through the spiritual levels, as awareness progressively stabilizes.

According to the Mahamudra tradition, realization is measured through four stages: one-pointedness, simplicity, one taste, and nonmeditation. In Dzogchen, one progresses through the four visions: manifest dharmata, increased visionary experience, consummate awareness, and exhaustion into dharmata.

If you ask what is the measure of realization of awareness (*rig pa'i rtogs tshad*) according to the Dzogchen teachings, it is never to move from the awareness wisdom (*rig pa'i ye shes*) that was introduced by your teacher. This is the measure of realization, as it is generally explained.

If you never meditate on your guru's introduction and fail to train in it, then you have just thrown it away, cast it aside, and forgotten it. From the moment you start to practice based on your guru's pointing-out instructions, awareness wisdom never changes. That is, it does not become something else. It is the same awareness that you have recognized from the beginning. You need not have any doubts in regard to it, nor do you need to have a lot of discursive thoughts about it, nor do you need to analyze and investigate it. It is always present and available to you, when you recognize it and practice.

Earlier, Jigme Lingpa spoke about the stages of intellectual understanding, actual experience, and realization. As a beginner, you gain some intellectual understanding, for example, after receiving introduction from your teacher. You hear what your teacher has said, and then for one hour you think you've understood, that you've got it. You think, "This is emptiness, this is clarity." Your ears feel very happy; you feel you have understood. This is a sign of having good karmic tendencies (*bag chags*), so it is not bad. Then the next day, due to various intervening factors, you will have completely forgotten it. You will be unsure about what was said, and you will have no confidence and certainty regarding it.

In Tibet there is the phrase *tra ye* (*phra yal*). It is related to a type of divination called *tra-bap* (*phra 'bebs*), which uses a mirror for prognostication. First one recites mantras over the mirror, then different consecrated grains are thrown upon it, evoking a variety of images and forms that appear in the mirror; the images or signs are known as *tra*. The diviner will then examine these images and signs and make his divination. Then, after a short while, the images will vanish, *ye;* hence the term *tra ye,* meaning "vanishing mirror images."

Intellectual understanding is similar to the analogy of mirror divination. At first you gain some understanding when you hear the words of your teacher. Then, due to different factors and circumstances, your understanding slips away. It does not remain for long. It is not stable, so it vanishes. But if you practice well, eventually this will no longer happen. To have actual experience (*nyongwa; myong ba*) of what the teacher pointed out is not like mere intellectual understanding. When you practice, the actual experience of what was pointed out by your teacher is still always with you. When we say "actual experience," in this instance it means to gain a clear and vivid presence of it in your mind (*gsal snang thob*). When your teacher speaks to you and imparts the teachings, the experience of this is in your heart (*snying gi nang la myong ba*). You can verify and confirm it. You can say, "Yes, that's how it is!"

There are many aspects related to actual experience, and they are not always stably present. Inner certainty is born from within your heart (*snying gi nang la nges shes skye*). Then even if someone tells you, "No, that's not it!" you will remain unmoved by their pronouncements. Your teacher has said to you that it is like this, and you have the confidence that this is so. As you have experienced it for yourself from within, you will not so easily lose the confidence it confers. Actual experience is superior to intellectual understanding; it is more profound. However, it will still have fluctuations, transitions, and transformations (*'pho 'gyur*). Experience does not always remain stably present. At some times, your meditation will be more like what we have been referring to as meditation experiences (*nyams*), but compared to mere intellectual understanding, this is still far superior.

So after the stage of actual experience, you are introduced to realization. There must be a qualified, authentic teacher; a genuine student endowed with faith and devotion; and the authentic oral advice of the lineage (*rgyud pa'i gdams ngag tshad ldan*). If all the necessary factors are gathered and present, then through the guru's introduction, realization can occur.

If you do not practice, nothing will happen. If you do, you will reach a point where you are free from confusion or mistakes. You will not entertain any doubts such as, "Is it this?" or "Isn't it this?" and will practice without errors or diversions. Whenever you meditate, you will directly see the essence of awareness (*rig ngo mthong ba*) in the clear mirror of mindfulness (*dran pa gsal ba'i me long*). Knowing this instruction, whenever you bring to mind the clear mirror of mindfulness, you will arrive at rigpa's own place of repose (*rig pa'i mal la bslebs yong*).

As I have emphasized throughout the teachings on Jigme Lingpa's *The Lion's Roar,* in the view of the Dzogchen teachings, it is important to be conscious of these three stages of intellectual understanding, actual experience, and realization. At the stage of intellectual understanding, there will be a lot of concepts about emptiness, and as Jigme Lingpa said in the text, "Nowadays there are a great many like this." He is referring to those who, for example, without having actual experience or any realization of emptiness, may say, "There is no such thing as positive or negative actions" and then throw everything aside. As explained, in these cases an array of errors and diversions will flourish like blossoming flowers. So according to the way of introducing the nature of mind in Dzogchen, there are these three stages of intellectual understanding, experience, and realization that need to be understood so that you can arrive at the correct understanding.

The teacher who gives the introduction must have received the oral advice of the lineage (*brgyud pa'i gdams ngag*). He or she should have actual experience (*nyams myong*) and be skilled and learned in the meaning of the tantras, should have no misconceptions regarding the nature of practice, and must be invested with the inconceivable qualities of experience and realization.

If one does not have such a teacher, even if the teacher is unlearned—as long as the student has purified the obscurations, accumulated merit, and has pure intentions and aspirations—even just meeting an ordinary teacher, it is possible for the student to be liberated. As it says in Jigme Lingpa's text, "Apparent objects are symbols and scriptures."[26]

There are an infinite number of ways in which beings have accumulated their individual karma, and there are beings of many different capacities. Sometimes even if the teacher doesn't do anything very significant, through the student's faith and devotion, he or she will have immediate recognition (*lam sang ngo shes 'gro kyi red*). Although this is possible, it is very rare.

The most frequent situation is that the student sees the teacher as a buddha, an enlightened being. The teacher is learned in the tantras, is entrusted with the oral advice of the lineage, and has deep practical experience of Dzogchen. A true teacher normally possesses these qualities in abundance. Also, the ideal student possesses great faith and devotion and has a vast and far-reaching mind (*blo rgya che ba*) and great discerning intelligence (*shes rab chen po*), and is thus an individual of the highest ability. In general, such a master and student need to come together for the perfect outcome to occur.

Still, there are some exceptions, like an account mentioned in the Vinaya tradition. At the time of the Buddha there was an old monk who had recently entered the sangha. As he was a novice, he had not yet had much time to study or reflect upon the dharma.

One day, as he was out on his daily alms round, he received a food offering from an aged woman. As was the custom, upon making the offering, she requested a dharma teaching from him. The monk was not at all learned, although he did have great faith in the Buddha and the dharma. So when he had to give a teaching to the elderly lady, which is known as "dedicating the merit of the sponsor," he thought, "I am advanced in years. I have nothing to teach. I am of no use to anyone." And he became rather dejected. At that moment, in the throes of his dilemma, the old monk found himself thinking aloud, and the words "not knowing anything is suffering!" slipped out.

The elderly woman thought this must be the monk's succinct teaching and thought to herself, "Oh, I did not realize that all compounded things are suffering; it is indeed true. I must contemplate this and understand it." She went off to meditate on these words and prayed to the Buddha and the monk. After some time, she saw the truth (*bden pa mthong*), and she realized the meaning of emptiness.

The news of her realization spread around the area. One elder abbot asked the old monk, "So what did you teach her?" The monk replied, "I didn't teach her anything." "But she saw the truth," the abbot insisted. The old monk answered, "That woman asked for a teaching, and I thought 'I don't know anything.' Then the words 'not knowing is suffering' just came out!"

One of the monks who was a close disciple of the Buddha also came to know of the event and went to ask the Buddha about it. The Buddha said, "Throughout her past lives she had accumulated meritorious positive karma and purified her karmic obscurations, and this is the reason for her realization."

In fact, that very same old monk also had a significant accumulation of merit and virtuous karma. He was unable to meet the Buddha when he was young, but did so in later life. When he heard that the elderly woman had reached realization through his words, he thought to himself that if he made efforts like she had, he too could attain liberation. Finally, the monk himself also gained realization, and it is said that he attained the level of an arhat.

These events can happen if there are special circumstances, and the story illustrates once again how beings of highest potential can be liberated. But as we continue to emphasize, ordinary beings will fall into errors and diversions, so they need the teachings in *The Lion's Roar*. As Jigme Lingpa instructs, it is important to distinguish between beings of the three capacities and to understand how they will attain liberation, so that they can be shown the appropriate path and taught Dzogchen in the manner that suits them. Finally, as is said, "Realization is like space, unchanging."

As Jigme Lingpa wrote in our last passage of *The Lion's Roar:*

> All that appears and exists is the mandala of the guru.
> Whatever arises is all-pervading primordial wisdom,
> And apparent objects are [experienced as] symbols and scriptures

In the text, the Tibetan phrase *yeshe cham dal* (*ye shes cham brdal*) or "all-pervading primordial wisdom" means that whatever arises and appears is the display of primordial wisdom (*ye shes kyi rol pa*).

This teaching is a summary of the complete path of Dzogchen, which I have been explaining in a concise way. In brief, let us keep in mind that Jigme Lingpa calls our attention to the famous quote "Realization is unchanging like space." First, the practitioner will have intellectual understanding; and to avoid becoming attached to that, what is the remedy? It is to not remain in mere intellectual understanding but to pray to your guru, receive the four empowerments, and merge your mind with the wisdom mind of your teacher. Then, further, to always endeavor diligently in meditation, free of any attachment to it (*sgoms la zhen pa med pa*). Gradually you will arrive at the stage of actual, direct experience.

During this period of practicing the instructions, there will be many types of meditation experiences, which are collectively known as those of bliss, clarity, and nonthought. As explained, they can lead to diversions in your practice. Again, do not remain with those experiences. Pray to your guru with open-hearted devotion, receive the four empowerments, and merge your mind with the guru's wisdom mind. Then try to stabilize your meditative composure (*nyamzhag tenpa; mnyam bzhag brtan pa*) and remain within awareness (*rig thog tu gnas*). This is how you will move through and pass beyond all these experiences.

When you have reached the end of your meditation practice (*sgoms nyams len mthar phyin*), you will arrive at realization; and with that you will be able to attain enlightenment. Even after reaching the stages of realization (*rtogs pa'i mtshams*), you have not yet attained complete enlightenment (*sangye pa; sangs rgyas pa*). So once again, you should pray to your teacher, receive the four empowerments, and merge your mind with the teacher's wisdom mind. Continuously, throughout the day and night, practice meditation according to these instructions.

Doing so, your realization will expand and unfold (*rtogs pa rgyes*), like the example of the phases of the moon. From the first day of the lunar month till the fifteenth day, the moon appears to increase in size. Of course, the moon has no good or bad qualities inherent in it and does not change size. But the example serves to illustrate that awareness (*rig pa*) goes through a process of developing its potential (*rtsal*), expanding and unfolding (*rgyas*), and then reaching its full potential for expression and coming to perfection or completion (*rdzogs*).

Until you attain ultimate realization, enlightenment within the youthful vase body (*gzhon nu bum sku*), you need to maintain this practice of the essence of awareness. On the path of stabilizing awareness, there is *tsal-wa* (*rtsal ba*), where one develops the potential and mastery of awareness; then there is *gyay-pa* (*rgyas pa*), the expanding and unfolding of this potential; and finally it is *dzog-pa* (*rdzogs pa*), brought to fullness, to perfect completion.

Initially, when you first recognize awareness, it is not so vast at all. It is small, like you are catching a glimpse of it. But finally, realization becomes as vast as the immensity of space, without fluctuations, transitions, and changes (*nam mkha' la 'pho 'gyur med rgya chen po*). In the vast expanse (*klong*) of the youthful vase body, all of samsara and nirvana are "beyond all effort and activity."

When you first catch a glimpse of realization (*rtogs pa mthong ba*), there is still some grasping and fixation (*'dzin ba*) present. But as the husk of fixation is removed (*'dzin pa'i shunpa bral*), awareness becomes more naked (*rjen*), limpid (*dvangs*), and without grasping (*'dzin pa med pa*). From there it continually expands and unfolds more and more (*gong nas gong du 'phel ba*).

As Jigme Lingpa writes in *The Lion's Roar*:

> **The [yogin's] wisdom mind, naturally at ease,**
> **Is beyond the activities of the levels and paths.**

> And from the primordially liberated vast expanse of samsara and
>   nirvana,
> In the interim [until all beings are enlightened],
> He will effortlessly and spontaneously
> Accomplish the benefit of the teachings and living beings.

In this teaching, we have spoken of the five paths or stages to complete enlightenment in relation to the three stages of understanding, experience, and realization. However, when the Dzogchen teachings speak from the ultimate viewpoint, it is said that there is no classification of the paths and spiritual levels (*sa lam*). The paths and levels are regarded as being complete within the essence of singularly liberated awareness (*rig pa gcig grol gyi ngo bo*). Ultimately, all the five paths and ten spiritual levels are complete in one single awareness (*rig pa chig rdzogs*). According to the ultimate understanding of Dzogchen, the definition of the levels or stages to complete enlightenment refers to the four visions (*nangwa zhi; snang ba bzhi*) of the path. All the qualities of the lower vehicles are perfected in these four visions.

A yogin who has truly realized Dzogchen awareness will have the ability at this time to spontaneously benefit the teachings and sentient beings. And as Jigme Lingpa explained earlier in *The Lion's Roar:*

> Then at the same time as the enclosure of your physical body
>   dissolves,
> Then just as when a vessel breaks
> And the space within it merges inseparably, as one with the
>   space outside,
> [The realized yogin] will manifest true enlightenment
> Within the youthful vase body,
> The primordial ground expanse of inner luminosity,
> Free from the investigating mind.
> This is the final, ultimate accomplishment!

When the limitation of the physical body collapses and dissolves (*zhig pa*), then simultaneously, like when a vase breaks and the space within the vase and the external space are indivisibly one, the yogin's mind becomes inseparable from the wisdom mind of the dharmakaya (*chos sku dgongs pa*). Within the primordial expanse of Samantabhadra, all becomes of a single taste (*ro gcig*). The ultimate attainment is complete enlightenment as the youthful vase body (*gzhon nu bum sku*), the primordial ground expanse of inner luminosity, which is beyond the domain of the investigating mind.

> In summary:
> Relative deluded appearances, the great falsehood,
> Have dissolved into the vast expanse
> Of the essential nature of awareness.
> Thus the mind play of discursive thoughts, like a child's dance,
> Has subsided within the continuity of mindfulness beyond
>   concepts.

All relative appearances are like illusions or dreams that deceive sentient beings. As Jigme Lingpa has fulfilled the enlightened realization of the essential nature of the vast expanse (*klong chen gshis kyi dgongs pa rdzogs*), he is telling us that all these relative, objective appearances are no longer able to deceive him. Thus all thoughts, which are the mind's play, a child's dance, finally come to rest within the ongoing state of mindfulness beyond concepts.

> As I am not intoxicated by stuporous sleep
> From imbibing the beer of good thoughts that pursue
>   a high view
> And bad thoughts that shackle in doubt,
> I remain at ease in naked ordinary awareness.

Jigme Lingpa says he does not drink the beer (*chang*) of "good" thoughts, like thinking he has reached the high view of Dzogchen and feeling proud about it. Nor does he drink the beer of the "bad" thoughts, such as those thoughts that entangle one in the chains of doubt due to superimposing concepts (*sgro 'dogs*). Not imbibing the beer of such thoughts, he is not intoxicated by the stuporous sleep of ignorance, and remains relaxed and at ease in naked ordinary awareness (*tha mal rig pa rjen pa lhod der gnas*).

> These profound and pithy vajra verses
> Of the wisdom mind transmission
> Will overpower, one hundred times over,
> The exaggerated claims of those who spout their theoretical
>   understanding;

> As well as the piercing torment of the treacherous passage
> Of stillness and movement.

These succinct and profound vajra words of the wisdom mind transmission (*dgongs brgyud*) will overpower the inflated pride of those who, though learned in texts and clever in speech, have not realized the natural state of Dzogpa Chenpo. And Jigme Lingpa's vajra words will likewise overpower the suffering and discouragement you may experience on the treacherous path of stillness and movement (*gnas rgyu'i 'phrang*), the play of the dualistic mind.

> Due to the auspicious connection of my previous accumulation
>   [of merit]
> And pure aspirations,
> Together with the kindness of the profound path of the vajra yoga,
> The knots of my central channel were released.
> And as a testimony of this, I wrote these oral instructions on the
>   vital points,
> Based on my own experience.

Due to Jigme Lingpa's accumulation of merit and prayers in his past lifetimes, and through meditating on the profound path of the vajra yoga, the knots of his wisdom channel were released, and he wrote this essential instruction based upon his own experience.

> When the roar of the summer thunder-drum resounds,
> It splits asunder the mouse-like hearts of pretentious learned ones.
> And as profound experience and realization have overflowed from
>   within,
> I was unable to conceal these words that spontaneously burst
>   forth.

This Dzogchen instruction, which is like the roar of the summer thunder-drum, splits asunder the faint hearts of the mouse-like conceited ones (*rlom sems*) who presume that they are learned or spiritually accomplished. As Jigme Lingpa has the stability of experience and realization, which overflowed spontaneously out of love for his students, he could not keep these instructions from them.

By this virtue,
Through sustaining the natural flow of mindfulness,
All of the nonvirtue accrued from straying into erroneous,
    restricted mindfulness
Is spontaneously purified within the innate continuity.

May all realize the Great Perfection!

The Lions Roar That Vanquishes Diversions and Errors was insistently requested many times by my attendant Dampa Longdrol Ying Rig, who is rich in the wealth of faith, generosity, and learning, while constantly maintaining the practice of the luminous Great Perfection due to his past karmic connection; and also by Kusum Ying Rig, whose mind abides in the three solitudes, and remaining in closed retreat, is focused on the practice of the Luminous Vajra Heart. Based on these requests, I, the Kusulu yogin, Padma Wangchen Yeshe Palgyi Rol Tsho (Powerful Lotus Wisdom Glorious Lake of Enjoyment), who consider myself familiar with the direct experience of the natural state (*mngon sum gyi gnas*) of the luminous Great Perfection, wrote this text during my retreat in the Great Secret Flower Cave of Ogmin Khadro Tshok Khang, "Feast Hall of the Akanishtha Dakinis," which is at the navel of Samye Chimpu. Do not show this text to those who have not received these instructions, or to those who, even if they have received them, hold wrong views; being intoxicated with the poisonous waters of pride, they thus lack the fortune to apply these vital points of the path. All those of you who are dedicated to practice, read this text again and again!

All those who have certainty may be given the reading transmission of it.

It is entrusted to the care of the sacred Nyingthig Protectors.
SAMAYA GYA GYA GYA

11. Spontaneous Songs

Great Peace

Letter from Chanteloube to Perigueux,
To Ani Damcho and Corinna, 1983

Peace, peace utterly great peace.
Three jewels, the place of refuge, great peace.
Swift path of the unsurpassable supreme secret, great peace.
One's own mind, the essence of dharmata, great peace.
If you meditate on the path of utterly great peace,
You will arrive in the state of great bliss, your own awareness.
Samsara and nirvana will be liberated in the vast expanse of great bliss,
And you will surely gain the great peace of total liberation.

Dakini Practice

TO MADELINE, PERIGUEUX RETREAT, FEBRUARY 1984

I pay homage at the feet of my father, the holy guru!
Listen here, Dechen Drolma!
You attained this free and well-favored human body, so difficult to find,
Met an authentically qualified noble guru,
And obtained the wish-granting gem of oral instructions.
How wonderful! Such great fortune!

The dharmakaya wisdom dakini
Is accomplished in the essence of the unborn nature of mind.
The sambhogakaya symbolic dakini
Is accomplished in the essence of the deity mandala.
The nirmanakaya dakini of signs
Pervades throughout the manifold worlds.
The three realms of existence are primordially pure
Within the dakini mandala. What a great wonder!
In the genuine, ultimate yoga
Samsara and nirvana abide as the mandala of the dakini.

Sustain the essence of your own awareness,
The self-originating ultimate dakini.
Since "the sustained" and "the sustainer" are not two,
Rest in natural clarity without grasping.
Remain in the continuity of the self-arising and self-liberating [of thoughts].
Release them in the continuum wherein
They disappear by themselves without needing to do anything.
Rest in the nature of the sky of dharmata,
The great ineffable state beyond concepts.

In brief, whatever perceptions manifest,
If you cut away all the bonds of attachment
To dualistic fixation, hopes and fears,
This can be understood to condense all the main points [of the practice].
So surely entrust this within your heart.

Thigle Gyachen, the Guru Practice of the Sealed Essence

To Corinna, Perigueux Retreat, October 1984

The most profound, immense expanse of the open sky
Is the marvellous wonder Longchen Rabjam, "All-Encompassing
    Vast Expanse."
The sun of Drimey Ozer, "Immaculate Light Rays," shines in your heart.
Through the oral instructions of the symbolic guru who points out,
I meet my true face as the ultimate guru, the one who is pointed out.
Invoking you with intense faith and devotion,
Bless my mind to be inseparable from your wisdom mind!

This is the way to practice Thigle Gyachen, the Sealed Essence.

Merging Three as One

Perigueux Retreat, November 1983

Pray by merging guru, deity, and dakini as one.
Practice by merging view, meditation, and conduct as one.
Sustain the essence of mind by merging ground, path,
    and fruition as one.
May it be virtuous!

The Signs of Spiritual Practice

PERIGUEUX RETREAT, AUGUST 1983

Homage to the king of self-originating wisdom!
This natural state of the mind
Is the primordially unborn nature.

When realized from the depth of your heart,
Compassion spontaneously wells forth
For all unprotected beings
Who have not recognized the essence of their mind;
And uncontrived, supreme bodhicitta arises.

Boundless faith and devotion are born
Toward the incomparable glorious protector gurus
Who are the supreme, oceanic fields of refuge;
And impartial pure perception will surely arise.

All you who seek the natural state of mind,
Know these as the true signs of spiritual practice

This is a message from the Tibetan stray dog, Jamyang Dorje.

NYOSHUL KHENPO PRACTICING SKY MEDITATION.
(PHOTOGRAPH COURTESY OF TERTÖN SOGYAL TRUST, UK.)

PEMA WANGYAL RINPOCHE, H.H. DUDJOM RINPOCHE,
AND NYOSHUL KHENPO AT THE END OF THE FIRST THREE-YEAR
RETREAT IN CHANTELOUBE, DORDOGNE, FRANCE, 1984.
(PHOTO COURTESY OF CHRISTIAN BRUYAT.)

NYOSHUL KHENPO BEFORE A SHORT MEDITATION
AT RINCHEN LING, PERIGUEUX, FRANCE, 1985.
(PHOTO COURTESY OF JOHN PETTIT.)

NYOSHUL KHENPO WITH H.H. DILGO KHYENTSE RINPOCHE
AT DILGO KHYENTSE'S RESIDENCE LA SONNERIE,
DORDOGNE, FRANCE.
(PHOTO COURTESY OF CHRISTIAN BRUYAT.)

NYOSHUL KHENPO WITH PEMA WANGYAL RINPOCHE
AT PROPOUTEL, FRANCE, 1990.
(PHOTO COURTESY OF RAPHAELLE DEMANDRE.)

NYOSHUL KHENPO PRAYING AT TIBET'S MOST FAMOUS
SHRINE, THE JOKHANG TEMPLE, IN LHASA.
(PHOTO COURTESY OF CORINNA CHUNG.)

Damcho Zangmo, Nyoshul Khenpo, and
Jetsun Jampa Chokyi resting on the way to Samye Temple.
(Photo courtesy of Corinna Chung.)

Nyoshul Khenpo, his wife Damcho Zangmo
(with glasses, to his right), and Jetsun Jampa Chokyi,
the wife of the late Kangyur Rinpoche,
crossing the Brahmaputra River to reach Samye Temple.
(Photo courtesy of Corinna Chung.)

APPENDIX 1: *A Wondrous Ocean of Advice for the Practice of Those in Retreat in Solitude*
BY JIGME LINGPA

Embodiment of all the glorious buddhas,
Lord of Compassion, Padmasambhava,
Remain upon the pinnacle of my diademed deep blue locks
And bless my mind.

L ISTEN, ALL OF YOU who possess faith, who keep samaya, and who strive from the depths of your hearts for spiritual ideals. In cyclic existence, without beginning or end, with your negative actions acting as the cause, you have fallen under the influence of adverse conditions. Everything you can think of [in samsara] is just an experience of fear and suffering. Beings of the six realms must experience this continually, like prisoners cast into a dark cell.

At present, if you have any physical illness or mental disturbance, or are in an undesirable situation, then you panic and are totally upset and paranoid about everything, like someone overcome by nausea. So how will it be when you experience the sufferings of the three lower realms? Alas! Now the only means of escape from these sufferings is to accomplish the ultimate goal of the supreme dharma; otherwise, there is no way out.

You may say, "Everything is an illusion," and then spend your day riding horses, drinking beer, and enjoying entertainments. Come evening, you don your cotton shawl [to show that you are practicing *tummo*], practice breathing like the noisy emptying and filling of a bellows, then play your bell and drum. You won't become enlightened by acting like this.

The cause of wandering in samsara is ego clinging. Nagarjuna writes in his *Letter to a Friend*, "'Desires bring destruction, like the kimba fruit,' the Munindra [the Buddha] said." They should be abandoned, as these chains bind all beings to the prison of samsara. In brief, regarding ego clinging: in clinging to your country, house, wealth, and possessions, you postpone the practice of dharma.

You praise your deity when you find a mere needle or some thread, and you get depressed if you lose even a pen or a shoelace. These are all external forms of ego clinging.

Seeing members of your own tradition as gods and those of other traditions as demons, and without examining your own qualities, you think, "Would I not be fit to take Shakyamuni Buddha's place?" All these are internal forms of ego clinging.

Clinging to the visualization in the development stage as being solid, having partiality in the generation of the bodhicitta, practicing the completion stage within a conceptual framework, you say all things are empty and lack self-nature, yet cling to the nature of emptiness, like a beautiful woman attached to her own body, and perceive it with a very tight and unclear mind, thinking, "No one has reached my level of meditation, so I don't need to ask for advice or consult anyone." Thus your life will be wasted in futility. These are all secret forms of ego clinging.

My frank advice is this: if you strongly renounce clinging to your country, wealth, and possessions, half of the dharma will already be accomplished.

Initially, by entering the door of the absolute teaching and having the capacity to cast off ego clinging like spit in the dust, I captured the citadel of the natural state. I began to gather an entourage of students, becoming a source of benefit to others, training disciples by means of my basic intention [of compassion], and giving teachings. I kept only some immediate necessities and just enough clothing to protect myself from the cold and didn't say, "I'll need this wealth for later," or "I'll need it if I'm sick or dying," or "I'll need it to perform ceremonies if I am sick," or "I must put something aside to be used for funeral offerings when I die."

Thus I didn't concern myself with worrying about my future means of support, but mainly made offerings to the three jewels, ransomed the lives of animals, served and respected the sangha, gave charity to beggars, and so forth.

I didn't waste the offerings of the living and [those made on behalf of] the dead by giving them to unworthy causes, nor did I hoard them like bees storing honey in a hive. Since I didn't carry great wealth with me, I felt no embarrassment before those who came to see me.

We will all die, remember that.

Since the dharma itself is free from partiality, try to have pure perception regarding everyone. If one examines all the traditions, each of them is indeed profound in its own way; but for me, the view of the Great Perfection was fine, and all the root downfalls were dissolved in space.

When laying the foundation of the preliminary practices, you should not forsake them by saying, "Everything is empty," thereby losing your actions in the view.

Then, for the actual practice, you should live in an uninhabited area without acquaintances, accompanied by your friend Awareness, and vow to maintain the flow of the uncontrived natural state.

If you hear good or bad news that stirs up hopes and fears, don't regard it as true. Neither reject nor accept it. Be like a dead person, to whom one can say anything.

Think how difficult it is to attain a human form, how difficult it is to meet the dharma, and about the rarity of true teachers.

Think about the many ways that Mara can enter.

Ponder the fact that everyone will die.

Think about the suffering and oppression endured by worldly people.

You should thus have the same revulsion for samsara that someone with liver disease has for greasy food. If you don't keep this in mind, then having good meals, a fine patron, warm clothes, a comfortable place, and pleasant conversations will only prepare you for worldly life; and before even beginning to practice the dharma, you will have already created obstacles. Furthermore, it is said, "You may raise your eyebrows and speak in a spiritual way about high realization, but if you haven't subdued the demons of ego clinging and attachment to pleasure, the signs will show in your behavior and can also be detected in your dreams." It is essential to understand this.

It is said: "Accepting offerings from the salary of a high official or from powerful people brings negative results."

If you think carefully about the source of their wealth and possessions, how can they possibly benefit your spiritual practice?

It is also said: "To misuse offerings is a razor blade to the life force. Overindulging in food cuts the life-vein of liberation."

Finally, this will be the weight that drags you to the depth of hell. So reflect on this well: rely only on alms for your sustenance, and give up flattering others.

As the buddhas of the past have said: take the proper amount of food, moderate the length of time you sleep, and maintain keen awareness.

If you eat too much food, your mental defilements will automatically arise; if you don't have enough, you'll beat your drum, chant, and perform village rites and only make your head spin. Then you'll say, "If I don't do this, I won't have enough food," and you'll become more frantic than a street dog. So be careful to eat the correct amount. Alcohol is the source of all faults, so drink only a cupful, no more. If you are unable to go without meat, eat only a suitable amount and practice food yoga in my advice in "How to Carry On Daily Activities" (*Spyod yul lam khyer*).

In describing how to undertake daily spiritual practice, it is of course difficult to set a single standard, as there are beings of high, mediocre, and inferior capacities. However, I will use as an example my own three years and five months [1756–59] in Palgyi Riwo. During this retreat, I awoke before dawn at the latest, rose very briskly, and expelled the stale breath nine times to separate the pure and impure essences of the wind element. After finishing the preliminary practices, I prayed so fervently that tears rolled from my eyes.

Then, for one session lasting till midmorning, I meditated on the prana practice of the completion stage from the extraordinary Drolthig Nyengyu. Initially, it was necessary to generate courage to bear the pains arising from the movements of prana; but after some time, all the blockages were spontaneously released, and the prana resumed its natural flow. Controlling the thirty-two channels of the left and the thirty-two channels of the right [at the navel center], I was able to detect the seasonal change in the lengths of day and night.

The ascending and descending pranas united, and a large, round vessel like a gourd was actually visible to the eye. This was the source from which my ordinary and extraordinary signs of the path were actualized.

So if you only hold the breath for a short time and have unclear visualization, it is important not to boast about your practice.

At midmorning I took tea or soup, and then offered sur, the burnt offering. Following that, I began a session of the approach and accomplishment practices.

In the development stage, the essence (*ngowo; ngo bo*) of the deity is free from grasping; its nature (*rangzhin: rang bzhin*), which is the deity's form, is luminous; and its capacity (*thugje; thugs rje*) is the clear concentration on the radiation and reabsorption of light rays. Only by maintaining an awareness of these will the development and completion stages be perfected.

Some lazy practitioners these days practice without making any effort, like an old man counting mani. This is not the correct way.

Going through these various practices, I finished this second session just after midday.

Then I offered water tormas, recited the "Confession of Downfalls," the "Spontaneous Accomplishment of Wishes," the "All-Victorious Ushnisha, Supreme Body of Wisdom," and so forth, and concluded with dharanis, mantras, and prayers from the "Daily Recitations."

Following this, if I had any writing to do, I quickly wrote about eight pages. Then, if I had nothing special in mind, I would meditate on the thögal practice. During lunch I blew many special mantras and dharanis on the meat, generated compassion, and offered prayers. Then I practiced food yoga by visualizing my aggregates and elements as deities and recited the sutra for purifying the offerings received.

Next, I did two or three hundred prostrations and recited prayers from the sutras and tantras.

Then I immediately sat down and practiced the meditation and recitation of my yidam intensively. Thus I was able to accomplish the practices of many classes of yidams. At dusk I performed a ganachakra feast offering, offered tormas, and finished the concluding practices and the dissolution of the completion stage. Then I made strong prayers to be able to perceive luminosity and also offered prayers, such as the "Spontaneous Accomplishment of Wishes," strongly and impartially for myself and all beings. After a session of prana meditation, I began sleep yoga.

Whenever I woke up, I didn't drift into confusion but one-pointedly kept my attention focused, and by so doing was able to make progress in my practice.

In brief, during these three years I always ate the same amount of food and wore only one cotton shawl. Not one word passed through the small inner door of my retreat, and when the retreat helpers came, they didn't go beyond that inner door. As I had a sense of renunciation and a weariness with samsara, and an acute awareness of the uncertainty of death, I didn't utter a word of gossip or meaningless talk.

However, my disciples, when you do retreat, you might have put a sign by your door, but your thoughts just wander; if there is a noise outside, you act like a watchman, and you listen to any babble. If you meet someone at the inner door, you discuss the news of China, Tibet, Mongolia, and everywhere else. Your six senses wander around outside, and you lose all the power of your retreat. You follow after external objects and perceptions, your accomplishments vanish outside, and you invite obstacles inside. If you fall into these habits, the time of your retreat will pass without your mind improving by a fraction. Never leave retreat just as ordinary as you were before.

You must develop determination so that whatever you are doing, the essential nature of your mind is ineffable, beyond the intellect, not too tight, not too loose; it is beyond meditation, yet without the slightest distraction. While in retreat, whether you are sick, in pain, or dying, practicing the development stage or completion stage, writing or reciting daily prayers—without changing, establishing, modifying, or spoiling this present awareness, you should never separate from it. Once you do separate from it, various thoughts may arise, and under their influence the pride of being the "great meditator" will increase.

You will think, "I know the dharma. I have met many lamas." You will expose the faults of your dharma friends, amass wealth, and create disturbing situations, passing your time doing many things without doing one properly. Brainless folk will say, "He is a person of great merit and immense benefit to beings." When you start eating the tsampa offered for tormas, it will be a sure sign that Mara has already possessed you.

As it is said:

> Commit your mind to the dharma.
> Commit the dharma to a frugal, humble life.
> Commit this frugal, humble life to the thought of death.
> Commit death to occur in a deserted place.

All dharma practitioners should take these four resolutions of the noble Kadampas as their crown jewel, and the obstacles (maras) will be unable to interrupt them.

Furthermore, if you speak of your experiences, realizations, or dreams, talk about dharma news and the difficulties of your retreat practices, or mention the faults of those who belong to the same lineage and hold the same view as yourself to people who do not have the same samaya, for instance, then your accomplishments will vanish and this behavior will serve only to expose your own flaws. So keep a low profile, be in harmony with everyone, wear tattered clothes, and do not be preoccupied with mundane concerns. In the depth of your being, you should have no fear, even of the Lord of Death.

Externally, by appearing even more peaceful than the King of Swans, Yulkhor Sung, you should be able to give other people a positive impression.

In brief, someone practicing dharma should rely only on himself and not take advice from anyone except a true teacher. Even parents' advice, however honest it may be, will not be right. Be like a wild animal escaping from a cage.

When you are practicing in retreat, never break your commitment; be like a stake driven into hard ground, firmly planted. If you receive bad news, or if bad circumstances arise, do not panic; you should be oblivious like a madman.

When you are with many people, do not let your mindfulness stray toward ordinary things.

You should train in perceiving all phenomenal existence as infinitely pure.

When you meditate on prana and the completion stage, you should never lose your concentration, just like someone threading a needle. Even if death should come upon you unexpectedly, then without any sadness or regret and with nothing left unfinished in your mind, you should be like an eagle soaring through the sky.

If you have these seven essential points, you will reach the ultimate accomplishment of the victorious ones, the buddhas of the past, and my wish will be fulfilled. Thus, you will make this human life meaningful, and, entering the gate of the supreme dharma, you will achieve the final result.

A LA LA HO!

I, the Dzogchenpa Longchen Namkhai Naljor, the Yogi of the Vast Space, wrote this heart advice, based on my own experience, for the powerful yogi practitioner Jalu Dorje, "Adamantine Rainbow Body," who became an excellent vessel for the Secret Mantra through his faith and devotion. I request you all to keep it by your pillow.

APPENDIX 2: THE TIBETAN TEXT OF
JIGME LINGPA'S *The Lion's Roar*

སྐྱེང་ཏིག་སྐོམ་པའི་བུ་བྲལ་གྱི་གོལ་ཤོར་ཚར་གཅོད་སེང་གེའི་ང་རོ་བཞུགས་སྟེ༔

ཡེ་ནས་མ་བསྒོམས་མ་བསྒྲུར་མ་བཅོས་ཤིང་༔༔མ་ཡེངས་མ་བཟུང་རིག་པའི་སྐྱིང་

པོ་ཅན་༔༔བདུང་བཞག་ཆེན་འཇོན་བྲོ་བྲལ་རྟོགས་པ་ཆེར༔༔རང་བབས་གཉུག

མའི་རྒྱུན་གྱིས་ཕྱག་བགྱིའོ༔འདེད་གསལ་རྒྱུད་སྤྱི་རྟོགས་པ་ཆེན་པོའི་བཅུད༔༔པ་ཌྭི

ཕུགས་ཏིག་མ་མཁའ་འགྲོའི་སྐྱིང་གི་ཁྲག༔རིམ་དགུའི་ཐེག་པ་ཀུན་ལས་འདས་པའི

དོན༔༔དགོངས་བརྒྱུད་ཁོ་ནའི་མཐུ་ལས་བཙོད་དུ་མིན༔དེ་ལྟ་ན་ཡང་སྐྱིང་པོའི

དོན་མཚོག་ལ༔༔གཅིག་ཏུ་གཞོལ་བའི་སྐྱེས་ཆེན་རྣམས་ཀྱི་དོན་༔༔རྟོག་དགོང

འཛུར་བཙོར་ཁྱིགས་བཅད་མ་ཡིན་པར༔༔སྟོང་ཆེན་དགོངས་པའི་མཛོད་ནས་འདི

བུས་སོ༔༔དེ་ལ་འདིར་སྟོན་གྱི་སྟོན་ལམ་དག་པས་མཚམས་སྦྱར༔རྟོགས་པ་དོན

གྱི་བརྒྱུད་པ་དང་ལུན་པའི་ལྔ་མ་དག་པ་མཚན་ཉིད་དང་ལུན་པ་ཞིག་དང་མཇལ༔

དེ་ལ་རྗེ་གཅིག་གི་དང་འདུན་དྲག་པོས་ཡིད་ཁྲིད་ཤེས་ཀྱི་བློ་ཁིལ་བས་གསོལ་བ

འདེབས༔ཤེས་ན་རྐྱེན་ཕོ་གོས་ཀྱི་བྲལ་ཏེ་ལྔ་མའི་རྟོགས་པ་སློབ་མ་ལ་འཕོས

ནས་རང་བཞིན་སློབ་བྲལ་རྟོགས་པ་ཆེན་པོའི་གནས་ལུགས་ཅིག་དང་དཔེ་ཡེས་མི

མཚོན་ལ༔༔གོ་མ་འགགས་ཤིང་༔རྒྱ་མ་ཆད༔ཕྱོགས་སུ་མ་ལྷུང་བ་དུ་ལྷའི

ཁྲིགས་ཆོད་ཀྱི་ཤེས་པ་སྤྲ་མ་བརྗེ་མདོག་མ་བསྒྲུར་པ་འདི་ཀ་སྐོམ་ལ་ཁྱིལ་གྱིས

སོང་ནས་སྐོམ་རྒྱའི་ཞེན་པ་དག༔༔ལྷ་སྐོམ་གྱི་སྐྱོག་ལས་གྲོལ་༔ངེས་ཤེས་ནང་ནས

སྐྱེ་སྟེ་སྐྱེ་མཁན་ཡུལ་མེད་དུ་སོང་ཚེ་བཟང་རྟོག་གིས་ཕན་མ་བཏགས་ཚེ་ཚེ་འན་རྟོག
གིས་གནོད་མ་བསྐྱལ་ཚེ་ལུང་མ་བསྟན་གྱི་མགོ་མ་བསྐོར་བར་དབྱིངས་རིག་ཆམ་
བརྡལ་དུ་སོང་ནས་ལམ་རྟགས་ཀྱི་ཡོན་ཏན་མངོན་དུ་འགྱུར་ཞིང་ཚེ་དེ་ལ་གོལ་ས་
དང་ཚེ་ནོར་ས་དང་ཚེ་འཕོར་ས་ཞེས་བྱའི་མིང་མེད་པ་ཞིག་ལགས་སོ་ཚེ་ཚེ་དེ་ལྟ་ནའང་
ཚེ་ཚོས་འདི་ཐེག་པའི་རྩེ་རྒྱལ་ཨེ་ཀུང་གང་ཟག་ལ་མཆོག་དམན་འབྱེད་གསུམ་སྣ་
ཚོགས་ཡོད་ཅིང་དབང་པོ་ཡང་རབ་འ་སྦྱག་ཚོགས་དཀར་བས་གདུལ་བྱ་དང་
འདུལ་བྱེད་ཀྱི་བར་དུ་འཛོལ་འཕོར་ནས་བསྒོམས་ཀྱང་ཡོན་ཏན་སྐྱེ་དཀར་བའི་སྐྱོན་
འདི་ནས་འཕོར་རོ་ཚེ་ཚེ་དེ་ལ་རིམ་སྐྱེས་པའི་དབང་དུ་བྱས་ན་སྲུགས་དམ་ལ་གོ་བ་
སྐྱོང་བ་རྟོགས་པ་གསུམ་མོ་ཡོད་པ་ཚོ་ཚོ་བྱུན་སོང་ཐེག་པའི་ལམ་རིམ་དང་སྦྱར་ན་ཚོ་
ཚོགས་ལམ་པས་གོ་ཚོ་ཚོ་སྦྱོར་ལམ་པས་སྐྱོང་ཚོ་མཐོང་ལམ་པས་རྟོགས་ཞེས་
མཁས་གྲུབ་རྣམས་གསུངས་པ་འདི་ཉིན་ཏུ་བཀའ་བཙན་པར་སྣང་ངོ་ཚོ་ཚོ་དེང་སང་
གི་དུས་སུ་ཐལ་ཆེར་གོ་བ་ལ་སྐོམ་རྒྱལ་མར་བཟུང་ནས་རྒྱས་འདེབས་སུ་ཕོར་བ
མང་ཚེ་དེ་ཇི་ལྟ་བུ་ཞིན་ཚ་ཞེས་པ་གསལ་སྟོང་གང་དུའང་མི་རྟོག་པའི་མཉམ་གཞག
སྦྱོང་སྦྱོད་འབོལ་འབོལ་འདི་སྐྱེས་དུས་བདེ་ཉམས་ཁོན་ཤས་ཆེ་ཚེ་འདི་སྐོམ་འདི་ཀ
ཡིན་ཚོ་འདི་ལས་ལྷག་པ་སུས་ཀྱང་མི་ཤེས་ཚ་ངས་འདི་ལྟ་བུ་རྟོགས་སྐྲམ་པའི་རང་
མཐོང་ཡང་སྐྱེ་བ་ཡོད་པས་འདིའི་ཆེ་ལྡ་མ་ཆད་ལྟན་གྱིས་མ་ཟིན་ན་ཚོ་ཇི་སྐད་དུ་
རྟོགས་ཆེན་ནས་ཚོ་གོ་བ་ལྷན་པ་འདད་སྟེ་གོག་ནས་འགྲོ་ཚོ་ཞེས་བཤད་པ་ལྟར་ཚོ་རྒྱེན་
བཟང་དང་དང་འཕུད་ཚེ་ཆུ་དང་ལོ་མ་སོ་སོར་བྱི་བ་མང་ཞིང་ཚོ་དེ་ཡང་རྒྱེན་ངན་
ལམ་དུ་སྦྱོངས་པ་ནི་ཆུང་ཟད་སྣ་མོད་ཚོ་བཟང་རྒྱེན་ལམ་དུ་སྦྱོངས་པ་ཉིན་ཏུ་དཀའ་
བས་རྟོགས་པ་མཐོན་པོར་རྣོམ་པ་དག་ཀྱང་ཚེ་འདིའི་ཆེ་ཐབས་འབའ་ཞིག་ལྱུར་
ཡིན་ཅིང་ཚོ་རྣམ་གཡེང་ལྱའི་བུའི་བདུད་ལ་ཞེན་པ་ཁོ་ནས་གང་བ་འདི་ནི་ཚོགས་
དྲག་རང་གྲོལ་གྱི་གནད་མ་རྟོགས་པས་ལན་ལ་ཚོ་དེང་སང་ནི་འདི་ལ་ཡ་མཚན་
དང་གྲུབ་རྟགས་སུ་བྱེད་པས་འདིར་སྐུ་བ་པོ་བུ་རོག་དཀར་པོར་ཟན་མོད་ཚོ་འོན་ཀྱང་

སྙིང་ནས་དམ་ཚོས་བྱེད་པ་དག་འདིའི་ཚོ་མཆན་མ་ཅན་གྱི་ལྱ་བ་ཐོམ་རོ་ཡི་བ་དེ་ལ་
སློམ་གོ་མི་གཅོད་པར་ཐུན་བཞིན་བླ་མའི་རྣལ་འབྱོར་ལ་རྩལ་འདོར་ཅེང་དབང་བཞི་
བླངས་རྗེས་ཐུགས་ཡིད་བསྲེས་པའི་ངང་ལ་རིག་པ་ཁ་ཡན་དུ་སློད་ལ་ཉམས་དེའི་ངོ་
བོ་གཏད་མེད་ཁྱངས་མེད་དུ་མ་སོང་བར་སྙིང་ལ་རྡོ་རུས་གདུག་གོ་སྙེ་དེ་བཞིན་དུ་
ཉམས་སྐྱོང་ལ་ཞི་གནས་ཞས་ཆེ་བའི་སྙིང་ཉམས་དང་ཕྲ་ལྷག་མཐོང་ཞས་ཆེ་བའི་
གསལ་ཉམས་སོགས་མདོར་ན་འགྱུ་དྲན་གྱི་མཆང་རིག་ཅིང་སོ་སོར་རྟོག་པའི་ཞིས་
རབ་ཀྱི་རྩལ་འབར་ནས་གནས་འགྱུ་གཉིས་ཀ་སློམ་དུ་ཁྱེར་ཞིས་པ་ཡོད་ཀྱང་རྩ་
ཞིས་མཁན་གྱི་རོ་བོ་ལ་ང་བདག་གི་འཛིན་སྣངས་ནས་སྙིང་དེ་བ་དང་རྩ་བཏག་
དཔྱད་བསམ་གཞིགས་ཀྱི་གཞིས་ལ་ཕོར་བ་སོགས་ཞན་དུ་ཀློག་དུ་གྱུར་པའི་ཞིས་
བྱའི་སློབ་པ་རྗམ་པོ་ཆེ་འདི་ན་ཡོད་པས་རྣམ་རྟོག་ལ་ཚོས་སྐྱའི་མེད་འདོགས་མི་ལྱ་
བར་དུ་ལྱར་གྱི་ཞིས་པ་གྲ་མ་ཉམས་ཞིང་བྱུར་མ་ཆག་པ་འདི་ཀ་ལ་སློམ་མཁན་གྱི་
གཉེན་པོ་དང་རུ་ལྱ་བའི་ཞིན་པས་མ་བཅིངས་པར་རང་ཐབ་ཁ་ཡན་དུ་ལམ་དུ་
འཁྱེར་བ་ཁོ་ན་ལས་ལྱག་པའི་མཉམ་གཞག་དང་རྗེས་ཐོབ་ཀྱི་གོ་བ་ལ་བཏག་དཔྱད་
ཀྱི་བུ་ཕོར་ན་ཉ་ལམ་གོལ་ས་དང་ཉ་ནོར་ས་དང་ཉ་ཕོར་ས་གསུམ་གྱི་འཕང་ཡོད་
དེ་ལ་དེ་དག་གི་ངོས་ཟིན་མ་ཞིན་ན་ཉ་ཡིན་པ་དང་མིན་པའི་སྣངས་མི་ཕྱིད་པས་
འདིར་དེ་དག་གི་མཆང་འཆད་ལ་ཉ་སྙོང་པ་ཉིད་ཅིས་པ་དེ་ཡེ་གདོད་མ་ནས་སྙོང་
ཞིང་བདག་མེད་པ་སྣོས་པའི་མཐར་བཞིའམ་བཀྲུད་དང་ཐུལ་བ་ད་ལྟའི་ཞིས་པ་བློ་
འདས་ཁ་ཡན་འདི་ཀ་རིག་པ་ལ་ཟེར་བ་དེ་མ་གོ་བར་ཉ་ཐེག་པ་འོག་མ་ལྱར་ཡོད་
མེད་དགག་སྒྲུབ་ཀྱི་བློས་དཔྱད་པའི་རྗེས་ཀྱི་ཅི་ཡང་མེད་པའི་སྙོང་པའམ་ཉ་རྒྱུད་སྡེ་
འོག་མ་ལྱར་སྦྲ ༀ ཕྱི་སྱགས་སོགས་ཀྱིས་སྙོང་པར་སྒྲངས་པའི་ཉིང་དེ་
འཛིན་གསལ་སྙོང་ཚ་མ་དུ་ཁས་ལེན་ཅིང་སྒྱུ་མ་ལྱ་བུའི་ལྱ་བ་ལྱར་སྐྱོང་ན་ནོར་སྱ་དེ་
བཞིན་དུ་ཞི་གནས་ཉི་ཕུ་རགས་ཀྱི་རྣམ་རྟོག་རང་སར་ཞི་སྟེ ༀ སེམས་ཉིད་འགྱུ་དྲན་
གྱི་རྒྱབས་དང་བྲལ་ནས་དངས་སིང་དེ་གནས་པའི་ཆ་རང་རིག་རང་གསལ་ལ་དེ་ཡིན་

པ་མ་གོ་བར་གནས་པ་དྲན་མེད་ནད་པོ་ལ་གོ་ན་ནོར༔ ལྷུག་མཐོང་ནི་གནས་འགྱུ་གཉིས་ཀ་རང་ངོ་རིག་པའི་ཤེས་པའི་རང་གདངས་གསལ་རིག་འཛིན་མེད་འདི་ཀ་ཡིན་པ་ལ༔ དེ་མ་གོ་བར་གནས་འགྱུ་ལ་བརྟག་དཔྱད་བྱེད་པའི་བློ་དང་ནོར་ས་ཡོད་༔ མཉམ་གཞག་དང་རྗེས་ཐོབ་ཅེས་པ་ལ་བཞེད་ལུགས་སྣ་ཚོགས་ཡོད་ཀྱང་༔ རྫོགས་ཆེན་རང་སྐད་དུ་གང་ཤར་གྱི་ངོ་བོ་དྲན་པའི་རྩིས་ཟིན་བཞིན་པའི་ངང་དུ་གནས་པ་ལ་མཉམ་གཞག་དང་༔ དེ་ཉིད་ཤེས་བཞིན་གྱི་ངང་དུ་སྤྱུལ་བསྒྱུར་སོགས་འགྱུ་བའི་ཆ་དེ་རྗེས་ཐོབ་ཡིན་པ་མ་གོ་བར༔ ལྟ་སྟངས་ཀྱི་སྟོང་པ་ལ་རྩེ་གཅིག་ཏུ་འཛོག་པ་ལ་མཉམ་གཞག་དང་༔ དེ་ལས་ལངས་ནས་གང་ཤར་ལ་སྒྱུ་མ་ལྟ་བུའི་སྟོང་ཉིད་ཀྱི་རྒྱས་འདེབས་བྱེད་པ་ལ་རྗེས་ཐོབ་ཏུ་འདོགས་པ་ནོར༔ ཡེངས་མེད་ནི༔ འཁྲུལ་འབྲུམས་ཀྱི་རྣམ་རྟོག་འོག་འགྱུར་ཤོར་བ་དང་ལུང་མ་བསྟན་དུ་མ་སོང་བར་ཡང་དག་གཉུག་མའི་དྲན་པ་ལ་ཟེར་གྱིས༔ ཡེངས་ཀྱི་དོགས་པའི་ཟློན་འཛུག་པ་དང་༔ སྤྱུག་བཙོར་འཛུར་དྲན་གྱིས་བཅིངས་ན་ནོར༔ ཐ་མལ་གྱི་ཤེས་པ་ནི་ད་ལྟའི་ཤེས་པ་སྐྱོན་ཡོན་གང་གིས་ཀྱང་མ་བསླད་པའི་རང་བབས་འདི་ཀ་རིག་པའི་རྒྱུན་གྱིས་སྐྱོང་བ་ལ་ཟེར་བ་མ་གོ་བར༔ འཇིག་རྟེན་ཐ་མལ་གྱི་རྣམ་རྟོག་རང་རྒྱུད་པ་ལ་ངོས་འཛིན་པ་ནོར༔ སྒོམ་མེད་ནི་གནས་ལུགས་ལྷུམས་སུ་ཚུགས་ནས་སྒོམ་མི་སྒོམ་གྱི་ཞེན་པ་དག་སྟེ་སེམས་ལ་བཟོ་བཅོས་དང་དམིགས་གཏད་གང་ཡང་མེད་པར་ཁྲེབ་གདལ་གྱི་དྲན་པའི་མཁར་ཚུགས་པ་ལ་ཟེར་གྱིས༔ བློས་བཏང་བའི་བཏང་སྒོམས་ཐ་མལ་དུ་སྤྱོད་པའམ༔ ཅི་ཡིན་འདི་ཡིན་མེད་པའི་ལུང་མ་བསྟན་དུ་རྒྱ་འབྲུམས་ན་ནོར༔ གང་ཤར་སྐྱོང་བ་ཟེར་བ་དེ༔ གང་ཤར་གྱི་རྣམ་རྟོག་དེ་ལ་ཅེར་གྱིས་བལྟས་ནས་དགག་པ་ཡང་མ་ཡིན༔ དེ་ལ་བརྟག་གཞིག་བྱེད་པ་ཡང་མ་ཡིན༔ དེའི་རྗེས་སུ་འབྲང་བ་ཡང་མ་ཡིན་པར་རྣམ་རྟོག་ཤར་མཁན་པོ་རང་གི་རིག་ཐོག་ཏུ་གློད་ནས་གནས་འགྱུ་ཟང་ཐལ་དུ་སྐྱོང་བ་ལ་ཟེར་བ་མ་གོ་བར༔ གང་ཤར་རང་དགར་རྗེས་སུ་འབྲང་ཞིང་རྟོག་དཔྱོད་བྱེད་ན་ནོར༔ དེ་བཞིན་དུ་གོལ་ས་གསུམ་ནི༔

བདེ་བ་ལ་ཞེན་ན་འདོད་ཁམས་ཀྱི་ལུར་སྐྱེ་ཞ་གསལ་བ་ལ་ཞེན་ན་གཟུགས་ཁམས་
ཀྱི་ལུར་སྐྱེ་ཞ་མི་རྟོག་པ་ལ་ཞེན་ན་གཟུགས་མེད་ཀྱི་ལུར་སྐྱེ་བས་གོལ་ས་ཞེས་བྱ་ལ་
ཞ་དེའི་དོས་འཛིན་དང་ནོར་ས་འཕད་ན་ཞ་བདེ་བ་ཞེས་བྱ་བ་དེ་རྩ་བའི་ལྷག་བསྩལ་
ཆེན་པོ་གསུམ་གྱིས་མ་བསྒྲུད་པར་གནས་ལུགས་དེའི་ངང་ལ་འབྲལ་མི་ཕོད་པ་ལྷ་
བུའི་དགའ་བདེའི་ཉམས་འཆར་བ་ལ་ཟེར་གྱིས་ཞ་ཟག་བཅས་འདོད་ཆགས་ཀྱི་བདེ་
བ་ལྷ་བུའམ་ཞ་ཡུལ་ཅན་གྱིས་བསྒྱུར་པའི་སྐྱིད་སྡུག་དག་དགའ་སྡེའི་རྣམ་རྟོག་
འཆར་བ་ལྷ་བུ་ལ་ཟེར་བ་མ་ཡིན་ཞ་གསལ་བ་ཞེས་པ་དེ་རྟགས་པའམ་བྱིང་
འཐིབས་ལྷ་བུའི་འགིགས་ཀྱིས་མ་བསྒྲུད་པར་རིག་པའི་རང་ཆའམ་འཆར་སྐྲ
འགག་མེད་དུ་གསལ་བ་ལ་ཟེར་གྱིས་ཞ་ཡུལ་སྣང་གི་ཁ་དོག་བཟོ་དབྱིབས་སོགས་
མ་ཚན་བཅས་ཀྱི་འཆར་སྐྲ་འཕྲུལ་སྣང་གི་རང་གཟུགས་ལ་ཟེར་བ་མ་ཡིན་ནོ་ཞ་ཞ་མི་
རྟོག་པ་ཡང་ཞ་རྣམ་རྟོག་མི་འགྱུ་དགུ་འགྱུ་ལ་འཕྲས་འབྱུལ་རྟོག་གི་གཡོ་འཕྱུགས་
དང་བྲལ་བའི་རྟོག་མེད་ནས་མཁའ་ལྷ་བུ་ལ་ཟེར་གྱིས་ཞ་དན་མེད་དུ་བཀྲལ་བ་ལྷ་
བུའི་ཆོར་བ་འགགས་པའམ་གཉིད་འཐུག་ལྷ་བུའི་སྨུན་ནག་ལ་ཟེར་བ་མ་ཡིན་ནོ་ཞ
མདོར་ན་ཉམས་གསུམ་པོ་འདི་ཡང་ལམ་རྟགས་ཀྱི་འཆར་ཚུལ་ཅམ་དུ་ཤུགས་
འབྱུང་དུ་བྱུང་བ་ཡིན་པ་མ་རྟོགས་ཞ་དེ་ཡོད་དུ་རེ་ནས་ཆེད་དུ་སྐོམ་པ་དང་ཞ་བྱུང་བ་
ལ་སྐོམ་རྩལ་མར་བཟུང་ནས་ཞེན་ཅིང་ཆགས་ན་ཁམས་གསུམ་དུ་གོལ་བའི་རྒྱུ་
ལས་མ་འདས་སོ་ཞ་ཞ་དེ་བཞིན་དུ་ཕོར་བཞི་ལ་སྡོང་པ་ཉིད་ཞེས་བྱའི་གཉིས་ལ་
ཕོར་བ་ཞ་སྡོང་པ་ཉིད་ལམ་དུ་ཕོར་བ་ཞ་སྡོང་ཉིད་གཉེན་པོར་ཕོར་བ་ཞ་སྡོང་ཉིད་རྒྱུ
འདེབས་སུ་ཕོར་བ་དང་བཞི་ཡོད་ཅིང་དེ་དག་རེ་རེ་ལའང་ཡེ་ཕོར་དང་འཕྲལ་ཕོར་
གཉིས་སུ་དབྱེ་བར་འཕད་ཀྱང་ཞ་མདོར་ཕྱིལ་གྱིས་དྲིལ་ན་དོན་དམ་པའི་སྡོང་ཉིད་ཀྱི
དེ་བོ་གདོད་ནས་རྣམ་པར་དག་པ་བྱས་ཆོས་དང་སྐོས་བཏགས་ཀྱི་སྤྲོག་ལས་གྲོལ་
བ་ད་ལྷའི་རིག་པ་ཀ་དག་ཕྱོགས་ཡན་ཆེན་པོའི་གནད་མ་གོ་བར་སྣང་བ་ལ་ཞ་སྡོང་
པས་རྒྱས་འདེབས་ལྷ་བུའི་སྡོང་པ་ལོགས་ནས་བསྒྲུབ་ན་གཉིས་ལ་ཕོར་བའི་ཞ་ཞ་དེ

བཞིན་དུ་རང་རིག་ཐ་མལ་ཤེས་པའི་ལམ་ཁྱེར་ལ་ཡིད་མ་ཆེས་ཤིང་རྒྱ་འབྲས་

དབྱེར་མེད་ཀྱི་རང་བཞིན་ཡེ་ནས་ལྷུན་གྲུབ་ཏུ་ཆད་བ་མ་ཤེས་པར་ར་ལམ་སྟོང་ཉིད་

སྣོམ་པས་འབྲས་བུ་ཆོས་ཀྱི་སྐུ་གཞན་ནས་འབྱུང་དུ་རེ་ནས་འབད་པས་བློས་

བཏགས་ཏེ་སྣོམ་པ་ནི་ལམ་དུ་འཁོར་བའི་རྩ་རྟེན་མོངས་པ་དང་རྣམ་རྟོག་གང་འཁར་

ཡང་དེ་ཁའི་ངོ་བོ་ཡེ་ནས་སྟོང་པ་ཉིད་ལས་མ་འདས་པས་སྟོང་རྒྱའི་ངོ་བོངས་དང་

རྩ་གཞིན་པོའི་སྟོང་ཉིད་གཞིས་སུ་མ་དགོས་པར་སྟང་བུ་ཁོ་རང་རིག་པས་ངོས་ཟིན་

པ་དང་མཉམ་དུ་སྒྱུལ་གྱི་མདུད་པ་ཞིག་པ་ལྟར་རང་གྲོལ་དུ་སོང་བའི་གནད་མ་གོ་

བར་རྩ་སྲུང་བུའི་རྣམ་རྟོག་དང་རྟེན་མོངས་ཀྱི་སྟིང་དུ་གཞིན་པོའི་སྟོང་ཉིད་ལོགས་སུ་

བསྣོམ་དགོས་ན་གཞིན་པོར་ཕྱེར་བའི་རྩ་རྒྱས་འདེབས་ལ་ཕྱེར་བ་ནི་སྟོས་བཅས་

དང་སྟོས་མེད་གང་ཡིན་ཀྱང་ཡེ་ནས་སྟོང་ཆེན་ཀུན་ཏུ་བཟང་མོའི་མཁའ་དབྱིངས་

སུ་གསལ་སྟོང་ཟུང་འཇུག་ཆེན་པོར་ལྷུན་གྲུབ་ཏུ་མ་ཤེས་པར་ཨ་འཐས་ཀྱི་སྣོམ་

མཁན་དང་དམིགས་མེད་དུ་སྟོང་བའི་འཛིན་སྣངས་ཟུང་དུ་མ་རྒྱད་པས་ཐབས་ཤེས་

ཡ་བྲལ་བ་དང་རྩ་ཐ་མལ་གྱི་རིག་པ་བློ་འདས་ཀྱི་རྒྱུན་དམིགས་མེད་ཀྱི་བུ་རས་མི་

སྟོང་བར་ཐོག་མའི་གོ་ཡུལ་དེ་ཡིད་ལ་བཞག་ནས་བསྣོམ་བུ་སྣོམ་བྱེད་མེད་དོ་ཞེ་ཞེ་

ཐམས་ཅད་སྟོང་པ་ཉིད་དོ་ཞེ་ཞེ་ཐམས་ཅད་ཆོས་སྐུའི་ཞེ་ཞེ་ལས་འབྲས་མི་བདེན་ནོ་ཞེ་

ཞེ་བློ་ཡིན་ནོ་ཞེ་ཞེ་རྣམ་རྟོག་ཡིན་ནོ་ཞེ་ཞེ་གང་ཡང་མ་གྲུབ་པོ་ཞེས་ཐག་ཆོད་ཀྱི་སྟོང་

ལུས་རྒྱས་འདེབས་པ་ལ་ཟེར་གྱིས་འདི་ནི་དེང་སང་ཤིན་དུ་མང་དོ་ཞེ་ཞེ་མདོར་ན་

སྣོམ་བདག་པོའི་ལག་ཏུ་འཕྱོད་ནས་རྣམ་ཀུན་མཆོག་ལྡན་གྱི་སར་བགྲོད་པ་ལ་ཕོར་

གོལ་ནོར་ས་གསུམ་གྱི་བསྐྱངས་ས་དང་འཕྱང་ཤིན་ཏུ་དོག་པས་རྣམས་སྦྱང་དེ་དག་

ལ་གདར་ཤ་མ་ཆོད་ན་ཁ་ཁྱེར་དང་ཆོག་ཁྱེར་མཁས་ཀྱང་རྩ་རྗེ་སྐྱད་དུ་རྟོགས་ཆེན་

ནས་རྩ་ཉམས་ན་བྱུན་འད་སྟེ་ཡལ་ནས་འགྲོ་ཞེ་ཞེ་ཞེས་པ་བཞད་པ་ལྟར་ཡུལ་གྱི་

རྒྱིན་བཟང་དང་ཕྱིན་བྱུས་ཀྱང་བློམ་ཆེན་པ་བསྒྲུས་ནས་རྒྱིན་ཐོག་ཏུ་འཆོལ་བ་དེས་

ལན་པར་གདའ་སྟེ་ཞེ་དེའི་ཕྱིར་གེགས་སེལ་བོགས་འདོན་གྱི་གནད་ཁྲིད་པར་ཅན་

གྱིས་མ་ཟིན་ན་མི་དང་མ་འཕྱད་པའི་བཅད་རྒྱ་དམ་པོ་བྱེད་པ་དང་། སྲུག་བཙོར་
བྱས་ཡུས་ཙན་གྱི་སེམས་འཛིན་ཡུས་གནད་དམ་པོས་འཆིང་བ་དང་། ལྷ་སྒོལ་པ་
དང་སྲུགས་བཟླ་བ་དང་། རྟ་རྒྱང་སྒོམ་པ་ལ་སོགས་སྲུག་པོ་སྲུས་བཅལ་ནས་ཉེས་པ་
གཅིག་ཡུས་ཐར་པ་བྱུང་རྒྱབ་གལ་ཐོབ་སྟེ་ཏུ་འཐགས་པ་སྲུད་པ་ལས་ཀྲུ་གང་ཞིག་
དཔག་ཆད་ལུ་བརྒྱ་ཡོད་པའི་རི་ཡི་སུལ་ཏུ་ཀྲུལ་གྱིས་གང་བར་ལོ་མང་བྱི་བར་
གནས་བྱས་ཀྱང་ཏུ་ཏུ་དབེན་པ་འདི་མི་ཤེས་པའི་བྱུང་རྒྱབ་སེམས་དཔའ་ནི་ཏུ་ཏུ་
ལྷག་པའི་ང་རྒྱལ་སྟེང་ནས་འགྲོ་བར་གནས་པ་ཡིན་ཏུ་ཏུ་ཞེས་གསུངས་སོ་ཏུ་ཏུ་དེའི་
ཕྱིར་ན་གང་ཁར་ལམ་འཁྱེར་གྱི་གནད་ཤེས་ནས་ལུས་ཀྱི་མཆམས་ཁད་ཏུ་སེམས་
ཀྱི་སྒྲུབ་པ་པོ་དབེན་པར་གནས་པའི་སྒྲུབ་པ་ཁོན་ལས་ཆད་ཆེ་བའི་ལམ་མེད་པས་
ལོ་མཆམས་བླ་མཆམས་ཀྱི་བྱས་ཡུས་ལ་རེ་ལྟོས་མི་འཆའ་བར་མི་ཆེ་ཁོ་ན་ལ་ཆད་
བཏུགས་ནས་གནས་ལུགས་མ་བཅོས་པའི་རྒྱན་སྐྱོང་བ་ལ་འབད་ཅེད་ཏུ་བཟང་དན་
གྱི་རྣམ་རྟོག་གང་ཁར་ཡང་རྣམ་རྟོག་གོ་སྒོམ་པའི་ཚེར་འཛིན་གྱི་ལྱན་པ་འདེབས་པ་
དང་སྲུང་བྱའི་སྙིང་དུ་གཉེན་པོའི་མི་བཅའ་རྒྱག་པ་སོགས་གང་ཡང་མི་བྱེད་པར་མི་
རྒྱན་གྱིས་གྱིས་པའི་ཅེད་མོ་ལ་བལྟ་བ་ལྟར་སྣང་མེད་སྲོས་བྲལ་གྱི་དང་དུ་ཉིན་
མཆན་བར་མེད་དུ་ལ་བརྩོ་བར་བྱས་པས་ལྷག་མཐོང་རྟོག་མེད་ཀྱི་ཅུལ་རྟོགས་ཏེ་ཏུ་
གནས་འགྱུ་དུན་རིག་བཟང་རྟོག་དན་རྟོག་ཏེ་ལྷ་བུ་འཆར་ཡང་རིག་སྟོང་བློ་འདས་
རྟོགས་པ་ཆེན་པའི་ཀློང་དུ་བཅན་ས་ཟིན་པས་ན་རྟོགས་ཆེན་ནས་ཏུ་རྟོགས་པ་ནམ་
མཁའ་འདྲ་སྟེ་འགྱུར་བ་མེད་ཏུ་ཏུ་ཅེས་པ་ལྟར་རྣལ་འབྱོར་པ་དེ་ལུས་ཐ་མལ་པ་ལྟར་
སྣང་ཡང་སེམས་ཆོས་སྐུ་བུ་ཙུལ་དང་བྲལ་བའི་དགོངས་པ་ལ་ལ་བཞུགས་པས་སྣང་
སྲིད་བླ་མའི་དཀྱིལ་འཁོར་གང་ཁར་ཡེ་ཤེས་ཆམ་བཟལ་ཡུལ་སྣང་བཟུང་དང་དཔེ་ཆ་
ཏུ་ས་ལམ་བུར་མེད་ལྷག་པ་དགོངས་པ་འཁོར་འདས་ཡེ་གྲོལ་གྱི་སྐྱོང་ནས་གནས་
སྐབས་སུ་བསྐྱེན་པ་དང་སེམས་ཙན་གྱི་དོན་འབད་མེད་ལྷུན་གྲུབ་ཏུ་འབྱུང་ཞིང་ཏུ་
ལུས་རྒྱའི་འཆིང་བ་ཞིག་པ་དང་དུས་མཆོངས་པར་བྱམ་ནང་གི་རྣམ་མཁའ་བྱམ་པ་

ཆགས་པ་དང་ལྡན་ཅིག་ཕྱིའི་རས་མཁན་དང་དབྱེར་མེད་རོ་གཅིག་ཏུ་གྱུར་པ་ལྟར༔
གདོད་མའི་གཞི་དབྱིངས་ནང་གསལ་དཔོད་བྱེད་ཀྱི་ཤེས་པ་དང་བྲལ་བའི་གཞོན་ནུ་
བུམ་པའི་སྐུར་མངོན་སངས་རྒྱ་བའི་བསྐྱབ་བུའི་མཐར་ཕྱག་གོ༔༔༔༔ དེར་སྐྱུར་
པ༔༔ཀུན་རྟོག་འཁྲུལ་བའི་སྣང་བ་རྟེན་པོ་ཆེ༔༔ཀློང་ཆེན་རིག་པའི་གཤིས་སུ་
ཕུབ་རྒྱུད་པས༔༔ གྱུ་དྲན་སེམས་ཀྱི་བུ་བྱེད་བྱིས་པའི་གར༔༔ཀློ་འདས་དྲན་
པའི་ངང་དུ་བཀག་ལ་ཞེ༔༔ལྟ་བ་མཐོན་པོར་སྐྱགས་པའི་བཟང་རྟོག་དང༔༔ཐེ་
ཚོམ་སྐྱོག་ཏུ་རྒྱུད་པའི་ངན་རྟོག་ཆང་༔༔བཏུངས་པའི་གདི་མུག་གཉིད་ཀྱིས་མ་
བཟི་བར༔༔ཐ་མལ་རིག་པ་རྟེན་པ་སྐྱོད་དེར་གནས༔༔གོ་ཡུལ་ཁ་ལྟར་འབྲམས་
པའི་ཉུད་གོག་དང་༔༔གནས་འགྱུའི་འཕུང་ལ་འཇོར་བའི་དུ:ཁ་སོགས༔༔
དགོངས་བརྐྱུད་རོ་རྟེའི་ཆོག་ཁྲན་ཟབ་མོ་ཡི༔༔ལུང་དུའི་གཏུམ་ཀྱིས་ལན་བརྒྱུར་
ཟིལ་ཀྱིས་མནན༔༔སྤྲིན་བསགས་སྤྲིན་ལས་དཀར་པོའི་རྟེན་འབྲེལ་དང་༔༔ཟབ་
ལམ་རྟེའི་རྣལ་འབྲོར་བཀའ་དྲིན་ལས༔༔དབུ་མའི་ཙ་མདུང་གྲོལ་བའི་ལགོ་
རྟེས་སུ༔༔ཉམས་སྐྱོང་གནད་ཀྱི་མན་ངག་འདི་ཁོྲས༔༔དེ་ལྟའི་དབུར་རྡོའི་ང་
རོ་བསྒྲགས་པ་ན༔༔མཁས་རྟོམ་ས་ཀུ་ཾ་ཡི་སྐྱིང་འགགས་ཀྱང་༔༔ཉམས་རྟོགས་
ཟབ་མོ་ཁོན་ནས་ལུད་པའི་ཕྱིར༔༔སྐྱོང་བཏོལ་གཏུམ་ལ་སྐྲ་གསང་བུ་མ་སྤྱ་བ༔༔
དགེ་དེས་རང་བཞས་དྲན་པ་སྐྱོང་བ་ལ༔༔ འཛུར་དྲན་འཚལ་བར་ཁོར་བའི་མི་
དགེ་ཀུན༔༔ཕྱགས་འབྱུང་གཙུག་མའི་དང་དུ་དག་ནས་ཀྱང་༔༔ཀུན་ཀྱིས་
རྟོགས་པ་ཆེན་པོ་རྟོགས་པར་ཤོག༔ ཅེས་གོལ་ཁོར་ཚར་གཅོད་མེད་གིའི་ངར་རོ་
ཅེས་བྱ་བ་འདི་ཡང་དང་གཏོང་ཐོས་པའི་ནོར་ཀྱིས་ཕྱུག་ཅེ་ཾ་འོད་གསལ་རྟོགས་
པ་ཆེན་པོ་ལ་འཕོ་ཞུད་མེད་པར་སྐྱོང་བའི་སྟོན་དགེའི་ལས་འཕོ་ཚན་ཚོས་དུང་དར་
པ་སྐྱོང་གོལ་དབྱེས་རིག་དང་༔༔དབེན་པ་གསུམ་ཀྱིས་རྒྱུད་བསྒམས་ཏེ་འདག་
བུར་ཁོན་ལ་གནས་པས་འོད་གསལ་རྟེ་རྗེ་སྐྱིང་པོའི་སྐྱབ་པ་ལ་བཙོན་པ་སྐྲ་གསུམ་
དབྱིངས་རིག་སོགས་ཀྱིས་ལན་གཅིག་མ་ཡིན་པར་ཡང་ཡང་བསྐུལ་འདེབས་བྱུང་

བར་བརྟེན་རྟེ་འོད་གསལ་རྟོགས་པ་ཆེན་པོ་མངོན་སུམ་གྱི་གནས་ལ་གོམས་པར་

རྟོམ་པའི་ཀུ་སུ་ལུའི་རྣལ་འབྱོར་པ། པཎྜིདབང་ཆེན་ཡེ་ཤེས་དཔལ་གྱི་རོལ་མཚོས་

རྟེ་དཔལ་གྱི་མཆིམས་ཕུའི་ལྷ་བ་འོག་མིན་མཁའ་འགྲོའི་ཚོགས་ཁང་གསང་ཆེན་

མེ་ཏོག་ཕུག་གི་མཚམས་མལ་དུ་བྲིས་པ་འདི་བྱིད་མ་ཐོབ་པ་དང་རྟེ་ཐོབ་ཀྱང་རང་

རྟེས་ཀྱི་དུག་ཆུས་སྒོས་ཞིང་ལམ་གྱི་གནད་མ་ལོངས་པའི་སྐལ་མེད་ལོག་ལྟ་ཅན་

གྱི་རིགས་ལ་བསྟན་པར་མི་བྱའི་རྟེ་རྟེ་སྒྲུབ་པ་སྙིང་པོར་བྱེད་པ་རྣམས་ཀྱི་ཡི་གེ་འདི་

ལ་ནན་ཏན་དུ་གཟིགས་ཤིག་རྟེ་ངེས་ཤེས་སྙེས་ཚད་ལ་ལུང་བྱིན་པ་ཡིན་ནོ་རྟེ་རྟེ་

སྙིང་ཏིག་གཉེན་པོའི་བཀའ་སྲུང་རྣམས་ལ་གཉེར་རོ་རྟེ་རྟེ་ས་མཱ༔ རྒྱ་རྒྱ་རྒྱ༔

NOTES

---

1. Chögyam Trungpa, *Mudra: Early Poems and Songs* (Boston: Shambhala Publications, 2001), 15.
2. These three are suffering beings, beneficial beings like parents, and beings with spiritual qualities, such as teachers and spiritual masters.
3. The two aspects of discipline are refraining from harmful actions and gathering virtuous actions.
4. The three buddha bodies.
5. Mindfulness of body, sensations, mind, and phenomena.
6. Subject, object, and action.
7. One gone to bliss, a buddha.
8. The intermediate state after death.
9. Pema Lingpa, 1450–1521. See Pema Lingpa, *The Life and Revelations of Pema Lingpa,* trans. Sarah Harding (Ithaca, N.Y.: Snow Lion Publications, 2003).
10. Longchenpa was a reincarnation of Pema Ledrel Tsal. See Nyoshul Khenpo, *A Marvelous Garland of Rare Gems,* trans. Richard Barron (Junction City, Calif.: Padma Publishing, 2005).
11. Jamyang Drakpa, as reported by Jokyab, in his commentary to *Light of Wisdom* (*Lamrim Yeshe Nyingpo; Lam rim ye shes snying po*), explains these terms as follows:

> The four measures of clarity [*gsal brtan tshad brgyad*] are: *distinct,* since the visible aspect of the particular deity's bodily form is clear and unblurred down to the black and white of the eyes; *alive,* since the deity is not in a state of lethargy devoid of the sharp cognizance of awareness, but rather endowed with the sharpness of awareness that is empty cognizance possessing an awake quality; *vibrant,* because the deities are also not made of mindless matter like a rainbow, but rather, even the pores on the body and every strand of hair on their heads are suffused with omniscient wakefulness so that they are radiantly present with the hundredfold qualities of their sense consciousnesses fully manifest; and *vivid* because these deities, as well, are not only concepts

of inferring that they may be such and such, but rather, they are vividly present in your experience as if in person.

The four measures of steadiness are: *unmoving* because of being unmoved by the general faults such as forgetfulness, laziness, and so forth; *unchanging* because of being unchanged by the specific faults such as fluttering or floating vision, and so forth; *utterly unchangeable* because the [visualization] is vividly clear not just for a short while but it does not become overpowered by even the most subtle thought even when composed throughout day and night; and *totally flexible* or *totally steady* when being thoroughly proficient no matter which sublime aspect you visualize such as the color of the bodily form, the face and arms, arriving and remaining, as well as the emanation and absorption of the rays of light.

When you have trained until you become adept in these eight measures of clarity and steadiness, you will experience everything as the mandala of the deity. This is the "experience of perfection," and known as "experience as the mandala of the deity," and it is the measure for having attained complete stability. (Padmasambhava, *Light of Wisdom*, vol. 2 [Hong Kong: Rangjung Yeshe Publications, 1998], 142n129)

12. All notes from Dilgo Khyentse Rinpoche are from recordings of Khyentse Rinpoche's teachings on Jigme Lingpa's *The Lion's Roar*, given in Boudhanath, Nepal. Dilgo Khyentse Rinpoche: Just as a patch on clothing will come off when the stitches wear out, likewise intellectual understanding will not last. Thinking you have realization of Dzogchen, you may cling to this notion. Then when negative conditions like strong emotions suddenly arise, the meditation is lost, and you become attached to activities involving the eight worldly concerns. You may experience favorable conditions such as your personal influence expanding, having a respected position, perhaps even everyone revering you as a great lama or great meditator. Or, you may experience difficult conditions where you are slandered and people speak ill of you. Meeting such diverse situations, there are many who will be separated from their "realization" of dharma, like water and milk are separated. For example, water is clear and has no flavor, whereas milk is white and tastes sweet. If you mix water and milk, they will blend together somewhat. A tortoise or a duck can separate them when drinking, and drink the milk while leaving the water. Like the example of separating water from milk, a practitioner may think he or she has realized Dzogchen, but when encountering positive and negative circumstances, the person and the dharma become separated, like water separates from milk.

13. Dilgo Khyentse Rinpoche: What are the six sense fields? They are the six sense organs and their objects. For example, you see a beautiful object and become attached to it; or you see something unpleasant and feel aversion. These perceptions should naturally self-liberate. If they don't, then you have not been able to

carry them onto the path, to integrate them with your practice.

14. Translator's note: It is said that the quality and purity of water improves the more it flows over rocks.

15. Dilgo Khyentse Rinpoche uses the word *gnad* meaning "vital point" or "key point" as his explanation for the word *mtsang* in our text, which can also mean "hidden flaw."

16. Dilgo Khyentse Rinpoche: You may have a little understanding of dharma texts, and think, "My meditation is empty, it is so clear. I benefit beings, I have great merit." When this occurs, it is called "straying into emptiness having the character of a knowable object" (*stong nyid shes bya'i gshis la shor ba*) This is the dualistic mind (*gnyis 'dzin sems*).

17. Dilgo Khyentse Rinpoche: This grave obscuration of conceptual knowing is very subtle. In fact, the Buddha has stated that in regard to the nature of emptiness (*stong pa'i rang bzhin*), if there is any fixation on the three spheres of subject, object, and action, then conceptual obscurations (*shes bya'i sgrib pa*) are present. If thoughts naturally arise and self-liberate, then we can truly say that "thoughts are dharmakaya." If they are not liberated upon arising, thoughts are not dharmakaya.

18. Dilgo Khyentse Rinpoche: In regard to the "immediate awareness, which is unimpaired and uncorrupted": There are what are known as "meditator's remedies." For instance, in the sutra tradition, if there is anger, one meditates on patience; if there is desire, one meditates on the unclean aspects of the object of desire; if there is dullness, one focuses on the exhalation of the breath; and so on. Here there is no need for a separate remedy. If you recognize the nature of your "ordinary mind," that is the remedy.

    If you claim, "This is my view, it is Madhyamaka," or "My view is Cittamatra," and so on, you are thus attached to the view and there is grasping and fixation present. So one should not be bound by clinging to one's philosophical view.

    As Jigme Lingpa mentions earlier, the actual view of the Great Perfection is *zang thal le* or "unimpeded open transparency," meaning that it pervades everything (*kun la khyab*). It is not bound by deliberate, restricted mindfulness (*ched 'dzin dran pa*), since it is "free and unbound (*kha yan*)." This is what is practiced on the path, also known as the meditation of naked awareness (*rig pa rjen pa la sgom pa*).

19. Dilgo Khyentse Rinpoche: At the time of meditation and postmeditation, having many theories (*go ba*) such as "My meditation is perfect" or "This time it was not OK." Or when experiences arise, you think, "This is an experience of bliss or this is an experience of clarity or nonthought."

20. Dilgo Khyentse Rinpoche: Both stillness and movement are recognized by awareness as its own essence (*rang ngo rang rig pa'i shes pa*).

21. Dilgo Khyentse Rinpoche: If we explain meditative equipoise and postmeditation, then to give the experiential meaning of "meditative equipoise" from the Dzogchen tradition: "Meditative equipoise" is when the naked essence of

awareness is recognized (*rig pa ngo rjen pa shes pa*). If we lose that naked aware-ness, this is what is meant by "postmeditation" in the Dzogchen teachings.

22. Dilgo Khyentse Rinpoche: In Dzogchen, what is the meaning of the term "ordi-nary mind" (*tha mal shes pa*)?

It is this immediate awareness (*da lta'i shes pa*), unspoiled by any defects such as afflictive emotions, or even by positive thoughts like conceptual devotion and compassion. This immediate awareness is natural and innate. As the saying goes, "If you leave water undisturbed, it will become clear." The practice is remaining with the continuity of awareness.

One may not understand this. Ordinary worldly thoughts like desire and aggression may arise, one thought following after the other, creating many more thoughts. Or you might have many positive thoughts arising in the same way. When this is happening, you may lose your meditative equipoise. It is an error if you mistake your ordinary thinking for the immediate awareness of Dzogchen.

23. In this passage of his commentary, Nyoshul Khen Rinpoche tells us that aware-ness is self-sustaining (*rang gnas*). Similarly, we find in Khen Rinpoche's song on Dakini Practice found in the last chapter of this book: "Since 'the sustained' and 'the sustainer' are not two, rest in natural clarity without grasping." Here, Rinpoche clarifies the point mentioned in his commentary to *The Lion's Roar* that awareness is self-sustaining (*rang gnas*), indicating that remaining in the continuity of awareness is free of any "meditator" who is "sustaining" this con-tinuity. As the great Nyingma master Mipham Rinpoche writes:

> When the lama's blessings enter, it is effortlessly realized.
> When the meaning of this is seen, one knows the way to sustain the
>   "unfabricated."
> Do not sustain it thinking, "I am sustaining my mind."
> Also do not think, "I am not sustaining it."
> Just let it be in its own place, and it will be naturally evident (*rang sar
>   chog ge zhog dang ngang gis gsal*).
> The yoga of the self-sustaining (*rang gnas*) natural flow (*rang babs*) is
>   the supreme meditation.

The short text from which this quote is excerpted is in a collection of Dzog-chen texts called *Thun min rdzogs chen skor gyi gdams pa phyogs bsdus zab don snying po sangs rgyas lag lag ster bzhugs*, pp. 133–34 (folios 29a4–b2). In the expanded redaction of the Complete Works of 'Ju Mipham series, Rdzong sar par ma, vol. 27 (Lama Ngodrup and Sherab Drimey: Paro, Bhutan, 2002).

24. Dilgo Khyentse Rinpoche: This is referring, for example, to when one is resting in the natural state in meditation and one does not feel able to part from it, or let go of it.

25. Dilgo Khyentse Rinpoche: "When you become attached to meditation experi-ences, there is the sense of a reified meditator having good and bad experiences,

happiness and sorrow. Some so-called great meditators are depressed if they have a bad experience and feel happy if a good experience occurs."

26. Dilgo Khyentse Rinpoche, private explanation of the text, given to Tulku Sangngak Rinpoche: "Due to the separation between the reified meditator (*sgom mkhan*) and the object of meditation (*sgom bya*), then skillful means and wisdom are divorced or disunited."

The object of meditation, or "that which is being meditated on" refers in this passage to the practice of Vajrayana visualization meditation. It is speaking of the point where all phenomena are purified into emptiness (*dmigs med du sbyong ba*) by using the mantra OM SVABHAVA SHUDDHA, etc. Here, the root text uses the term *dmigs med*, which means "free of reference points," but in this case it is synonymous with "emptiness" (*stong pa nyid*)); so it is speaking of purifying phenomena into emptiness.

In such practices, conceptual fixation (*blo'i 'dzin stang*) is present, which Jigme Lingpa refers to as "a conceptual way of dissolving all phenomena into emptiness." On the other hand, within awareness (*rig pa*), the meditator and the object of meditation are already primordially indivisible and naturally empty.

INDEX